Popular Mechanics

THE BOY MECHANIC MAKES TOYS

Popular Mechanics

THE BOY MECHANIC MAKES TOYS

159 GAMES, TOYS, TRICKS *and* OTHER AMUSEMENTS

HEARST BOOKS

A DIVISION OF STERLING PUBLISHING CO., INC.

NEW YORK

Library of Congress Cataloging-in-Publication Data

The boy mechanic makes toys : 200 games, toys, tricks, and other amusements / The editors of Popular mechanics.
 p. cm.
"...contains 200 original PM projects, some dating back to 100 years ago. Some are quaint like homemade skis while others are just as fun now. This is for entertainment as much as instruction."
Includes index.
ISBN-13: 978-1-58816-639-5
ISBN-10: 1-58816-639-2
1. Toy making. 2. Handicraft. I. Popular mechanics magazine.
TT174.B68 2007
745.592--dc22

        2006023489

Book design by Barbara Balch

Published by Hearst Books
A Division of Sterling Publishing Co., Inc.
387 Park Avenue South, New York, NY 10016

Popular Mechanics and Hearst Books are trademarks of Hearst Communications, Inc.

www.popularmechanics.com

For information about custom editions, special sales, premium and corporate purchases, please contact Sterling Special Sales Department at 800-805-5489 or specialsales@sterlingpub.com.

Distributed in Canada by Sterling Publishing
C/o Canadian Manda Group, 165 Dufferin Street
Toronto, Ontario, Canada M6K 3H6

Distributed in Australia by Capricorn Link (Australia) Pty. Ltd.
P.O. Box 704, Windsor, NSW 2756 Australia

Manufactured in China

Sterling ISBN 13: 978-1-58816-639-5
   ISBN 10: 1-58816-639-2

CONTENTS

FOREWORD

Anyone who has ever seen children amuse themselves with the boxes their presents came in understands that there is no imagination like a youthful one. Kids don't see those boxes as mere disposable containers: Instead, they envision a car, a plane, a time machine, and so much more.

Today's explosion of electronic toys, games, and devices has created a new universe of imagination and given kids the ability to put themselves in incredible make-believe worlds. This technology is nothing short of fantastic and opens up new avenues for imaginative fun. But that doesn't mean that old-fashioned ingenuity and craftsmanship are lost. The following pages are filled with sparks to fire the young imagination—straight from the pages of *Popular Mechanics* circa the early 1900s.

Some of these projects, such as the homemade skis, are delightfully quaint. Magic tricks that can amaze friends and family are just as wonderful today as they ever were. Some of these projects help the young mechanic learn science while having fun, as is the case with the myriad motors and gizmos in Chapter 2. And, of course, when you select projects from the halls of history, you're bound to wind up with a few whacky examples. We include odds and ends, such as the sailing canoe, as much for entertainment as instruction.

Given the wide range of projects in these pages, it's a sure bet there's something here for kids of all ages.

The young child will no doubt be enchanted by the idea of a toy donkey whose head and tail move as it's pulled along. Older kids will be intrigued by the idea of making their own "parlor cue alley" game, or a ukulele they can really play. And anyone can delight in the idea of a tree swing that moves in great exhilarating circles.

It is, however, important to point out what may already be obvious: These projects have not been updated. We've left them largely as they first appeared. Anyone attempting any projects in this book should do so only under adult supervision, and only when using all appropriate safety precautions. The materials and methods called for in these projects reflect the limited technology of the times, and only modern tools, techniques, and safeguards should be used in making any project.

But, fortunately, the projects don't have to be created to offer a wealth of amusement for anyone willing to bring a little imagination to their reading. An intriguing history lesson of early-twentieth-century enterprise and ingenuity requires no tools. Just flip the page and let the fun begin.

The Editors of
Popular Mechanics

{ CHAPTER 1 }

MAKING MAGIC

—

SLICK TRICKS

— A FINGER-TRAP TRICK —

You can fool your friends with the little joker made to trap a finger. It consists of a piece of paper, about 6 in. wide and 12 in. or longer. To prepare the paper, cut two slots in the one end as shown and then roll it up in tube form, beginning at the end with the cuts, then fasten the end with glue. The inside diameter should be ½ in.

When the glue is dry, ask someone to push a finger into either end. This will be easy enough to do, but to remove the finger is a different matter. The end coils tend to pull out and hold the finger. If the tube is made of tough paper, it will stand considerable pull.

IT IS EASY TO INSERT A FINGER IN THE TUBE, BUT TO GET IT OUT IS ALMOST IMPOSSIBLE.

— A Ring-and-Egg Trick —

This trick consists in borrowing a ring and wrapping it in a handkerchief from which it is made to disappear, only to be found in an egg, taken from a number on a plate.

Obtain a wedding ring and sew it into one corner of a handkerchief. After borrowing a ring from a member of the audience, pretend to wrap it in the center of the handkerchief, but instead wrap up the one concealed in the corner, retaining the borrowed one in the hand. Before beginning the performance, place in the bottom of an egg cup a small quantity of soft wax. When getting the cup, slip the borrowed ring into the wax in an upright position. An egg is then chosen by anyone in the audience. This is placed in the egg cup, the ring in the bottom being pressed into the shell. With a buttonhook break the top of the shell and fish out the ring. The handkerchief is then shaken out to show that the ring has vanished.

— A Matchbox Trick —

All that is required to perform this trick is a box of safety matches. Four matches are removed and three of them arranged as shown in the sketch. The performer then tells his friends that he will light the fourth match and set the cross match on fire in the center, then asks which match of the standing ones will light first. Most people will not stop to think and will guess either one or the other. As a matter of fact, after the cross match is set on fire, it soon burns the wood away, and the pressure of the two side matches will

cause it to spring out so that neither catches fire.

— VANISHING HANDKERCHIEF TRICK —

The necessary articles used in performing this trick are the handkerchief, vanishing wand, a long piece of glass tubing about ½ in. shorter than the wand, and a paper tube closed at one end and covered with a cap at the other. The handkerchief rod, shown at *C,* is concealed in the paper tube *A* before

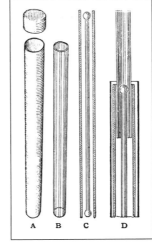

the performance. The glass tube *B,* after being shown empty, is put into the paper tube *A* so that, unknown to the spectators, the handkerchief rod now is within it. The handkerchief is then placed over the opening of the tube and pushed in by means of the wand. In doing this, the handkerchief and the rod are pushed into the wand, as shown in *D.* After the wand is removed, the cap is placed over the paper tube, and this is given to someone to hold. The command for the handkerchief to vanish is given, and it is found to be gone when the glass tube is taken out of the paper cover. This is a novel way of making a handkerchief vanish. It can be used in a great number of tricks and can be varied to suit the performer.

— DEVICE FOR A FINGER TUG-OF-WAR GAME—

Considerable pleasure is afforded by this tug-of-war game. Two contestants, one at each end, take hold of the rollers with their forefingers and thumbs and endeavor to move the pointer to their respective ends. The game is fun for people of all ages, and they will all want to try it.

The device should be made strong enough to stand up to wear and tear. The top and bottom are boards, ½ by 8 by 24 in. Four blocks, 3 in. high and 2½ in. square, are fastened between them at the corners with screws. The rollers are set in the blocks and held by small nails passing through them and against the inner faces of the blocks. The pointer is made of a strip of brass, bent to a rectangle around the top board, in line with numbers from 9 to zero and back to 9 (scores for each contestant). Cords extend from the pointer inside the box and are tied to the rollers.

— THE DIE-AND-BOX TRICK —

The die-and-box trick, often performed on the stage, is a very interesting and mystifying one. The apparatus, however, is simple. It consists of a box, die, a piece of tin in the form of three adjacent sides of the die, and a hat. The die and box are constructed entirely of wood, ⅛ in. thick; the piece of tin can be cut from

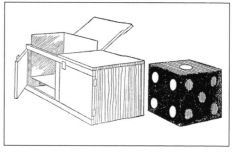

WITH THE FALSE DIE IN PLACE
THE BOX APPEARS TO BE EMPTY.

any large coffee can. The box is closed by four doors, as shown in *Fig. 1,* two of which are 2¾ in. square, and the others, 3⅛ by 3¼ in. The first two are the front doors and are preferably hinged with cloth to the two uprights *A* and *B.* Small pieces of tin are fastened on the doors at *C* and *D,* to provide a means to open them. The other doors are placed on top and are hinged to the back, as shown.

The die is 3 in. square on all sides, and is constructed of two pieces, 3 in. square; two pieces, 2¾ by 3 in., and two pieces, 2¾ in. square. These are fastened together with ½-in. brads. The tin, forming the false die, is cut out as shown in *Fig. 2,* and is then bent on the dotted lines and soldered together on the joint formed by the two edges *E* and *F.* All parts should be painted a dull black with white spots on the die and false die.

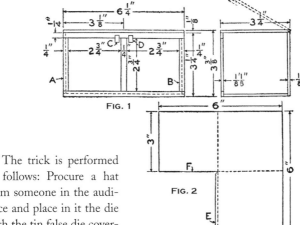

THE BOX WITH DOORS ON ONE SIDE AND
THE TOP, AND THE FALSE-DIE PATTERN.

The trick is performed as follows: Procure a hat from someone in the audience and place in it the die with the tin false die covering three sides of a block, at the same time telling the audience that the block will be caused to pass from the hat into the box, the latter being placed some distance away. Inform the audience that it would be more difficult for the die to pass from the box into the hat. Remove the tin piece from the hat and leave the die, holding the surfaces of the false die toward the audience. This will give the impression that the die has been removed. Set the hat on the table above the level of the eyes of the audience. With the back of the box toward the audience, open one top door and insert the tin piece in the right-hand compartment so that one side touches the back, another the side, and the other the bottom of the box. Close the door and open the two doors of the opposite compartment, which, when shown, will appear to be empty. Tilt the box to this side and open the doors of the side opposite to the one just opened, which, of course, will be empty. This should be done several times until someone asks that all doors be opened at the same time. After a few more reversals and openings, open all doors and show it empty, then take the die from the hat.

— WIRELESS LIGHTED LAMP DECEPTION —

Window displays of a puzzling nature usually draw crowds. A lighted globe lying in full view, yet apparently not connected to any source of electricity, could easily be arranged as a window display, deceiving the closest observer. A mirror, or window glass, backed with some opaque material, should be used for the foundation of the device. For the display lamp, it is best to use a 25- or 40-watt tungsten, as these will lie

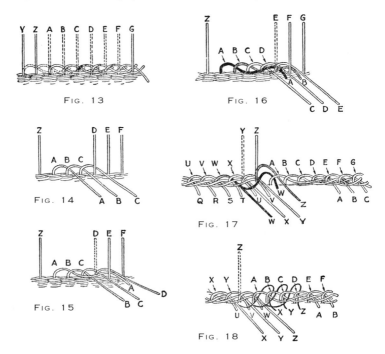

FIG. 13

FIG. 16

FIG. 14

FIG. 15

FIG. 17

FIG. 18

A SIMPLE BREAKDOWN ROLE FOR THE TOP.
ALSO A METHOD OF FORMING A ROLL BETWEEN
THE FIRST AND SECOND SPOKES, WHERE ONLY THREE
SPOKES ARE TURNED DOWN BEFORE THE
THROWING-ACROSS PROCESS BEGINS.

flatter on the glass than the larger sizes, and the deception will not be as easily discovered. The place where the brass cap of the lamp touches the glass should be marked and a small hole drilled through to the wire connecting the tungsten filament to the plug on the top of the lamp. At any suitable place, a hole should be drilled in the glass plate, no larger than is necessary, to permit two small cotton-covered magnet wires to pass through. One of the wires should be looped, passed through the hole in the cap, and hooked onto the bare wire connecting with the plug on top of the lamp. The other wire should be fastened to the brass cap near the drilled hole, after

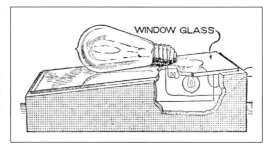

AN ELECTRIC LIGHTBULB
LIGHTED ON A PIECE OF GLASS
MAKES A GOOD WINDOW ATTRACTION.

which the lamp may be placed in position and the two wires connected to a source of electricity. If proper care has been taken and no crosses occur, the lamp will light. And if the display is placed in the proper surroundings, it will prove very deceiving. To protect against a fuse blow-out from a short circuit, it is advisable to run another lamp in series with the display lamp as shown.

— THE MAGIC CLOCK HAND —

The hand, or pointer, is the only working part needed to perform this trick. A clock face can be drawn on any piece of white paper and a pin stuck in its center on which the hand revolves. The hand *A* is cut from a piece of sheet brass and may

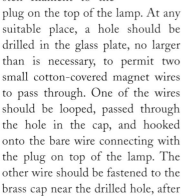

be in any form or design desired. It must, however, balance perfectly on the axle, which passes through a ¼-in. hole in the center, or else the magic part will fail. The illustration shows a good design with dimensions that will cause it to balance

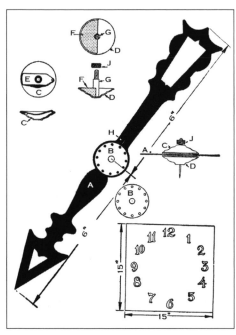

center. This disk is soldered to the hand where both ¼-in. holes will coincide. It is necessary to procure two washers, *C* and *D,* which are embossed—raised—in the center, and about 1¼ in. in diameter. These can be purchased from a dealer in curtain rods, and are the washers used on the ends of the rods. A careful mechanic can raise the center portion of a brass disk by beating it over a hole with a ball-peen hammer.

One of the washers, *C,* has a spring, *E,* soldered at one end, and the other carries a small projection that will engage the holes in the disk, *B.* The projection can be made by driving the metal out with a center punch, set on the opposite side.

The washer, *D,* is provided with a lead weight, *F,* and a ¼-in. stud, *G,* is soldered in the center. The stud has a ¹⁄₁₆-in. hole drilled through its center for the pin axle. The weight is made by filling the washer with melted metal, which when cold is removed and sawn in two. One piece is then

well; however, this can be adjusted by removing some metal from the end that is heavier with a file or tinner's snips, or a bit of solder may be stuck to the lighter end.

A disk, *B,* is cut from a piece of sheet brass, 1⅛ in. in diameter. Twelve ³⁄₃₂-in. holes are drilled at equal distance apart near the edge, and a ¼-in. hole is drilled in its stuck in the washer with shellac. The stud is ⅞ in. long with the upper part, about ¼ in. in length, filed, or turned down, smaller, and threaded. Just below the thread, or on the shoulder, the body is filed square to fit a square hole filed in the face of washer *C* carrying the spring. This square hole and stud end are necessary for both washers to turn together.

The dial can be made of a piece of thick cardboard, or thin wood, with the numbers 1 to 12 painted on, like a clock face. A pin, ¹⁄₁₆ in. in diameter, or an ordinary large pin, is run through the center so that it will project on the face side on which the hand is to revolve.

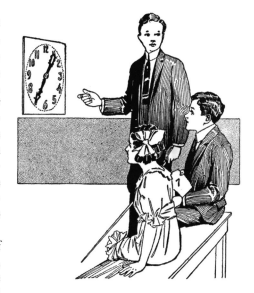

A NUMBER IS MENTIONED AND THE PERFORMER GIVES THE WASHERS A TWIST TO SET THE CONCEALED WEIGHT SO THAT THE HAND WHEN HUNG ON THE DIAL WILL BE DRAWN TO POINT OUT THE NUMBER SELECTED.

The washer *D* with the weight is placed on the rear side of the hand with the fixed stud running through the hole in the center of the hand; then the washer *C* is placed on the square part of the stud, and the nut, *J*, which should have a round, knurled edge, is turned on the threads. This will cause the projection on the spring *E* to engage one of the small holes on the disk *B*. In turning the two washers, *C* and *D*, with the thumb and first finger of the right hand, the projection snapping into the holes of the disk *B* can be felt. The hand is placed on the pin of the clock face, and the washers are turned so that the weight will make it point to 12. Scratch a mark on the hand at *H*. Also mark a line on the front washer at this point. These lines are necessary, as they enable the performer to know how many holes to snap the spring over to have the hand point at any desired number.

By reversing the hand it will point to a different number; for instance, if set for 8 and put on the pin backward, it will point to 4, and so on with other settings. The dial can be held in the hand, hung on a stand, or fastened to a wall, and can be used to the day of the week, time of day, cards selected, etc. The audience can call for any number on the clock face, and the setting of the disks is an easy matter while holding the hand, or pointer, in the hands, so that it cannot be detected.

— THE MYSTIC CLIMBING RING —

The performer hands out a wand for examination and borrows a finger ring. He holds the wand in his hand, point upward, and drops the ring on it. Then he makes hypnotizing passes over the wand with the other hand, and causes the ring to climb toward the top, stop at any place desired, pass backward, and at last fall from the wand. The wand and ring are examined again by the audience.

To produce this little trick, the performer must first provide himself with a round, black stick, about 14 in. long, a piece of No. 60 black cotton thread, about 18 in. long, and a small bit of beeswax. Tie one end of the thread to the top button on the coat and to the free end stick the beeswax, which is stuck to the lower button until ready for the trick.

After the wand is returned, secretly stick the waxed end to the top of the wand, and then drop the ring on it. Moving the wand slightly from oneself will cause the ring to move upward, and relaxing it causes the ring to fall. In the final stage remove the thread and hand out the wand for examination.

CRAZY CARDS

— THE "X-RAY" PACK OF CARDS —

This trick is a "mind-reading" stunt that is worked on a new principle and is very puzzling. A full pack of cards is shown and half of them are handed out, the other half being kept by the performer. A spectator is asked to select any card from those he holds, and insert it in the pack held by the performer, while the latter's eyes are closed or his head is turned. Without manipulating the pack in any way, the performer places it against his forehead and instantly names the card chosen by the spectator.

The cards held by the performer are prepared for the trick by cutting a slot ⅛ in. wide and 1 in. long in one corner of 25 cards, with the sharp point of a penknife, in such a manner that all the slots coincide. In presenting the trick the performer keeps all the prepared cards, and also one card that has no slot, the latter being kept on top of the pack so that the slots cannot be seen by the spectators. The performer's thumb is held over the slots when the bottom of the pack is shown. A spectator is asked to insert a card face down into the cards the performer holds in his hand. When this is done, the thumb is lifted from the slot as the cards are raised to the forehead, when the performer can look through the pack and see the index on the card the spectator has selected. After the forehead "stall," the performer announces the card selected. The trick is repeated by "fanning" out the cards and extracting the card named.

— THE ENCHANTED CARD FRAME —

Amystifying card trick, in which the performer makes use of the enchanted card frame shown in detail in the illustration, is performed as follows: A pack of playing cards is given to one of the spectators, who selects a card, noting the number and suit. The card is then placed in an envelope and burned by the spectator. The performer takes the ashes and loads them into a pistol, which he aims at a small frame, shown as empty, and set upon a table a few feet distant. The frame is covered with a handkerchief, and the pistol is fired at a frame. On removing the handkerchief the selected and destroyed card appears in the frame, from which it is taken at the back.

The trick is performed as follows: A forced deck is prepared having 24 like cards, and the backs of the cards are held to the spectators when a card is selected. The frame is made of molding 2 in. wide, mitered at the corners, and of the size indicated, the opening being 6⅜ by 7½ in. The general views of the frame in normal position and inverted are shown in *Figs. 1* and *5*. A pocket is cut in the lower edge of the frame at the back,

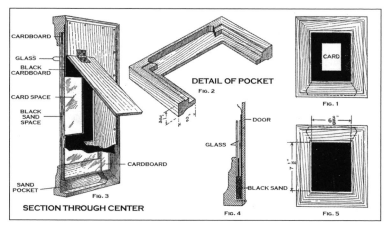

A POCKET IS CUT INTO THE FRAME AND FILLED WITH BLACK SAND,
OBSCURING THE CARD WHEN THE FRAME IS INVERTED.

as shown in detail in *Fig. 2.* A pane of glass is fitted into the frame, and on the three edges other than the one having a pocket, ⅛ in. thick strips of cardboard are glued as a bearing for the second piece of glass, as shown in *Fig. 4.* The back of the frame is fitted with a cover of thin wood, and a hinged door is arranged in the center of the back, as shown in *Fig. 3.*

A mat of black cardboard is fitted into the frame to form a background behind the card, *Fig. 1.* The pocket at the bottom is filled with black sand—that used by sign painters is satisfactory—and the frame is ready to receive the card for the performance of the trick. One of the cards from the forced deck is placed in the frame. By inverting the latter the sand is caused to run between the glass partitions, concealing the card on the black mat behind it. In this condition it is exhibited to the spectators and then placed upon the table. A handkerchief is thrown over it. The pistol is one of the toy variety and a cap is fired in it. In picking up the frame the performer turns it over, while removing the handkerchief, so that the black sand runs back into the pocket in the frame.

— A Magic Change Card —

Procure two cards, the 5 of diamonds and the 5 of spades, for example. Bend each exactly in the center, with the face of the cards in, and then paste

A CARD HAVING TWO FACES, EITHER OF WHICH CAN BE SHOWN TO THE AUDIENCE INSTANTLY.

any card on the back, with its face against the two ends of the bent cards. The two opposite ends will then have their backs together, and these are also pasted. The illustration clearly shows this arrangement.

To perform the trick pick up this card, which is placed in the pack beforehand, and show to the audience both the front and back of the card, being sure to keep the center part flat against one end or the other, then pass the hand over the card, and in doing so catch the center part and turn it over. The card can be changed back again in the same manner.

— Two Effective Card Tricks —

The first trick involves the use of four cards, which are "fanned" out to show a corresponding number of kings. The performer repeats the magical "abracadabra," and, presto! The same hand has changed to four aces when it is again displayed—a third pass, and only blank cards are shown. Six cards are required for this trick, three of which are unprepared, the other three being "prepared." The three unprepared cards are the king, ace, and blank card shown in *Fig. 1*. The three other cards are prepared by pasting a part of the remaining three kings over a corner of the aces of their corresponding suits as shown in *Fig. 2*. In the presentation of this trick, the four kings are first displayed to the audience. The real king being on the top, the cards are fanned as in *Fig. 3*, so as to show only the kings on the corners of the other three cards. Then, the performer picks up the ace of spades, which has been left face up on the table, and announces that he will place it directly behind the king of spades, which he does. He then lays the king of spades on the table. The cards are then closed up and turned over so that the cards are held at

what is the top of the cards in the first presentation of the four kings. Then, the cards are fanned out to show the four aces, as in *Fig. 4*. The index numbers in the corners of the aces should be erased or covered up, otherwise it will be impossible to show the blank cards.

The manipulator now states that by placing a blank card, which he picks up from the table where the aces of spades are, the spots will disappear from all of the cards. The ace of spades is placed on the table, the blank card taking its place. The cards are then closed and fanned out, the hand showing four blank cards, as in *Fig. 5*.

In the second trick, an ace of diamonds is held in one hand and ace of spades in the other, but while held in full view of the audience, the cards change places. The prepared cards are made from two aces of diamonds, from which the corner index pips and letters have been erased. An ace of spades is also required, the center of which is cut from the rest of the card as indicated in *Fig. 6*, which shows the appearance of the three prepared cards. In presenting this particular trick, an ace of diamonds is

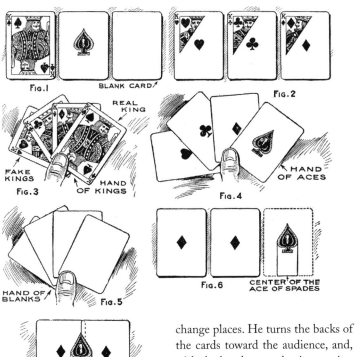

FIG. I BLANK CARD

FIG. 2

REAL KING

FAKE KINGS

FIG. 3 HAND OF KINGS

HAND OF ACES

FIG. 4

HAND OF BLANKS FIG. 5

FIG. 6 CENTER OF THE ACE OF SPADES

THE FAKE SPADE IS SLIPPED FROM ONE CARD TO ANOTHER

FIG. 7

held in each hand, but only one of them is visible to the audience, the other being concealed underneath the ace that has been cut from the card. The performer then announces his intention of making the cards change places. He turns the backs of the cards toward the audience, and, with the hands apart, begins moving the cards back and forth, bringing them a little closer to each other at each pass. Finally, when the edges touch, as in *Fig. 7,* the false center from the card is slipped over and onto the other card; this done, the cards are moved back and forth, gradually separating them, and their faces are again turned to the audience, when, to all appearances, the cards have changed positions.

— Mind-reading Effect with Cards —

Five cards are shown, and one person is asked to think of two cards in the lot, after which the performer places the cards behind his back and removes any two cards, then shows the remaining three and asks if the two cards in mind have been removed. The answer is always yes, as it cannot be otherwise.

To prepare the cards, take any 10 cards from the pack and paste the back of one card to another, making five double cards. Removing any two cards behind the performer's back reduces the number of cards to three, and when these are turned over they will not have the same faces so that the ones first seen cannot be shown the second time even though all five cards were turned over and shown.

— Mechanical Trick with Cards —

The following mechanical card trick is easy to prepare and simple to perform: First, procure a new deck and divide it into two piles, one containing the red cards and the other the black ones, all cards facing the same way. Take the red cards, square them up, and place in a vise. Then, with a plane, plane off the upper right-hand corner and lower left-hand corner, as in *Fig. 1*, about 1/16 in.

Then take the black cards, square them up, and plane off about 1/16 in. on the upper left-hand corner and lower right-hand corner, as in *Fig. 2*.

Next, restore all the cards to one pack, taking care to have the first card red, the next black, and so on, every

CARD TRICK

alternate card being the same color. Bend the pack so as to give some spring to the cards, and by holding one thumb on the upper left-hand corner all the cards will appear red to the audience; place your thumb in the center at top of pack and they will appear mixed, red and black; with thumb on upper right-hand corner all cards appear black. You can display either color called for.

Money Magic

— Trick of Taking a Dollar Bill from an Apple —

A rather pleasing, yet puzzling, deception is to pass a dollar bill into the interior of an examined lemon or apple. This can be accomplished in several ways, either mechanically or purely by sleight of hand. The mechanical method, of course, is the easier and just as effective. In performing, a plate with three apples is first exhibited, and the audience is given choice of any one for use in the experiment. The selected one is tossed out for examination and then returned to the performer, who places it in full view of the spectators while he makes the dollar bill vanish. Taking the knife he cuts the apple into two pieces, requesting the audience to select one of them. Squeezing this piece he extracts the dollar bill. The entire secret is in the unsuspected article—the table knife.

The knife is prepared by boring out the wooden handle to make it hollow. Enough space must be made to hold a dollar bill. The knife lies on the table with the fruit, the open end facing the performer. After the bill

THE DOLLAR BILL IS HIDDEN IN THE KNIFE HANDLE THAT CUTS THE APPLE.

has been made to vanish and the examined apple returned to the entertainer, he takes it and cuts in half. One of the halves is chosen, the performer impaling it on the end of the knife blade and holding it out to view. While still holding the knife he turns the blade downward and grasps the half apple and crushes it with a slight pass toward the knife handle end where the bill is grasped along with the apple, which makes a perfect illusion of taking the bill out of the apple.

As to the disappearance of the dollar bill, there are many ways in which this may be accomplished. Perhaps the method requiring the least practice is to place the bill in the trousers pocket, and then show the audience that the pocket is empty. This can be done by rolling the bill into a small compass, and pushing it into the extreme upper corner of the pocket where it will remain undetected while the pocket is pulled out for inspection. Other combinations can be arranged with the use of the knife, which is simple to make and very inexpensive.

— DROPPING COINS IN A GLASS FULL OF WATER —

Take a glass and fill it to the brim with water, taking care that the surface of the water is raised a little above the edge of the glass but not running over. Place a number of nickels or dimes on the table near the glass and ask your spectators how many coins can be put into the water without making it overflow. No doubt the reply will be that the water will run over before two coins are dropped in. But it is possible to put in ten or twelve of them. With a great deal of care the coins may be made to fall without disturbing the water, the surface of which will become more and more convex before the water overflows.

— A MYSTERY COIN BOX —

The effect of this trick is as follows: A small metal box, just large enough to hold a half dollar and about ½ in. high with a cover that fits snugly over the top, is passed out to be examined. When handed back to the performer he places it on the finger ends of his left hand and a half dollar is dropped into it and the cover put on. The box is then shaken to prove that the coin is still there. The performer then taps the box with his fingers and picks it up with the other hand and the coin will appear to have fallen through the bottom. Both the coin and box are then handed out for examination.

This seemingly impossible effect is made when the performer places the cover on the box. The box is resting on the fingers of the left hand and the cover is held between the thumb and forefinger of the right hand, but just before placing the cover on, the box is turned over with the right thumb, and the cover is placed on the bottom instead of the top.

The trick can be done within a foot of the spectators without their seeing the deception. It is a good plan to hide the box with the right hand when placing the cover, although this is not necessary.

— OLD-TIME MAGIC: CHANGING A BUTTON INTO A COIN —

Place a button in the palm of the left hand, then place a coin between the second and third fingers of the right hand. Keep the right hand faced down and the left hand faced up, so as to conceal the coin and expose the button. With a quick motion bring the left hand under the right, stop quick and the button will go up the right-hand coat sleeve. Press the hands together, allowing the coin to drop into the

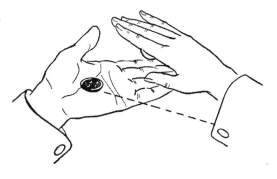

MAKING THE CHANGE

left hand, then expose again, or rub the hands a little before doing so, saying that you are rubbing a button into a coin.

— Coin and Tumbler Trick —

The accompanying sketch shows how a good trick may be easily performed by anyone. Lay a piece of heavy paper that is free from creases on a board or table. Secure three tumblers that are alike and stick a piece of the same heavy paper over the openings in two of them, neatly trimming it all around the edges so as to leave nothing of the paper for anyone to see. Make three covers of paper as shown in *Fig. 1* to put over the tumblers. Place three coins on the sheet of paper, then the tumblers with covers on top of the coins, the unprepared tumbler being in the middle. Now lift the covers off the end tumblers, and you will see that the paper on the openings covers the coins. Replace the covers, lift the middle one, and a coin will be seen under the tumbler, as the opening of this tumbler is not covered. Drop the cover back again and lift the other tumblers and covers bodily, so that the spectators can see the coins, remarking at the same time that you can make them vanish from one to the other. The openings of the tumblers must never be exposed so that anyone can see them, and a safe way to do this is to keep them level with the table.

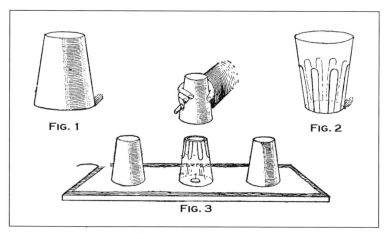

FIG. 1

FIG. 2

FIG. 3

THIS IS A GOOD TRICK.

SLEIGHT *of* HAND

— STRING-AND-BALL TRICK—

Stopping of a ball on a string at a desired point is a technique understood by almost every person, but to make one that can be worked only when the operator so desires is a mysterious trick. Procure a wooden ball, about 2 in. in diameter, and cut it into two equal parts.

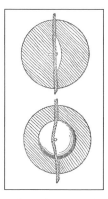

Insert a small peg in the flat surface of one half, a little to one side of the center, as shown, and allow the end to project about ³/₁₆ in. The flat surface of the other half is cut out concave, as shown, to make it ½ in. deep. The two halves are then glued together, and a hole is drilled centrally on the division line for a string to pass through.

To do the trick, hold an end of the string in each hand tightly and draw it taut with the ball at the top, then slacken the string enough to allow the ball to slide down the string. To stop the ball at any point, pull the string taut.

Before handing the ball out and string for inspection, push the string from each side of the ball and turn it slightly to throw it off the peg. This will allow the string to pass freely through the ball, and it cannot be stopped at will. To replace the string, reverse the operation.

— MAGIC SPIRIT HAND —

This magic hand is made of wax and given to the audience for examination, along with a board that is suspended by four pieces of common picture-frame wire. The hand is placed upon the board and answers, by rapping, any question asked by members of the audience. The hand and the board may be examined at any time and yet the rapping can be continued, though surrounded by the audience.

The secret of this spirit hand is as follows: The hand is prepared by concealing in the wrist a few soft iron plates, the wrist being afterward bound with black velvet as shown in *Fig. 1*. The board is hollow, the top being made of thin veneer (*Fig. 2*). A small magnet, *A,* is connected to a small flat pocket-lamp battery, *B*. The board is suspended by four lengths of picture-frame wire, one of which, *E,* is connected to the battery and another, *D,* to the magnet. The other wires, *F*

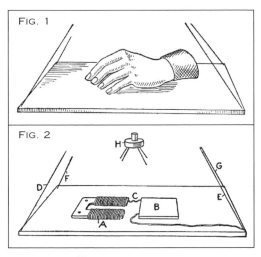

WAX HAND ON BOARD
AND ELECTRICAL CONNECTIONS

and *G,* are only holding wires. All the wires are fastened to a small ornamental switch, *H,* which is fitted with a connecting plug at the top. The plug can be taken out or put in as desired.

The top of the board must be made to open or slide off so that when the battery is exhausted a new one can be installed. Everything must be firmly fixed to the board and the hollow space filled in with wax, which will make the board sound solid when tapped.

In presenting the trick, the performer gives the hand and board with wires and switch for examina-

tion, keeping the plug concealed in his right hand. When receiving the board back, the plug is secretly pushed into the switch, which is held in the right hand. The hand is then placed on the board over the magnet. When the performer wishes the hand to move he pushes the plug in, which turns on the current and causes the magnet to attract the iron in the wrist, and will, therefore, make the hand rap. The switch can be made similar to an ordinary push button so the rapping may be easily controlled without detection by the audience.

— THE MAGIC THUMB TIE —

The prestidigitator crosses his thumbs and requests someone from the audience to tie them together with a piece of tape, as shown in the drawing. A hoop is then thrown at the performer and, to the surprise of the audience, it is seen hanging upon one of his arms, although his thumbs are still securely tied.

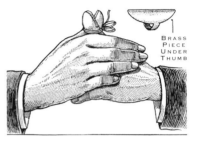

BRASS PIECE UNDER THUMB

"THERE ARE TRICKS IN ALL TRADES:"
CATCHING A HOOP ON THE ARM WITH THE THUMBS TIED TOGETHER IS ONE OF THE MAGICIAN'S TRICKS.

The explanation of this, like most other tricks of legerdemain, is simple. A piece of sheet brass or heavy tin is made into the ring shown in the small drawing, to fit over the right thumb. The broad portion is next to the ball of the thumb; when the thumbs are crossed, the ring is on the underside of the thumb and quite invisible to the person tying the knot. To minimize the possibility of detection, the ring is painted a flesh color. When the hoop is thrown, the performer quickly removes his thumb from the ring, catches the hoop on his arm and slips his thumbs back into the ring too rapidly to be detected.

POWERFUL ILLUSIONS

— CORKS-IN-A-BOX TRICK —

Procure a pillbox and a clean cork. Cut two disks from the cork to fit in the box and fasten one of the pieces centrally to the inside bottom of the pillbox with glue.

To perform the trick, put the loose disk in with the one that is fast and then open the box to show both corks. Close the box and in doing so turn it over, then open and only one cork will be seen. Be careful not to show the inside of the other part of the box with the cork that is fastened.

— Mystery Sounding Glass —

Procure a thin, tapering drinking glass, a piece of thin, black thread about 2 ft. long, and a long lead pencil. Cut a small groove around the pencil near one end. Make a slip noose in each end of the thread and slip one into the notch and place the thin glass in the other with the thread near the top. When the pencil is revolved slowly the thread will be wound on it slightly and it will slip back with a jerk that produces a ring in the glass. This may be kept up indefinitely. The movement necessary is so small that it is imperceptible. The glass can be made to answer questions by two rings for "yes" and one ring for "no."

— A One-Piece Bracelet Cut from a Calling Card —

A trick that will amuse and interest both old and young can be performed with a calling card, cigarette paper, or other similar material, cut with a scissors or knife, as indicated in the diagram. The card is shown, and the performer announces that he will pass his hand through the card, making a bracelet of it. He

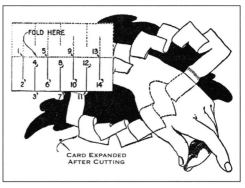

CARD EXPANDED AFTER CUTTING

IT IS HARD TO IMITATE A QUICK AND SKILLFUL PERFORMANCE OF THIS SIMPLE TRICK.

will, of course, be challenged, and proceeds as follows: He folds the card lengthwise and cuts through two thicknesses from 1 to 2, 3 to 4, etc.; then opens the card, and cuts from 1 to 13. By stretching the paper, as shown in the sketch, the hand may be passed through the card readily. The spectators are soon trying to duplicate the trick.

— AN ELECTRIC ILLUSION BOX —

The accompanying engravings show a most interesting form of electrically operated illusion consisting of a box divided diagonally and each division alternately lighted with an electric lamp. By means of an automatic thermostat arranged in the lamp circuit causing the lamps to light successively, an aquarium apparently without fish one moment is in the next instant swarming with live goldfish; an empty vase viewed through the opening in the box suddenly is filled with flowers, or an empty cigar box is seen and immediately is filled with cigars.

The electric magic boxes are shown and made of metal and finished with oxidized copper. But for ordinary use they can be made of wood in the same shape and size. The upper magic boxes as are shown in the engraving are about 12 in. square and 8½ in. high for parlor use and the lower boxes are 18 in. square and 10½ in. high for use in window displays. There is a partition arranged diagonally in the box as shown in the plan view, which completely divides the box into two parts. One-half the partition is fitted with a plain, clear glass as shown. The partition and interior of the box are rendered non-reflecting by painting them matte black. When made of wood, a door must be provided on the side or rear to make changes of exhibits. If the box is made large enough, or in the larger size mentioned, openings may be made in the bottom for this purpose. The openings can also be used to perform the magic trick of allowing two people to place their heads in the box and change from one to the other.

The electric globes are inserted as shown at LL through the top of the box, one in each division. When the rear part is illuminated, any article arranged within that part will be visible to the spectator looking into the box through the front opening, but when the front part is illuminated, and the back left dark, any article placed therein will be reflected in the glass, which takes the same position to the observer as the one in the rear. Thus a plain aquarium is set in the rear part and one with swimming fish placed in the front, and with the proper illumination one is changed, as it appears, into the other. When using as a window display, place the goods in one part and the price in

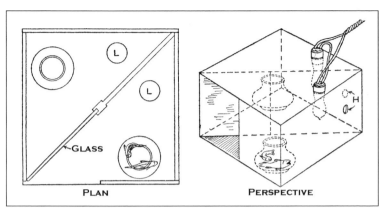

CONSTRUCTION OF MAGIC BOXES

the other. Many other changes can be made at the will of the operator.

Electric lamps may be controlled by various means to produce different effects. Lamps may be connected in parallel and each turned on or off by means of a hand-operated switch or the button on the lamp socket. Or, if desired, a hand-operated adjustable resistance may be included in the circuit of each lamp for gradually causing the object to fade away or reappear slowly.

Instead of changing the current operated by hand, this may be done automatically by connecting the lamps in parallel on the lighting circuit and each connected in series with a thermostatic switch plug provided with a heating coil that operates to automatically open and close the circuit through the respective lamp.

When there is no electric current available, matches or candles may be used and inserted through the holes *H*, as shown in the sketch.

— A TRUNK MYSTERY —

Doubtless every person has seen the trunk mystery, the effect of which is as follows: A trunk, mounted upon four legs, is brought out on the stage and proven to be empty by turning it all the way around to show that there is nothing on the back. Then pieces of plate

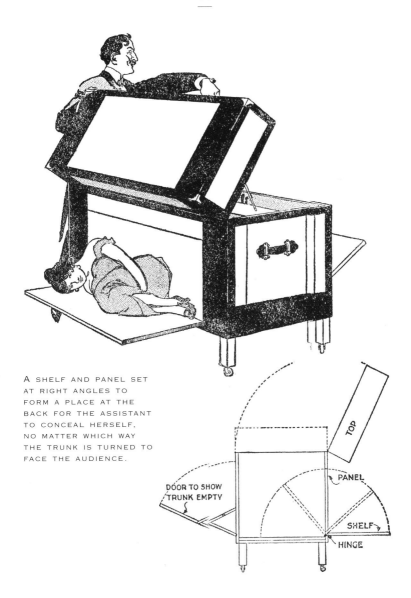

A SHELF AND PANEL SET
AT RIGHT ANGLES TO
FORM A PLACE AT THE
BACK FOR THE ASSISTANT
TO CONCEAL HERSELF,
NO MATTER WHICH WAY
THE TRUNK IS TURNED TO
FACE THE AUDIENCE.

TOP

PANEL

DOOR TO SHOW
TRUNK EMPTY

SHELF

HINGE

glass are placed along the back, sides, and front, the trunk is closed and given a swift turn and then opened. To the amazement of all, a lady steps out appearing to come from nowhere. The secret of this trick is very simple, and the trunk can be made up very cheaply.

In the back of the trunk there is a movable panel with a shelf exactly the same size as the panel attached to its bottom, forming a right angle. The corner of the right angle is hinged to the bottom of the trunk. The back panel can be turned in until it rests on the bottom of the trunk and, when this is done, the shelf part rises and takes its place, making the back of the trunk appear solid.

When the trunk is brought out upon the stage, the assistant is crouching on the shelf. The trunk can then be shown empty. This is all very simple until the trunk is turned around, when it takes skill not to give the trick away. As soon as the performer starts to turn the trunk around, the assistant shifts her weight on the panel, thus causing it to fall inward and bring the shelf up to make the back appear solid. The assistant is now in the trunk, and the back can be shown clear of any apparatus. When the trunk is turned to the front, again, the lady repeats the previous operation in the opposite direction, thus bringing her body to the back of the trunk again.

To make the trick appear more difficult, glass plates are made to insert in the ends, front and back of the trunk. In making the trunk, the back should be the same size as the bottom. Fit the piece of glass for the back into a light frame, similar to a window frame. This frame is hinged to the bottom of the trunk and is ½ in. smaller all around than the back of the trunk. This is so that the two pieces of glass can be put in the ends and also allow the back frame and glass to fall flush in the bottom of the trunk. A few rubber bumpers are fastened in the bottom of the trunk to ensure the glass falls without noise. The best way to work this is for the performer to let the frame down with his right hand while he is closing up the front with his left.

As soon as the trunk is closed, the assistant again shifts her weight to cause the panel to fall in. The trunk can be turned to show the back or whirled around and turned to the front again, then opened up, whereupon the assistant steps out, bows to the audience, and leaves the stage.

— A Mystic Fortune-teller —

Fortune-telling by means of weights striking glasses or bottles is quite mysterious if controlled in a manner that cannot be seen by the audience. The performer can propose two strikes for "no," and three for "yes" to answer questions. Any kind of bottles, glass, or cups may be used. In the bottles the pendulum can be suspended from the cork, and in the glasses from small tripods set on the table.

THE ROCKING OF THE TABLE IS CAUSED BY THE PRESSURE OF AIR IN THE BULB UNDER THE FOOT, THE MOVEMENT CAUSING THE PENDULUM TO SWING AND STRIKE THE GLASS.

The secret of the trick is as follows: A rubber tube with a bulb attached to each end is placed under a rug, one bulb being located under one table leg and the other near the chair of the performer set at some distance from the table where it can be pressed with the foot. Someone selects a pendulum. The performer gazes intently at it, and presses the bulb under his foot lightly at first. Then, by watching the swaying of the pendulum selected, he will know when to give the second impulse, and continue until the weight strikes the glass. As the pendulums are of different lengths they must necessarily swing at different rates per second. The impulses must be given at the proper time or else the pendulum will be retarded instead of increased in amplitude. A table with four legs is best, and the leg diagonally opposite that with the bulb beneath it must not touch the carpet or floor. This can be arranged by placing pieces of cardboard under the other two legs.

— Rubber-Band-Change Trick —

The trick of changing a rubber band from the first and second fingers to the third and fourth, if done quickly, can be performed without detection by the audience. The band on the first two fingers is shown to the spectator as in *Fig. 1*, with the back of the hand up. The hand is then turned over and the band drawn out quickly, as shown in *Fig. 2*, in a manner as to give the impression that the band is whole and on the two fingers. While doing this, quickly fold all the fingers so that their ends enter the band, and turn the hand over and let go the band, then show the back with the fingers doubled up. In reality the fingers will be in

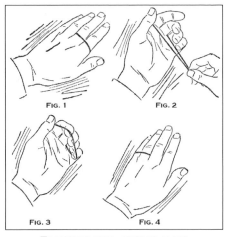

TRANSFERRING RUBBER BAND
FROM THE FIRST TWO FINGERS
TO THE LAST PAIR, LIKE MAGIC.

the band, as in *Fig. 3*, and the back will still show the band on the first two fingers. Quickly straighten out all the fingers, and the band will snap over the last two fingers.

— Old-time Magic: The Growing Flower —

This trick is performed with a widemouthed jar that is about 10 in. high. If an earthen jar of this kind is not at hand, use a glass fruit jar and cover it with black cloth or paper so that the contents cannot be seen. Two pieces of wire are bent as

shown in *Fig. 1* and put together as in *Fig. 2*. These wires are put in the jar, about one-third the way down from the top, with the circle centrally located. The wires can be held in place by carefully bending the ends, or using small wedges of wood.

Cut a wire shorter in length than the height of the jar and tie a rose or several flowers on one end. Put a cork in the bottom of the jar and stick the opposite end of the wire from where the flowers are tied through the circle of the two wires and into the cork. The dotted lines in *Fig. 3* show the position of the wires and flowers.

To make the flowers grow in an instant, pour water into the jar at one side of the wide mouth. The cork will float and carry the wire with the flowers attached upward, causing the flowers to grow, apparently, in a

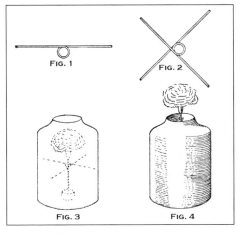

FLOWER GROWS INSTANTLY.

few second's time. Do not pour in too much water or you will raise the flowers so far that the wire will be seen.

— OLD-TIME MAGIC: BALANCING FORKS ON A PIN HEAD —

Two, three, or four common table forks can be made to balance on a pinhead as follows: Procure an empty bottle and insert a cork in the neck. Stick a pin in the center of this cork so that the end will be about 1½ in. above the top. Procure another cork about 1 in. in diameter by 1¾ in. long. The forks are now stuck into the latter cork at equal distances apart, each having the same angle from the cork. A long needle with a good sharp point is run through the cork with the forks and ½ in.

of the needle end allowed to project through the lower end.

The point of the needle now may be placed on the pinhead. The forks will balance, and if given a slight push they will appear to dance. Different angles of the forks will produce various feats of balancing.

— COMIC CHEST EXPANDER FOR PLAY OR STAGE USE —

A device used in an amateur vaudeville sketch with good effect, and that is interesting for play purposes and magic tricks of various kinds, is made of a 1/32-by-9-by-14-in. piece of sheet spring brass, rigged as shown. In the center, near the upper edge, a small pulley is soldered. At the center of the bottom edge a small hole is drilled. In it is fastened one end of a 4-ft. string that runs up through the pulley. The other end is fastened to a strap to fit around the leg just above the knee. At the two upper corners of the brass sheet two slots are cut to accommodate similar straps, as fastenings. When the wearer stands in a normal position the chest is as usual, but by straightening the body and slightly moving the strapped leg back, the brass sheet is bowed outward, giving the appearance indicated.

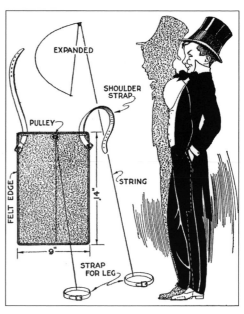

THE PERFORMER'S CHEST "SWELLS WITH PRIDE" WHEN HE DRAWS ON THE STRING BY SHIFTING HIS POSITIONS.

— A Trick "Letter" —

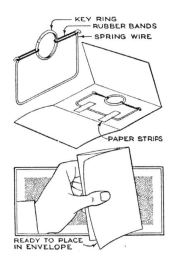

Endless amusement can be obtained from the simple device illustrated, which is attached to an ordinary sheet of letter paper, folded up and placed in an envelope. On opening the supposed "letter," the recipient gets something of a surprise when the ring revolves rapidly.

A U-shaped piece of spring wire is fastened to the paper by paper strips. An iron washer, or ring of the type shown, is held across the open part of the "U" by rubber bands. In use, the rubber bands are twisted so that as soon as the letter is opened they begin to untwist and the ring to revolve, causing it to whiz and whir as though there were something very much alive in the letter.

{ CHAPTER 2 }

THE SCIENCE
of FUN

AMAZING MOTORS

— A SIMPLE MOTOR CONTROLLER —

The controller described here is very similar in operation to the types of controllers used on electric automobiles, and its operation may be easily followed in the diagrammatic representation of its circuits, and those of a two-pole series motor to which it is connected, as shown in *Fig. 1*. The controller consists of six flat springs, represented as small circles and lettered *A, B, C, D, E,* and *F.* These make contact with pieces of narrow sheet brass mounted on a small wood cylinder, arranged so that it may be turned by means of a small handle located on top of the controller case. The handle can be turned in either direction from a point called neutral, which is marked *N.* When the cylinder of the controller is in the neutral position, all six contact springs are free from contact with any metal on the cylinder. The contacts around the cylinder in the six different horizontal positions are lettered *G, H, J,*

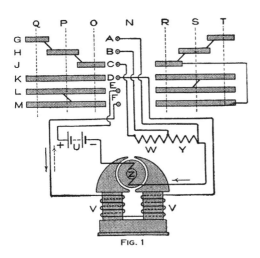

Fig. 1

DIAGRAM OF THE ELECTRICAL CONNECTIONS
OF A CONTROLLER TO A TWO-POLE
SERIES MOTOR.

If the cylinder was rotated to the position marked *O*, the circuit could be traced from the positive terminal of the battery *U*, as follows: To contact spring *E*, to strip of brass *L*, to strip of brass *M*, to contact spring *F*, through the field windings *V V*, to contact spring *D*, to strip of brass *K*, to strip of brass *J*, to contact spring *C*, through resistance *W* and *Y*, to armature *Z*, through armature to the negative terminal of the battery. Moving the cylinder to the position *P* merely cuts out the resistance *W*, and to the position *Q*, cuts out the remaining resistance *Y*. The direction of the current through the armature and series field, for all positions of the cylinder to the left, is indicated by the full-line arrows. Moving the controller to the positions marked *R*, *S*, and *T* will result in the same changes in circuit connections as in the previous case, except the direction of the current in the series field windings will be reversed.

K, *L*, and *M*. There are three different positions of the controller in either direction from the neutral point. Moving the cylinder in one direction will cause the armature of the motor to rotate in a certain direction at three different speeds, while moving the cylinder in a reverse will cause the armature to rotate in the opposite direction at three different speeds, depending upon the exact position of the cylinder. These positions are designated by the letters *O*, *P*, and *Q*, for one way, and *R*, *S*, and *T*, for the other.

The construction of the controller may be carried out as follows: Obtain a cylinder of wood, 1¾ in. in diameter and 3⅛ in. long, preferably hardwood. Turn one end of this cylinder down to a diameter of ½ in., and drill a ¼-in. hole through its center from end to end. Divide the circumference of the small-diameter portion into eight equal parts and drive a small nail into the cylinder at each division point, the nail being placed in the center of the surface lengthwise and perpendicular to the axis of the cylinder. Cut off all the nail heads so that the outer ends of the nails extend even with the surface off the outer, or larger size, end.

Divide the large end into eight equal parts so that the division points will be midway between the ends of the nails, and draw lines the full length of the cylinder on these points. Divide the cylinder lengthwise into seven equal parts and draw a line around it at each division point. Cut some ⅛-in. strips from thin sheet brass and mount them on the cylinder to correspond to those shown in *Fig. 1.* Any one of the vertical division lines drawn on the cylinder may be taken as the neutral point. The pieces may be mounted by bending the ends over and sharpening them so that they can be driven into the wood. The various strips of brass should be connected electrically, as shown by the heavy lines in *Fig. 1,* but these connections must all be made so that they will not extend beyond the outer surface of the strips or brass.

A small rectangular frame is made, and the cylinder is mounted in a vertical position in it by means of a rod passing down through a hole in the top of the

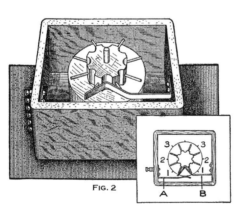

FIG. 2

UPPER-END VIEW OF THE CONTROLLER SHOWING THE MANNER OF ATTACHING THE SPRINGS.

rectangle, through the hole in the cylinder, and partly through the bottom of the rectangle. The upper part of the rod may be bent so as to form a handle. The rod must be fastened to the cylinder in some convenient way.

Make six flat springs similar to the one shown at *A, Fig. 2,* and mount them on the inside of the rectangle so that they will correspond in their vertical positions to the strips of brass on the cylinder. Six small binding posts mounted on the outside of the box and connected to these springs serve to make the external connections, and they should be marked so that they may be easily identified.

A flat spring, ¼ in. wide, is made similar to the one shown in *B, Fig. 2.* Mount this spring on the inside of the rectangle so that it will mesh with the ends of the nails in the small part of the cylinder. The action of this spring is to make the cylinder stop at definite positions. The top of the case should be marked so that the position of the handle will indicate the position of the cylinder. Stops should also be provided so that the cylinder case cannot be turned all the way around.

— Motor Made of Candles —

A tube of tin or cardboard, with an inside diameter that allows it to accommodate a candle snugly, is hung on an axle in the center that turns in bearings made of wood. The construction of the bearings is simple, and they can be made from three pieces of wood as shown. The tube should be well balanced. Pieces of candle are then inserted in the ends, also well balanced. If one is heavier than the other, light it and allow the tallow to run off until it rises; then light the other end. The alternate dripping from the candles will cause the tube to tip back and forth like a walking beam. It will keep going automatically until the candles are entirely consumed.

TALLOW DRIPPING FROM THE ENDS ALTERNATELY LESSENS THE WEIGHT OF THE ARMS AND CAUSES THE TUBE TO TIP.

— How to Wind Wire
on Electrical Apparatus —

Beginners are bound to find it difficult to reproduce in a home-made apparatus the mathematical regularity and perfection of the winding on the electrical instrument coils found in the supply stores. But they can achieve a professional and workmanlike finish with the help of a simple contrivance and a little care and attention to details

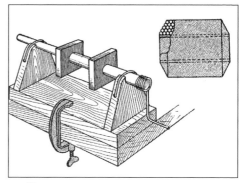

WINDING A COIL OF WIRE SO THAT THE LAYERS WILL BE EVEN AND SMOOTH.

before beginning. Experimental work suddenly takes on a new interest.

At the outset let it be stated that wire should never be wound directly on the iron core, not only because it cannot be done satisfactorily in that manner, but because the home mechanic often desires to remove a coil from a piece of apparatus after it has served its purpose. It is therefore advisable to make a bobbin, which consists of a thin, hard tube with two ends. The tube may be easily formed by wrapping a suitable length of medium-weight paper on the core, having first coated it with ordinary fish glue, excepting, of course, the

first 2 or 3 in. in direct contact with the core. Wind tightly until the thickness is from $1/32$ in. to $1/16$ in., depending upon the diameter of the core, and then wrap with string until the glue hardens, after which the tube may be sandpapered and trimmed up as desired.

Where the wire is not of too small a gauge and is not to be wound to too great a depth, no ends will be necessary. This is true if each layer of wire is stopped one-half turn before the preceding one, as indicated in the accompanying sketch, and is also thoroughly shellacked. With ordinary care magnet wire may be wound in this manner to a depth of over one-half inch.

The tube having been made ready—with or without ends as may be necessary—the small winding jig illustrated is made. All that is essential is to provide a suitable means for rotating by hand a slightly tapering wood spindle, upon which the tube is pushed. The bearings can be just notches made in the upper ends of two standards, through each of which a hole is drilled at right angles to the length of the spindle, so that some string or wire may be laced through to hold the spindle down. A crank may be formed by winding a piece of heavy wire around the larger end of the spindle. A loop of wire or string should be attached at some convenient point, so that the crank may be held from unwinding while adjusting matters at the end of each layer, or while making a connection. There should also be provided a suitable support for the spool of wire, which is generally placed below the table to good advantage. Much depends, in this sort of work, upon attention to these small details. After which it will be found that the actual winding will require very little time.

— How to Make a Toy Steam Engine —

A toy engine can be easily made from old implements that can be found in nearly every house.

The cylinder *A, Fig. 1,* is an old bicycle pump cut in half. The steam chest *D* is part of the piston tube of the same pump, the other parts being used for the bearing *B,* and the crank bearing *C.* The flywheel *Q* can be any small-sized iron wheel— either an old sewing-machine wheel, pulley wheel, or anything available. We used a wheel from an old high chair for our engine. If the bore in the wheel is too large for the shaft, it may be bushed with a piece of hardwood. The shaft is made of heavy steel wire, the size of the hole in the bearing *B.*

The base is made of wood, and has two wood blocks, *H* and *K,* ⅜ in. thick, to support bearing *B* and valve crank *S,* which is made of tin. The hose *E* connects to the boiler, which will be described later. The clips *F* are soldered to the cylinder and nailed to the base, and the bearing *B* is fastened by staples.

The valve motion is shown in *Figs. 2* and *3*. In *Fig. 2* the steam is entering the cylinder, and in *Fig. 3* the valve *B* has closed the steam inlet and opened the exhaust, thus allowing the steam in the cylinder to escape.

The piston is made of a stove bolt, *E, Fig. 2*, with two washers, *F*, and a cylindrical piece of hardwood, *G*. This is wound with soft string, as shown in *Fig. 3*, and saturated with thick oil. A slot is cut in the end of the bolt *E* to receive the connecting rod *H*. The valve *B* is made of an old bicycle spoke *C*, with the nut cut in half and filed down as shown, the space between the two halves being filled with string and oiled.

The valve crank *S, Fig. 1*, is cut out of tin, or galvanized iron, and is moved by a small crank on the shaft. This crank should be at right angles to the main crank.

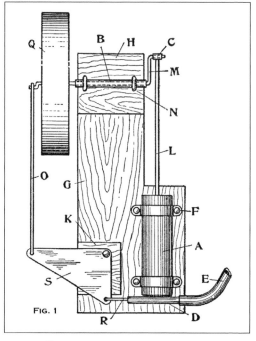

FIG. 1

THE STEAM ENGINE ASSEMBLED.

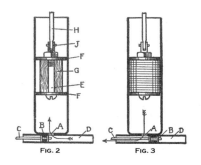

FIG. 2   FIG. 3

VALVE MOTION AND
CONSTRUCTION OF PISTON.

The boiler, *Fig. 4,* can be an old oil can, powder can, or a syrup can with a tube soldered to it, and is connected to the engine by a piece of rubber tubing. The heat from a small gas stove will furnish steam fast enough to run the engine at high speed.

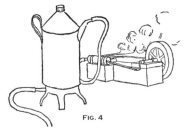

FIG. 4

ENGINE IN OPERATION.

— WORM GEARS FOR TOY MACHINERY —

Every youngster who owns a small battery motor delights in rigging up hoists, mills, and all manner of "machinery" for the motor to drive. Because these motors necessarily run at high speed and have only a very small torque, or turning force, it is always necessary to have some sort of speed-reduction gear. This is usually a system of large and small pulleys using strings as belts. A better arrangement is to use worm gearing, and the fine thing about this is the fact that a speed reduction of 100 to 1 is just as easy to obtain, or perhaps easier, than a 10-to-1 reduction. And because the speed is much reduced, the turning force is greatly increased. This means that a very small motor will, when provided with a worm-gear drive, operate mechanism it could

not even turn by means of the strings running over small V-pulleys.

In worm gearing, the driving member, or "worm," is nothing but a screw; a special kind of thread is used on large screws made for this purpose, but this is not at all necessary for small worms to drive toys. Any bolt or machine screw that has a good, full thread will do for the driving worm, provided that the proper gear, or worm wheel, can be obtained to serve as the driven member. The worm wheel must have a number of teeth equal to the desired speed ratio, one with 50 teeth giving a reduction of 50 to 1, when used with an ordinary single-thread screw.

The only special tool needed for cutting worm wheels is an ordinary machinists' tap. It should be of some

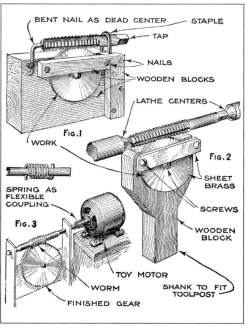

BENT NAIL AS DEAD CENTER — STAPLE

— TAP

— NAILS

— WOODEN BLOCKS

LATHE CENTERS

FIG. 1

WORK

SPRING AS FLEXIBLE COUPLING

FIG. 3

FIG. 2

SHEET BRASS

SCREWS

WOODEN BLOCK

TOY MOTOR

WORM

SHANK TO FIT TOOLPOST

FINISHED GEAR

TWO FIXTURES ARE SHOWN FOR CUTTING SMALL WORM WHEELS; THE FIRST IS FOR USE BY HAND AND THE SECOND WITH A LATHE. THE LAST PICTURE SHOWS HOW THE WORM DRIVE IS CONNECTED.

wire nail, and a large wire staple are the only other materials needed. *Fig. 2* shows how the work is done in a lathe; any lathe having a cross feed can be used. It may be remarked that although the shank of the wooden block may be held quite rigidly in the tool post, some kind of bracing block will have to be wedged under the forward end of the block to prevent chattering.

The blank for the worm wheel is merely a disk of sheet brass or soft iron, with a hole in the center. It can be turned out of the sheet, or filed if no lathe is handy. The diameter need not be determined accurately, unless the speed reduction must be exact. The rule for determining the diameter of the worm wheel is to multiply the pitch (distance between teeth) by the number of teeth wanted, and take $7/22$ of the result. Thus, for a 100-tooth wheel to fit a ¼-20 worm, the diameter would be

common size, such as ¼-20, and the worm or screw must, of course, be of the same pitch, in this case, 20 threads to the inch.

Two methods of cutting the worm wheel are illustrated. *Fig. 1* shows a fixture that can be made of three wooden blocks nailed together. A screw for holding the gear blank, a

100 x $^1/_{20}$ x $^7/_{22}$, or 1$^{13}/_{22}$ in. In practice, the diameter should be somewhere near 1⅝ in., the main thing being to get the disk as nearly round as possible. In the hand fixture, shown in *Fig. 1*, the feed is obtained by striking light blows on the heavy staple. The staple should at first be driven in just so far that the teeth of the tap scratch the edge of the blank. The tap is then revolved with a bit brace or wrench; when it has made 100 revolutions the blank will be scratched clear around. As the turning is continued, notice whether the tap teeth have worked into the scratches previously made or are cutting new ones. If the latter is the case, apply a little backward or forward pressure with the hand on the blank. As the turning is continued and the tap is fed in with an occasional blow on the staple, so that the teeth will revolve in the grooves previously cut, and not cut double-pitch.

Fig. 3 gives an idea as to how the motor is connected to drive the slow-speed shaft by means of the worm and wheel. There must be plenty of play between the worm and gear, as the simple teeth of this type will not work well if pressed tightly together. The worm in *Fig. 3* is made by turning or filing down a screw or bolt having the proper thread, so that journals are formed on the ends. The thread is also filed off for the sake of appearance, except at the center, where it meshes with the gear.

— Toy Sand Engine —

A toy sand engine that will provide the amateur mechanic with some interesting applications of mechanical movements and give endless entertainment to the children can be made from a few easily obtained parts. The machine is operated by the weight of sand, which runs from the bin at the top into the hods. As only one of the hods is filled at a time, one of the crossheads and connecting rods is forced down alternately, the small flywheel preventing the device from stopping on dead center. As the hod reaches the lowest point of its travel, one end of it comes into contact with the tripper, which overbalances the load and dumps the sand.

The hods are alternately filled with sand from the overhead bin by a slide valve that, when the engine is

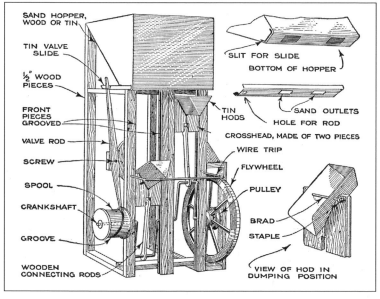

SAND HOPPER, WOOD OR TIN

TIN VALVE SLIDE

½" WOOD PIECES

FRONT PIECES GROOVED

VALVE ROD

SCREW

SPOOL

CRANKSHAFT

GROOVE

WOODEN CONNECTING RODS

TIN HODS

SLIT FOR SLIDE
BOTTOM OF HOPPER

SAND OUTLETS
HOLE FOR ROD

CROSSHEAD, MADE OF TWO PIECES
WIRE TRIP
FLYWHEEL
PULLEY

BRAD
STAPLE

VIEW OF HOD IN DUMPING POSITION

A TOY ENGINE, IN WHICH SOME WELL-KNOWN MECHANICAL MOVEMENTS ARE APPLIED. THE SAND HODS ARE AUTOMATICALLY FILLED FROM THE BIN BY A SLIDE-VALVE ARRANGEMENT, SIMILAR TO THAT USED ON STEAM ENGINES.

started, is automatic in action. The valve consists of a strip of tin with two openings that correspond to similar openings in the bottom of the bin. These openings are so spaced that when one hod is receiving sand, the opening on the opposite side is closed and the hod on that side is descending. The valve slides horizontally and is operated by a valve rod pivoted to a bracket on the frame. The valve is timed to open and close the sand openings by a grooved cam firmly secured to the end of the crankshafts. An old spool forms the basis for the cam, and an elliptical groove is cut into it large enough to take the end of the valve rod. The cutting and proportioning of this cam so as to have the slide valve open and close at the proper time will probably require more or less experimenting before the valve is properly "timed." The nearer the cam groove comes to the ends of the spool, the greater the travel of the valve rod. The upper end of the valve rod fits into a hole provided for it in the end of the slide valve. The valve should be "timed" so that it will remain open until the hod that is being filled with sand is halfway down. Also, the valve should be adjusted so that just before one hod is being tripped at the end of its travel, the other hod begins to receive sand.

— MAKING A STATIONARY ENGINE PROPEL ITSELF —

Different jobs for the stationary engine—first at the well, in the pasture, and then at the barn a half-mile away—prompted the farmer to rig the engine so as to eliminate the necessity of loading and unloading it into a wagon for each trip.

The photograph shows at a glance the details of this arrangement. The

LOADING EVEN A SMALL STATIONARY ENGINE FOR TRANSPORT TO DIFFERENT JOBS WAS TOO BOTHERSOME FOR THIS FARMER, SO HE MADE THE ENGINE HAUL ITSELF.

power of the engine is conveyed to the old mower wheel at the rear, which provides traction. A clutch pulley is keyed to the shaft of the rear wheel. The inner periphery of this is provided with studs that serve as gear teeth and engage with the link chain, to which power is delivered through a horizontal jackshaft connected to the engine pulley by a short belt. The engine is steered by manipulating the long lever shown, which is connected to the front axle by iron rods.

— A QUICKLY MADE TOY ELECTRIC MOTOR —

The illustration shows a small electric motor of such simple construction that it can be easily made from odds and ends found in any amateur workshop. Cut six strips, ½ in. wide and 3½ in. long, from an old tin can, and bend them together in a U-shape. This forms the magnet *A.* The outside piece should be a trifle longer than the others so that its ends can be turned over the other ends to keep them all in place. Screw this down on a small wood base. At one side of

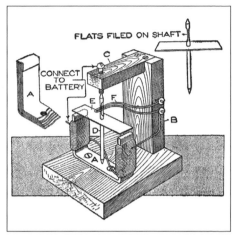

THE MOTOR IS CONSTRUCTED OF PIECES OF TIN, A NAIL, AND SOME WOOD BLOCKS.

the wood base, fix an upright, *B*, and on top, a light wood bracket, *C*, to take the upper bearing of the motor. The shaft *D* is simply a wire nail with the head filed off and filed to a point. Drive it through a 1½-in. length of the same kind of material as used for the magnet. This forms the rotating armature *E*.

Make a slight indentation with a center punch or strong nail, exactly in the center of the base portion of the magnet to take the lower end of the shaft. For the upper bearing, file

the end of a brass screw off flat and make a similar indentation with a center punch, or by a few turns of a small drill. This screw should be adjusted in the bracket until the shaft rotates freely with the armature just clearing the tips of the magnet. Wind about 40 turns of fairly thin cotton-covered copper wire—No. 24 or 26 gauge is suitable—around each limb of the magnet, first covering the latter with paper, to prevent the possibility of short-circuiting. The windings should be in opposite directions so that the connecting piece of the wire from one coil to the other passes across diagonally as shown in the illustration.

The brush *F* is formed by doubling up one of the free ends of the windings after removing the cotton covering and fixing it firmly with two screws to the side of the upright. After attaching, it should be bent until the outer end bears lightly on the shaft. Remove the shaft and at the point where the brush touched, file two flat surfaces on opposite sides of the nail in a direction at right angles to the longitudinal centerline of the armature. On replacing the shaft the brush should be adjusted so that it makes contact twice in a revolution and remains clear at the flat portions. Connect to a battery, one wire to the screw at the top of the motor and the other end to the open end of the windings. Give the armature a start and it will run at a terrific speed.

Gizmos *and* Gadgets

— How to Make an Experimental Lead Screw —

Often in experimental work a long narrow, parallel screw is desired for regulating, or moving, some part of the apparatus in a straight line. A simple way of making such a screw is to tin thoroughly a small straight rod of the required length and diameter. After wiping off all the surplus solder while it is still hot, wrap the rod with a sufficient length of bright copper wire and fasten the ends. This wire is then securely soldered in place by running the solder on while

A COPPER WIRE WRAPPED AROUND AND SOLDERED TO A STRAIGHT ROD FOR A LEAD SCREW.

holding the screw over a blue gas flame. To make the solder run freely, brush frequently during the heating with a small mucilage brush dipped into the soldering acid. An even pitch can be secured by winding on two wires side by side at the same time, the second one being unwound before soldering.

— BUILDING A SIMPLE RADIO RECEIVER —

This receiver is a popular one for reception from broadcasting stations; it gives excellent results for distances up to 250 miles and can be built at small cost. Under average conditions, telegraphic signals can be received within a radius of 1,500 miles, on wavelengths from 150 to 400 meters. The instruments are mounted on a 3/16-in. Bakelite panel, fastened to a wooden base by two angle irons. The variable condenser used is of .001-mf. capacity and is of the panel-mounting, 43-plate type. The variocoupler may either be bought ready-wound, or the knock-down parts are wound and assembled. The stationary Bakelite or cardboard tube is wound with 40 turns of No. 20 single cotton-covered magnet wire and six taps are taken off at approximately equal steps; these taps are led off to the contact points of the primary switch, as shown. The secondary, or rotor, of the variocoupler is wound with 34 turns of No. 26 single cotton-covered wire, 17 turns on each half, and the leads are brought out through the hollow shaft to a pair of binding posts. The tube socket is mounted on the base, at the left of the variocoupler; in front of the

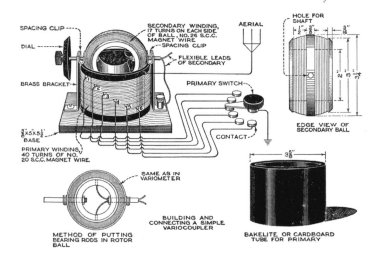

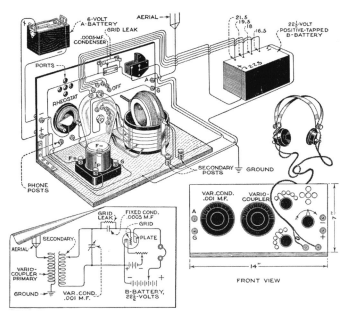

A SIMPLE AND EASILY MADE RECEIVER FOR BROADCASTING-STATION
WORK. IT HAS A WAVELENGTH RANGE OF 150 TO 400 METERS, AND
A WORKING RADIUS FOR TELEPHONE WORK OF 250 MILES. TELEGRAPH
STATIONS CAN BE HEARD AT A DISTANCE OF 1,500 MILES.
STANDARD INSTRUMENTS ARE USED THROUGHOUT.

socket, the 6-ohm battery-type rheostat is placed, and above it several holes are drilled through the Bakelite for observing the brilliancy of the tube filament when in operation. The binding posts for the earphones are located in the panel directly in front of the socket. The switch for the primary of the variocoupler is mounted on the panel, at the right of

the socket, looking at it from the rear. The switch lever is connected to the ground post. Above the primary switch is located the B-battery switch, which has the "off" point at the right; this switch is for the purpose of varying the B-battery voltage on the plate of the detector tube. The grid condenser is placed on the panel above the variocoupler; this condenser is of standard type with a capacity of .0005 mf. The grid leak has a resistance of 2 megohms, and is of the ordinary type, obtainable from any dealer in radio supplies. Six binding posts are placed on the panel, one for the aerial, one for the ground, two for the A battery, which is a 6-volt, 40- or 60-ampere-hour type, and the other two are for the earphones. The B battery is a positive-tapped 22 ½-volt unit of standard make. The taps are connected to the B-battery switch taps on the panel; the various voltages are plainly marked on the battery unit and should be connected to the switch in the order shown.

Use No. 18 insulated fixture wire for the circuit and carefully solder every connection. Bare, tinned copper wire, with varnished cambric tubing, or "spaghetti," slipped over it, can be used, but the fixture wire is cheaper and serves just as well. The detector tube used is a UV-200. The dials for the variable condenser and variocoupler are of standard make.

The proper aerial to use with this type of receiver is one wire, 125 to 150 ft. long, placed from 30 to 50 ft. above the ground. The phones should be wound for at least 2,000 ohms resistance. If desired, the instruments can be placed in a cabinet, to make a neat and compact set, at the same time protecting the various parts from dust. Many operators prefer the variable condenser in series with the aerial with a receiver of this type, instead of across the secondary, as shown in the diagram, as closer tuning may be had for the radiophone broadcasting stations. Try both ways to find out which best suits the aerial used, as under varying conditions the results will differ.

List of Materials

1 variable condenser, .001-mf. capacity
1 grid condenser, .0005-mf. capacity
1 UV-200 detector tube
1 tube socket
6 binding posts
2 angle irons
1 battery rheostat
1 Bakelite panel, 3/16 by 7 by 14 in.
1 wood base, ½ by 6 by 14 in.
1 variocoupler
2 switch levers
12 contact points
1 22 ½-volt B-battery unit
1 storage battery; 6 volt, 40 or 60 ampere-hour
1 pair 2,000-ohm phones

— An Electrical Dancer —

The modification of the well-known mechanical dancer shown in the illustration is based on the principle of the electric bell. While the amusing antics of the mechanical dancer are controlled by the hand, the manikin shown is actuated by the electromagnet.

The mechanism is contained in a box. It consists of an electromagnet with a soft-iron armature carried by a spring. A wire from the battery goes to the magnet. The other terminal of the magnet connects with the armature spring at $L1$. The spring is bent at a right angle at its other end, $L2$, and carries a platform, $L3$, strengthened by a smaller disk underneath. The dancer performs upon this platform.

A contact spring, S, is carried by the armature spring. A. Contact screw, C, is adjustable in its contact with the spring S. A wire runs from the contact screw to the binding post B, to which the other battery wire is connected.

The current keeps the platform in constant vibration, causing the dancer to "dance." By means of the screw C, the action of the current may be varied, and the "dancing" will vary correspondingly.

The figure is made of wood with very loose joints and is suspended so that feet barely touch the platform.

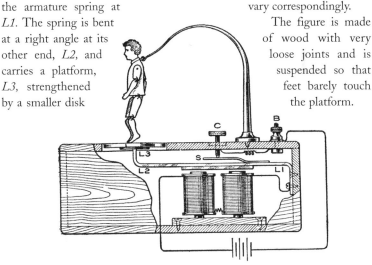

WHEN THE CONTACT IS MADE THE FIGURE DANCES.

— How to Make a Heliograph —

THE HELIOGRAPH AS IT IS USED BY NEIGHBORING BOYS TO SEND MESSAGES ON A CLEAR DAY BY FLASHING THE SUN'S RAYS FROM ONE TO THE OTHER. THE MESSAGES CAN BE READ AS FAR AS THE EYE CAN SEE THE LIGHT.

The heliograph used in the army provides a good method of sending messages using the reflection of the sun's rays. There are stations in the mountains from which messages are sent by the heliograph for great distances, and guides carry them for use in case of trouble or accident. The wireless telegraph delivers messages by electricity through the air, but the heliograph sends them by flashes of light.

The main part of the instrument is the mirror, which should be about 4 in. square, set in a wood frame and swung on trunnions made of two square-head bolts, each ¼ in. in diameter, and 1 in. long. These bolts are firmly held to the frame with brass strips, ½ in. wide and 3 in. long. The strips are drilled in their centers to admit the bolts, and then drilled at each end for the screw that fastens them to the frame. This construction is clearly shown in *Fig. 1*.

A hole is cut in the center of the frame backing and a small hole, not over ⅛ in. in diameter, is scratched through the silvering on the glass. If the trunnions are centered properly, the small hole should be exactly in line with them and in the center.

A U-shaped support is made of wood strips, ⅜ in. thick and 1 in. wide, the length of the uprights being 3½ in. and the crosspiece

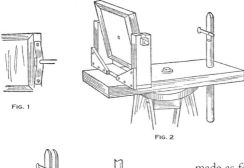

FIG. 1

FIG. 2

FIG. 3   FIG. 4

DETAIL OF THE PARTS FOR MAKING
THE MIRROR AND SIGHT ROD THAT
ARE PLACED ON A BASE
SET ON A TRIPOD TOP,
THE WHOLE BEING ADJUSTED
TO REFLECT THE SUN'S RAYS IN
ANY DIRECTION DESIRED.

for this bolt should be exactly below the peephole in the mirror and run through one end of the baseboard, which is ¾ in. thick, 2 in. wide, and 10 in. long.

At the opposite end of the base, place a sighting rod, which is made as follows: The rod is ½ in. in diameter and 8 in. long. The upper end is fitted with a piece of thick, white cardboard, cut ¼ in. in diameter and having a projecting shank 1 in. long, as shown in *Fig. 3*. The rod is placed in a ½-in. hole bored in the end of the baseboard, as shown in *Fig. 2*. To keep the rod from slipping through the hole, a setscrew is made of a small bolt with the nut set in the edge of the baseboard as shown in *Fig. 4*.

The tripod head is formed of a wood disk, 5 in. in diameter, with a hole in the center, and three small blocks of wood, 1 in. square and 2 in. long, nailed to the underside, as shown in *Fig. 5*. The tripod legs are made of light strips of wood, ⅜ in. thick, 1 in. wide, and 5 ft. long. Two of these strips, nailed securely together to within 20 in. of the top, constitute one leg. The upper unnailed ends are

connecting their lower ends a trifle longer than the width of the frame. These are put together, as shown in *Fig. 2,* with small brackets at the corners. A slot, ½ in. deep and ¼ in. wide, is cut into the upper end of each upright to receive the trunnions on the mirror frame. Nuts are tightly turned on the bolt ends to clamp the standard tops against the brass strips on the mirror frame. The cross strip at the bottom is clamped to the base with a bolt, 1½ in. long. The hole spread to slip over the blocks on the tripod top. These ends are bored to loosely fit over the headless nails driven partway into the block ends. One tripod leg is shown in *Fig. 6*.

The screen, or shutter, is mounted on a separate tripod and is shown in *Fig. 7*. Cut out two slats from hardwood, ⅜ in. thick, 2½ in. wide, and 6 in. long, and taper both edges of these slats down to ³/₁₆ in. Small nails are driven into the ends of the slats and the heads are filed off so that the projecting ends will form trunnions on which the slats will turn. Make a frame of wood pieces, ¾ in. thick and 2½ in. wide, the opening in the frame being 6 in. square. Before nailing the frame together bore holes in the side uprights for the trunnions of the slats to turn in. These holes are 1¾ in. apart. The frame is then nailed

together and also nailed to the tripod top. The shutter is operated with a key very similar to a telegraph key. The construction of this key is shown in *Fig. 7*. A part of a spool is fastened to a stick that is pivoted on the opposite side of the frame. The key is connected to the slats in the frame with a bar and rod, to which a coil spring is attached, as shown in *Fig. 8*. *Fig. 9* shows the positions of the tripods when the instrument is set to flash the sunlight through the shutter. The regular telegraph code is used in flashing the light.

To set the instrument, first turn the cardboard disk down to uncover the point of the sight rod, then sight through the hole in the mirror and adjust the sight rod so that the tip end comes squarely in line with the receiving station. When the instrument is

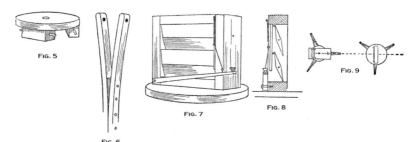

THE PARTS IN DETAIL FOR MAKING THE TRIPODS AND THE SHUTTER FOR FLASHING THE LIGHT, AND DIAGRAM SHOWING THE LOCATING OF THE TRIPODS TO DIRECT THE LIGHT THROUGH THE SHUTTER.

properly sighted, the shutter is set up directly in front of it and the cardboard disk is turned up to cover the end of the sight rod. The mirror is then turned so that it reflects a beam of light with a small shadow spot showing the center made by the peephole in the mirror, which is directed to fall on the center of the cardboard sighting disk. It will be quite easy to direct this shadow spot to the disk by holding a sheet of paper 6 or 8 in. in front of the mirror and following the spot on the paper until it reaches the disk. The flashes are made by manipulating the key operating the shutter in the same manner as a telegraph key.

— An Easily Constructed Ball-bearing Anemometer —

An anemometer is an instrument that measures the velocity of the wind. The anemometers used by the weather bureau consist of four hemispherical cups mounted on the ends of two horizontal rods that cross at right angles and are supported on a freely turning vertical axle. Because the concave sides of the cups offer more resistance to the wind than do the convex sides, the device is caused to revolve at a speed that is proportional, approximately, to that of the wind. The axle, to which the rotary motion is transmitted from the cups, is connected to a dial mounted at the foot of the supporting column. This dial automatically records the rotations. The reproduction of such a registering mechanism would be rather complicated. Hence, in the arrangement to be described, none will be used. Therefore, one of these improvised anemometers mounted on a high building will indicate by the changing rapidity of its revolutions only the comparative, not the real, velocity of the wind.

In constructing the instrument, straight, dished vanes will be used instead of hollow cups. The vanes operate almost as effectively and may be combined more readily into a sturdy rotating unit. A bicycle front hub is utilized to make a wear- and noise-proof bearing having minimum friction. Each of the four wings is formed from a piece of galvanized iron, measuring 4½ by 10 in., with one end cut to a curve as shown. Use tinners' rivets to fasten a

4-in. length of ¾- by ¹⁄₁₆-in. strap iron to each wing. Form each of the strips into a trough-shaped vane, measuring 2¼ in. from edge to edge—this being the distance between the spoke flanges of a bicycle hub. Some cylindrical object of suitable diameter will serve as a form for bending. Place the ends of the support strips between the spoke flanges and rivet them securely. The rivets pass through the spoke holes. Some trial-and-error may be required to ensure a symmetrical arrangement of the parts. Solder the curved end of each wing to the inner surface of the adjacent wing. Place a tin cap—a salve-box lid will do—under the upper locknut on the hub to exclude rain from the bearing.

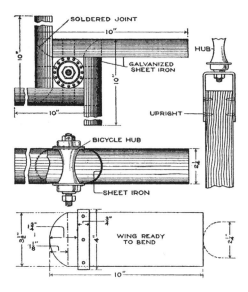

THIS ANEMOMETER IS MADE FROM GALVA-NIZED SHEET IRON, A BICYCLE HUB, AND A FEW IRON STRAPS. PRACTICE IN OBSERVING ITS MOTION WILL ENABLE ONE TO ESTIMATE FAIRLY CLOSELY THE WIND'S VELOCITY.

The supporting upright may be a heavy wooden rod or a piece of iron pipe. A yoke of 1 by ⅛-in. strap iron, held to the top of the upright with screws, is provided for the attachment of the hub. The locknut on the hub clamps it to the yoke. Apply a coat of metal paint to the iron parts that are exposed. Mount the device sufficiently high to give the wind free access to it from all directions. The curve at one end of each wing is an irregular one. Hence, its accurate construction involves a knowledge of sheet-metal pattern drawing. However, if it is made of a form similar to that shown it will fit sufficiently well to permit a good soldered joint.

— A Simple Motion-picture Machine —

The drum *A* is a piece of wood, 1¾ in. long and 1¹¹/₁₆ in. in diameter, supported on the end of a round stick, *B*. The stick can be made in one piece with the drum if a wood lathe is at hand, but a piece cut from a curtain pole and a lead pencil inserted in a hole bored in the end will answer the purpose. Be sure to make the diameter of the drum 1³/₁₆ inches.

Provide a base piece, *C*, ½ in. thick and 2 in. square, and fasten a piece of cardboard having a slit *E*, as shown. The cardboard should be 2 in. wide and 2½ in. high, the slit being cut ½ in. in width, ¼ in. from the top and ¾ in. from the bottom. A hole is bored in the center of the block to admit the standard *B* easily.

The next step is to provide the picture and attach it to the drum. A picture of a boy pounding cobble-

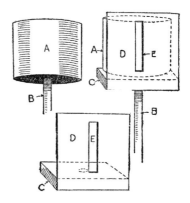

THE PARTS FOR MAKING THE REVOLVING DRUM FOR HOLDING THE STRIP OF PICTURES.

stones is shown in the sketch, in *F*, which should be made on a strip of paper 4⅜ in. long. This is glued or attached with rubber bands to the drum. The drawing can be enlarged in pen and ink. Or it can be reproduced as it is if a hand camera is at hand, and a print used on the drum.

THE DIFFERENT POSITIONS OF THE PICTURE WILL APPEAR IN ACTION WHEN TURNING WITH THE DRUM.

It is only necessary to put the parts together, grasp the base in one hand and turn the support *B* with the other. Then, looking through the slot *E,* the viewer will see the boy pounding the stones. Various pictures can be made and the strips changed.

— AN INTERESTING WATER TELESCOPE —

A water telescope is easy to make and will offer much pleasure in exploring plant or animal life in comparatively shallow water. The device is made by fitting a heavy glass disk into the end of a round metal tube, about 2 in. in diameter. The glass is fitted between two rings of metal, prefer- ably with a small flange set against the glass. Waterproof cement is used to fix the glass between the rings. To use the "telescope," rest it on the other side of a boat or other convenient place at the water, and set the lower end containing the glass under the water. Remarkably clear views may be had in this way.

— HOW TO MAKE A WONDERGRAPH —

An exceedingly interesting machine is the so-called wondergraph. It is easy and cheap to make and will furnish both entertainment and instruction for young and old. It is a drawing machine, and the variety of designs it will produce—all symmetrical and ornamental and some wonderfully complicated—is almost without limit. *Fig. 1* is a diagram of the machine shown in the sketch. This is the easiest to make and gives as great a variety of results as any other.

Fasten three grooved circular disks with screws to a piece of wide board or a discarded box bottom, so as to revolve freely about their centers. They may be sawed from pieces of thin board or, better still, three of

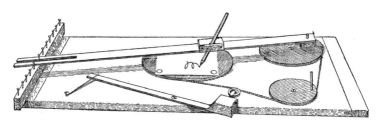

AN EASILY MADE WONDERGRAPH

the plaques so generally used in burnt-wood work may be bought for a small amount of money. Use the largest one for the revolving table *T. G* is the guide wheel and *D* the driver with attached handle. Secure a piece of a 36-in. rule, which can be obtained from any furniture dealer. Nail a small block, about 1 in. thick, to one end and drill a hole through both the ruler and the block. Pivot them by means of a wooden peg to the face of the guide wheel. A fountain pen or a pencil is placed at *P* and held securely by rubber bands in a grooved block attached to the ruler. A strip of wood, *MN*, is fastened to one end of the board. This strip is made just high enough to keep the ruler parallel with the face of the table, and a row of small nails are driven partway into its upper edge. Any one of these nails may be used to hold the other end of the ruler in

position, as shown in the sketch. If the wheels are not true, a belt tightener, *B*, may be attached and held against the belt by a spring or rubber band.

After the apparatus is adjusted so that it will run smoothly, fasten a piece of drawing paper to the table with a couple of thumbtacks, adjust the pen so that it rests lightly on the paper, and turn the drive wheel. The results will be surprising and delightful. The accompanying designs were made with a very crude combination of pulleys and belts, such as described.

The machine should move at a speed that will cause the pen to move over the paper at the same rate as in ordinary writing. The ink should flow freely from the pen as it passes over the paper. A very fine pen may be necessary to prevent the lines from running together.

The dimensions of the wondergraph may vary. The larger designs in the illustration were made on a table, 8 in. in diameter, which was driven by a guide wheel, 6 in. in diameter. The size of the driver has no effect on the form or dimensions of the design, but a change in almost any other part of the machine has a marked effect on the results obtained. If the penholder is made so that it may be fastened at various positions along the ruler, and the guide wheel has holes drilled through it at different distances from the center to hold the peg attaching the ruler, these two adjustments, together with the one for changing the other end of the ruler by the rows of nails, will make a very great number of combinations possible. Even a slight change will greatly modify a figure or give an entirely new one. Designs may be changed by simply twisting the belt, thus reversing the direction of the table.

If an arm containing three or four grooves to hold the pen is fastened

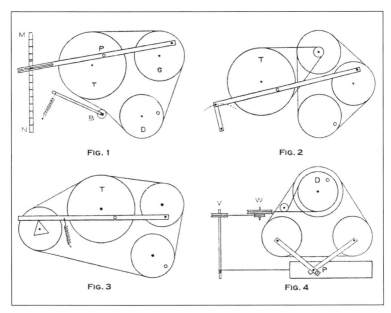

DIAGRAMS SHOWING THE CONSTRUCTION OF WONDERGRAPHS

SPECIMEN SCROLLS MADE ON THE WONDERGRAPH

to the ruler at right angles to it, still different figures will be obtained. A novel effect is made by fastening two pens to this arm at the same time, one filled with red ink and the other with black ink. The designs will be quite dissimilar and may be one traced over the other or one within the other according to the relative position of the pens.

Again change the size of the guide wheel and note the effect. If the diameter of the table is a multiple of the guide wheel, a complete figure of few lobes will result as shown by the one design in the lower right corner of the illustration. With a very flexible belt tightener an elliptical guide wheel may be used. The axis may be taken at one of the foci or at the intersection of the axis of the ellipse.

The most complicated adjustment is to mount the table on the face of another disc, table and disc revolving in opposite directions. It will go through a long series of changes without completing any figure and then will repeat itself. The diameters may be made to vary from the fraction of an inch to as large in diameter as the size of the table permits. The designs given here were originally traced on drawing paper 6 in. square.

Remarkable and complex as the curves produced in this manner are, they are but the results obtained by combining simultaneously two simple motions as may be shown in the following manner: Hold the table stationary and the pen will trace an oval. But if the guide wheel is secured in a fixed position and the table is revolved a circle will be the result.

So much for the machine shown in *Fig. 1*. The number of the modifications of this simple contrivance is limited only by the ingenuity of the maker. *Fig. 2* speaks for itself. One end of the ruler is fastened in such a way as to have a to-and-fro motion over the arc of a circle and the speed of the table is geared down by the addition of another wheel with a small pulley attached. This will give many new designs. In *Fig. 3* the end of the ruler is held by a rubber band against the edge of a thin triangular

piece of wood that is attached to the face of the fourth wheel. By substituting other plain figures for the triangle, or outlining them with small finishing nails, many curious modifications such as are shown by the two smallest designs in the illustrations may be obtained. It is necessary, if symmetrical designs are to be made, that the fourth wheel and the guide wheel have the same diameter.

In *Fig. 4*, *V* and *W* are vertical wheels that may be successfully connected with the double horizontal drive wheel if the pulley between the two has a wide flange and is set at the proper angle. A long strip of paper is given a uniform rectilinear motion as the string attached to it is wound around the axle *V*. The pen *P* has a motion made of two simultaneous movements at right angles to each other produced by the two guide wheels. Designs such as shown as a border at the top and bottom of the illustration are obtained in this way. If the vertical wheels are disconnected and the paper fastened in place the well-known Lissajou's curves are obtained. These curves may be traced by various methods, but this arrangement is about the simplest of them all. The design in this case will change as the ratio of the diameters of the two guide wheels are changed.

These are only a few of the many adjustments that are possible. Frequently some new device will create a figure that is apparently like one obtained in some other way. Yet, if you watch the way in which the two are commenced and developed into the complete design you will find they are formed quite differently.

The average boy will take delight in making a wondergraph and in inventing the many improvements that are sure to suggest themselves. In any event it will not be time thrown away, for, simple as the contrivance is, it will arouse latent energies which may develop along more useful lines in later years.

— A Perpetual Calendar —

It is necessary only to set this calendar the first of each month, by sliding the insertions up or down, to get the proper month or week. The calendar, as it is shown, is set for January 1916. Saturday is the first day and the Friday the seventh, and so on. It is not confusing and can be read either by the day or date. If the day is known it will show the date, and if the date is known it will show the day. The illustration clearly shows the parts, which can be cut from heavy paper or cardboard.

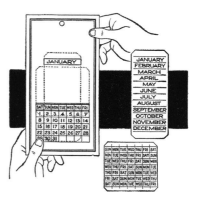

IT IS NECESSARY ONLY TO CHANGE THE SLIDING PIECES TO SET THE CALENDAR FOR EACH MONTH.

— Improvised Postcard Projector and Enlarging Camera —

An outfit that may be used for either projecting picture postcards or enlarging photographic neg-

atives was assembled as delineated in the illustration. An ordinary camera is required to provide the lens and bellows in combination with a dark box that can be built in the home workshop. The method of construction is this:

Make a box about 8 in. square out of ½-in. planed softwood stock. Nail the sides, but omit for the present the top and the bottom. The two openings thus left will be called the front and the back. Mount an 8-by-8-by-½-in. board, *D*, on the back with hinges, for a door.

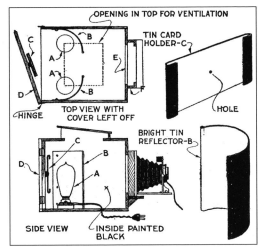

AN ORDINARY SMALL CAMERA, FITTED WITH THIS ATTACHMENT, BECOMES AN ENLARGING AND POSTCARD-PROJECTING CAMERA.

Provide a hook to hold it shut. Cut a square hole, of the same size as that of the opening in the back of the camera that is to be used, in another 8-by-8-in. piece, *E*. This will constitute the front board. This front board is cut so that it fits in between the sides of the box instead of on the ends, as does the back. In the top, cut a square hole for ventilation. A hood is provided over this hole to prevent light being thrown forward.

When using the arrangement as a projector or magic lantern, two

40-watt tungsten lamps, *A*, are required. Each lamp is mounted in a porcelain receptacle attached to the floor of the box with screws. A lamp cord, one end connecting the two lamps in multiple and the other fitted with an attachment plug, passes through a hole in the floor of the box. Form the two reflectors, *B*, of 8-by-7-in. bright tinned sheet-iron pieces, each having holes along one of its edges to allow for attachment. The reflectors are bent to a semicircular contour before mounting. The card holder is detailed in *C*. It is a piece of tinned sheet iron bent to the form shown so that it will hold a postcard. A hole is drilled in its center for a screw pivot. It can then be fastened to the center of the back door and can be turned into position for either horizontal or vertical pictures. A washer is inserted on the screw between the holder and the door. The thickness of the camera body having been determined, a slide is fastened to the front board, as in the diagram, to support this body.

Before it can be used as a projector it must be adjusted to operate with the camera of the type and size available. The adjustment must be made in a darkened room with one of its walls a white screen on which the image will be projected. This is done as follows: Remove the back from the camera and place the camera in the slide without extending the bellows. Open the shutter. Insert a card in the hold *C*. Light the tungsten lamps. Now move the front board, with the camera carried on it, back and forth within the box until the components are in focus. That is, until the most distinct image obtainable is reproduced on the screen. Then, illuminate the previously darkened room and nail the front board in the position thus determined. These

adjustments having been made, paint the box flat black inside and out. Everything should be painted black except the reflecting surfaces of the tin reflectors and the incandescent-lamp bulbs. The front board having been fastened, subsequent focusing can be affected by shifting the lens board of the camera longitudinally. The image of any sort of a picture that will fit in the holder can be reproduced. Colored postcards will project in their natural tints.

To make enlargements with the same box, a few minor changes are necessary. When used for enlargements the tungsten lamps, which are required for projection, are not used. They may, however, remain in the box and can be disconnected from the circuit by unscrewing them a few turns. The negative or film that is to be enlarged is held in the opening *E*. Where a film is to be reproduced, it is held between two pieces of glass that are fastened to the inside of the front board with small clips. If a glass negative is used, the two additional glass plates are unnecessary. If the negative does not fill the opening in the camera, a mask cut from heavy black paper will be required to cut off the light.

The light for the enlargement is

furnished by another tungsten lamp mounted in a porcelain receptacle that is screwed to a board that constitutes a base. This light source is moved about in the house until it is directly in back of the opening E in the front of the box and until the light is distributed equally over the entire negative. To focus, move the camera backward or forward. While focusing, use a yellow glass, or ray screen, to cover the lens. When focusing has been completed, the shutter is closed and the ray screen removed. Then stop down the lens to bring out detail, and expose.

— A HOMEMADE MAGIC LANTERN —

The essential parts of a magic lantern are a condensing lens to make the beam of light converge upon the slide to illuminate it evenly, a projecting lens with which to throw an enlarged picture of the illuminated slide upon a screen, and some appliances for preserving the proper relation of these parts to each other.

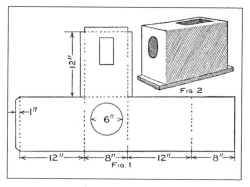

LANTERN HOUSE

The best of materials should be used and the parts put together with care to produce a clear picture on the screen.

The first part to make is the lamp house, or box, to hold the light. The illustration shows the construction for an electric light, but the same box may be used for a gas or oil lamp, provided the material is of metal. A tin box with dimensions close to those given in the diagram may be secured from your local grocer. But if such a box is not found, one can be made from a piece of tin cut as shown in *Fig. 1*. When this metal is bent at right angles on the dotted lines it will form a box as shown in *Fig. 2*, which is placed on a baseboard, ½ to ¾ in. thick, 8 in. wide,

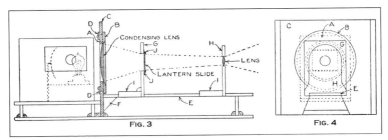

MAGIC-LANTERN DETAILS.

and 14 in. long. This box should be provided with a reflector located just in back of the lamp.

Procure a plano-convex or biconvex 6-in. lens with a focal length of from 15 to 20 in. and a projecting lens 2 in. in diameter with such a focal length that will give a picture of the required size. Or you can use a lens of 12-in. focus enlarging a 3-in. slide to about 6 ft. at a distance of 24 ft.

The woodwork of the lantern should be ½-in., well-seasoned pine, white wood, or walnut, and the parts should be fastened together with wood screws, wire brads, or glue, as desired. The board on which the condensing lens is mounted should be 16 in. wide and 15 in. high, battened on both ends to keep the wood from warping. The board is centered both ways. At a point 1 in. above the center, describe a 9-in. circle with a compass and saw the wood out with

a scroll or keyhole saw. If a small saw is used and the work carefully done, the circular piece removed will serve to make the smaller portion of the ring that holds the condensing lens. This ring is actually made up from two rings, *A* and *B*, *Fig. 3*. The inside and outside diameters of the ring *B* are ⅜ in. greater than the corresponding diameters of ring *A*, so when fastened together concentrically an inner rabbet is formed for the reception of the lens and an outer rabbet to fit against the board *C*. This is the board in and against which it rotates, being held in place by buttons, *DD*.

A table, *E*, about 2 ft. long, is fastened to the board *C* with brackets, *F*, and supported at the outer end with a standard. The slide support *G* and the lens slide *H* are constructed to slip easily on the table *E*, the strips *II* serving as guides. Small strips of tin, *JJ*, are bent as shown and fastened at the top and bottom of the rectangular opening cut in the support *G* for holding the lantern slides.

All the parts should be joined together snugly and the movable parts made to slide freely. When all is complete and well sandpapered, apply two coats of shellac varnish, place the lamp house on the bottom board behind the condensing lens, and the lantern is ready for use.

The proper light and focus may be obtained by slipping the movable parts on the board *E*. When the right position is found for each, all lantern slides will produce a clear picture on the screen, if the position of the lantern and screen is not changed.

Spy Lab

— A Simple Cipher Code —

Have you ever needed a secret code in which to couch the contents of a message intended for the eyes of one person alone? If you have, you will remember the difficulties that were experienced in making up the code and enciphering your letter. Here is a cipher code that may be mastered in a few minutes; one that is most difficult to decipher by any person other than those having the key words, and that is very simple when once understood.

It is commonly known as the "Play Fair" code and is in use in some of the foreign military services. It is a substitutive cipher that operates with one or more key words, two letters in the code being substituted for each two letters in the text of the message. In preparing the cipher code by this method the key words are selected by the correspondents and their location in the cipher square mutually agreed upon. A large square divided into 25 smaller squares is drawn, as shown in *Fig. 1,* and the letters of the key words entered into their proper spaces, the remaining spaces being filled by other letters of the alphabet. The key words must not contain duplicate letters. The letters *I* and *J* are considered as one and entered in the same space, the letter *I* being invariably used in enciphering.

Suppose that the two words "grant" and "field" have been selected for the key, the same to be entered respectively in the spaces on the first

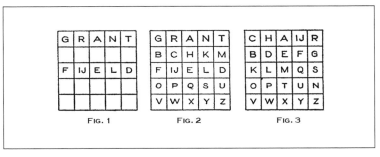

THE CIPHER CODE ILLUSTRATED IN THESE DIAGRAMS
MAY BE ADAPTED FOR WIDE USES BY THE SUBSTITUTION
OF APPROPRIATE KEY WORDS FOR THOSE SHOWN.

and third horizontal lines of the square. Then the basis of the construction would be as indicated in *Fig. 1.* Now fill in the remaining fifteen spaces of the square with other letters of the alphabet, beginning at the blank space at the left of the second line, entering the letters in rotation and not using any letter of the key words. The completed cipher would then appear as shown in *Fig. 2.*

The text of the message to be sent is then divided into groups of two letters each and the equivalent substituted for each pair. Where two like letters fall in the same pair the letter *X* is inserted between them and when the message is deciphered this additional letter is disregarded. If one letter is left over after the last pair, simply add an *X* to it and make a pair.

Suppose it is desired to send this message in the cipher: "Will you meet me as agreed?" Having three pairs of the same letter, it will be necessary to break them up by placing the letter *X* between them. The message will then be paired off as follows:

WI LX LY OU ME XE TM EA SA GR EX ED

The message may now be enciphered, after considering three simple rules for guidance: Every pair of letters in the square must be either in the same vertical line, the same horizontal line, or at the diagonally opposite corners of a rectangle formed by the smaller squares within the large square.

In the first case, *R* and *P* are in the same vertical line (the second). The next letter below in each case is substituted for *R* and *P,* which are *C* and *W.* If the pair consists of *K* and *Y* (fourth vertical), substitute *L* for *K* and go to the first horizontal line (the second), and thus substitute the next letters to the right, which are *C* and *K.* If the pair consists of *P* and *U* (fourth horizontal), substitute *Q* for *P* and then go back to the first vertical line (fourth horizontal) and substitute *O* for *U.* In the third case, *R* and *S* are at the opposite corners of a rectangle. Each letter of the pair is substituted by the letter in the other corner of the rectangle on the same horizontal line with it. Then *R* would be represented by *N,* and *S* would be represented by *P.* To illustrate further, *NE* would be represented by *AL; BZ* would be represented *MV; TP* by *RU.*

The message may now be enciphered, applying the rules:

> WI LX LY OU ME XE TM EA SA
> GR EX ED
> RP EY SN PO HD AQ MD QH QN
> RA QA LF

In sending this message, to make it more difficult for the inquisitive cipher expert, divide the substituted letters into words of five each and give him the added task of deter-

mining whether the cipher used is the transposition or the substitution method. The message ready to hand to the telegrapher would read:

> RPEYS NPOHD AQMDQ
> HQNRA QALFX

In deciphering a message the method is reversed. Take the message as received, divide the letters into pairs, and disregard the final *X,* which was put in to make a five-letter word. Then apply the key reversed. Practice it on the message at left to get the system with respect to letters occurring at the end of the lines. Where the letters of a pair are in the same vertical line, substitute for each the letter above; where they are in the same horizontal line, substitute the letter to left; where they are in the corners of a rectangle, substitute the letters at the opposite corners on the same horizontal line. To test the understanding of the system, the message given in *Fig. 3,* with the key words "chair" in the first horizontal line and "optun" in the fourth line, may be deciphered. The message to be deciphered is as follows:

> FQVUO IRTEF HRWDG APARQ
> TMMZM RBFVU PICXM TRMXM
> AGEPA DONFC BAXAX.

— DRAWER LOCKED
BY SECRET DOWEL PIN —

The secret lock shown in the drawing was fitted to a drawer whose lock was rendered useless by the loss of the key. Simply drill a hole through the under rail and into the panel of the drawer. Insert a loosely fitting hardwood dowel pin, or a steel nail into this hole. A thin metal button keeps the pin in position. To remove the pin and unlock the drawer, the clip is turned to one side that causes the pin to drop out. Not being easily discovered, such a lock may be applied, for additional

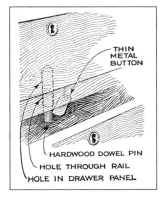

THIN METAL BUTTON

HARDWOOD DOWEL PIN
HOLE THROUGH RAIL
HOLE IN DRAWER PANEL

safety, to drawers whose locks are easily "jimmied."

— AN EFFECTIVE COMBINATION LOCK
EASILY MADE —

The combination lock described has been used for years on lockers and letter boxes in a large public building. The details are for a lock with three disks and, in *Fig. 4,* the use of two disks is suggested. The lock is made as follows: From a piece of 3/16- or 1/4-in. hardwood, saw out three disks, *A, Fig. 1,* from 1 to 4 in. in diameter, according to the size of lock desired. For one with 2-in. disks, as shown, cut slots, *B,* 1/2 in. wide and deep, in the edge

of the disks. For axles use 3/8- by 2-in. hardwood dowels, *C,* with a six-penny headless wire nail in one end, leaving about 1/4 in. of it exposed.

The case of the lock is shown in *Fig. 1.* It is made large enough to mount the disks, as shown. Fasten strips a trifle thicker than the disks around the edges of the inside surface of the lid. Place the disks in the positions shown, drilling small holes in the baseboard for the nail axles. The bolts *D* and the piece *E* are made of hardwood, fastened with a lap joint. On each side of the bar D fasten cleats F to hold it in position. The hand H moves in a slot in the lid, and is fixed to the bar, E.

The door, or lid, on which the lock is to be used is provided with openings, J, as shown in Fig. 3. The axles, C, project through openings, as bearings. When the windows J, through which the combinations are read, are made, place the ends of the bolts in the slots of the

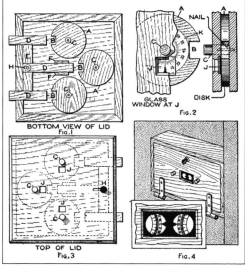

THIS WOOD COMBINATION LOCK GIVES GOOD SERVICE AND IS EASILY MADE.

disks and screw the lock in position. Mark on each disk the point exactly in the center of the window, enabling one to work the combination temporarily. To lock the device, push the handle to the left and turn the axles. To unlock it, turn the axles until the pencil marks appear in the middle of the windows, and throw the bolts.

Next make paper dials, K, of a diameter shown in Fig. 2. Divide the circumference into from 50 to 100 equal parts, according to the size of the dial, and draw radii, as shown.

Number at least every fifth point. Fasten one of the dials to the face of each disk, A, with small thumbtacks, placing the combination numbers selected exactly over the pencil marks made in setting the temporary combination. Verify the combination before locking it. Unless the slots in the disks are a little wider than the ends of the bolts, the combination must be very closely adjusted. A line on the glass or a point of a black paper will be an aid in setting the combination, as shown in *Fig. 2*. The combination may be changed by setting the dials in new positions. The large number of combinations possible makes it very difficult for someone to decipher the actual combination. For most purposes, two disks are sufficient in a lock of this kind.

— How to Transfer Drawings —

The young draftsman can avoid soiling drawings transferred with carbon paper by substituting a piece of unfinished paper, the surface of which has been covered with a thin coating of lead rubbed from the pencil. If an error is made in the tracing, or under pressure is applied with the hand, the resulting impressions may be removed readily with an eraser.

If a copy of a drawing is desired, and it is not necessary that the same relative left and right position be maintained, the original pencil drawing may be placed face downward on a sheet of paper and the back of it rubbed with a bone paper knife, or other smooth, rounded object. By going over the impression and making a reverse of it in the same way, a copy of the original in the same relations may be obtained.

— A Combination Electrically Operated Door Lock —

The illustration shows a very useful application of an ordinary electric door lock in the construction of a combination lock and alarm to be operated from the outside the building.

The three numerals, 1, 2, and 4, or any other combination of numbers constituting the house number on a door, are made of some kind of insulating material and fastened in place on a base of insulating fiber, or wood, about ¼ in. thick. Fasten the numbers by means of ordinary brass-headed tacks, as indicated by the black dots. The tacks will extend through the base a short distance so that the electrical connections may be made by soldering wires to them, as shown in the diagram, alternate tacks being connected together with the exception of three; for instance, *A, B,* and *C.*

The terminals of the leads that

are connected to alternate tacks are in turn connected to the terminals of a circuit composed of an ordinary vibrating bell, *D*, and battery, *E*. If any two adjacent tack heads are connected together (except tacks *A,* *B,* and *C*) the bell circuit will be completed and the bell will ring, which will serve as an indication that someone is tampering with the circuit. The person knowing the combination connects the tack heads *A*

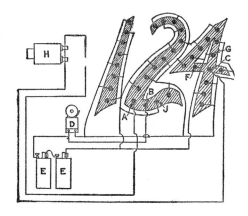

THE BRASS TACK HEADS HOLDING THE NUMERALS IN PLACE CONSTITUTE THE COMBINATION POINTS.

and *B,* and at the same time connects the tack head *C* with *F* or *G,* or any other tack head that is connected to the plus side of the battery, whereby a circuit will be completed through the lock *H* and the door opened. A metallic substance, such as a knife, key, or finger ring, may be used in making the above indicated connection, and there will be no need to carry a key for this particular door so long as the combination is known.

The base upon which the numbers are mounted and through which the points of the tacks protrude should be mounted on a second base that has a recess cut in its surface to accommodate the wires and points of the tacks.

The combination may be made more or less complicated, as desired, by connecting the tacks in different ways and by using a separate battery for the bell and lock. The circuit leading to the door lock, if there is one already installed, may be used and then no extra circuit is needed.

Such a device has been used on a private-desk drawer with entire satisfaction. The battery was placed in the back end of the drawer, and if it happened to fail, a new one could be connected to the points *B* and *J* so that the drawer could be opened and a new battery put in.

— SIMPLE MACHINE FOR TRANSMITTING WRITING —

An interesting and novel construction for amateur or boy mechanics is a telautograph or writing telegraph machine. The instruments, as shown, are duplicates with the exception of the placing of the rubber bands. They can be made in different sizes, and sat-

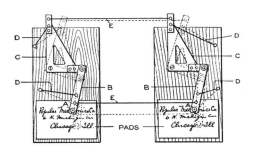

A MESSAGE WRITTEN ON THE PAD WITH A PENCIL IS TRANSMITTED TO THE OTHER PAD AT A CONSIDERABLE DISTANCE AWAY.

isfactory results were obtained by making the base 7 by 12 in., the arm *B,* 5 in. long and ¾ in. wide, and the triangle *C,* 6 in. by 3½ in. A hole is bored in the arm *B,* slightly smaller than the pencil to be used, and a slot sawed from the edge to hole so that when the pencil is forced into the hole it will be tightly gripped, as in *A.* The arm *B* is fastened to triangle *C* to move freely. The triangle is fastened to the base and can also move freely. The rubber bands *D* are stretched tightly to hold the moving parts in position. The strings *E* should be strong and stretched taut.

The larger diagram shows the instruments placed in parallel position. The smaller diagram shows how

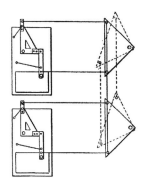

they can be placed one above the other. An unruled pad is fastened to the base of each instrument with thumbtacks. The operation may be traced by noting the successive action of the parts when the pencil on the pad at the left is moved in writing a message. The pivoted triangle communicates the action to the string *E*, which actuates the other triangle and its lever system. The rubber bands serve to steady the action. The instruments may be arranged a short distance apart for play or experimental purposes or set in rooms on different floors by making suitable pulley connections for the cords.

— USEFUL PERISCOPE THAT A BOY CAN MAKE —

Mention of periscopes is quite common in the reports from European trenches; such a device in a simple form can be made easily by boys who have fair skill with tools. The illustration shows a periscope that may be used for play and has other practical uses as well. In a store or other place where a person on duty cannot watch all parts of the establishment, such a device is convenient in that it will reflect persons entering the door. As a toy or for experimental purposes the periscope shown has

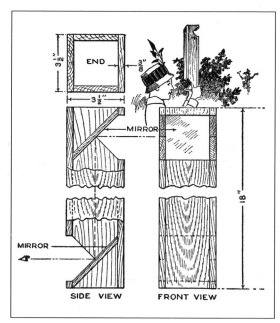

THIS SIMPLE PERISCOPE IS USEFUL BOTH FOR PLAY AND PRACTICAL PURPOSES.

many possibilities, and will appeal to youngsters.

It consists of a square box, 18 in.

long, and open at the ends. It is 3 ½ in. wide and made of wood, ⅜ in. thick. A mirror is fitted at an angle of 45 degrees near one end of the box or tube, as shown in the sketch. The front of the mirror is opposite a three-cornered opening in the box that extends across one side. The opposite end of the tube is also fitted with a mirror in the same manner, except that the front of the mirror faces to the opposite side of the box at which there is also an opening. In using this device, the user sights from the point indicated by the eye. The image is reflected in the mirror at the top and thrown onto the lower mirror, where it may be seen without exposing the head above the level of the lower opening. It is this application of reflection by mirrors that makes it possible for soldiers to see distant objects without exposing themselves to fire, by the use of the periscope.

— A Flashlight Telegraph on a Kite Line —

An ordinary pocket flash lamp is prepared in the following manner: A brass spring, as shown in the sketch, is bound tightly to the flash lamp with a cord. Two wires, one at each end, are twisted around the lamp's body, forming two loops at the top. The kite string is run through the loops and over the spring. The lamp is then placed near the kite. The ordinary pull on the kite string does not close the spring, but a sharp jerk will pull the string in contact with the push button and its slight pressure causes an instant flash of the light. By this method words may be spelled out in the telegraph code.

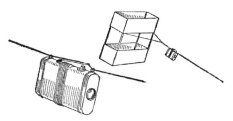

THE FLASH OF THE LIGHT ON THE STRING
MAY BE READ AS FAR AS IT CAN BE SEEN.

— A Handy Portable Lock —

Travelers who feel insecure behind the flimsy or disabled locks that may be found in many out-of-the-way hostelries—and in some city hotels—can use a detachable lock of the type shown in the drawing, and sleep with the assurance that anyone trying to force the door to which it is attached will arouse the occupant of the room. A ⅛-in. steel plate is cut to the form and dimensions given, and the two points are bent over and sharpened. Several slots are cut through the plate, and a metal wedge, or key, is provided to fit them. In use, the sharpened points of the lock are forced into the wooden door jamb against the stop strip; then the door

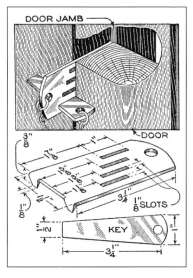

is closed, and the wedge pushed home tightly in the proper slot.

— ❖ ❖ ❖ —

{ CHAPTER 3 }

THE REALLY GREAT OUTDOORS

—

A CANOE ADVENTURE

— PONTOONS FOR STABILITY IN THE CANOE —

To sleep in a canoe has always been considered the equivalent of making an appointment with the coroner, because the craft is likely to capsize with a sudden shifting of weight. However, one may sleep aboard a canoe in safety and also stand upright to "play" a gamey fish, or make a difficult landing, by equipping the craft with pontoons.

Two false thwarts are first provided; these should make a snug fit between the inside of the gunwales, one at the position of the center thwart and the other at the rear off the forward seat. The length of these thwarts will depend upon the beam of the boat at those points and, as shown in *Figs. 1* and *2,* should come flush with the top of the gunwales. Angle-iron braces underneath hold the thwarts in place and make them readily removable; the guides are attached with screws down the exact center of each, the heads of the screws being countersunk. Eight iron straps are provided, made as shown in *Fig. 3*. Four are attached to each thwart, as in *Figs. 1* and *2*, the outer ones coming directly over the gunwales. A hole is drilled through

each side of the center straps to accommodate pins.

The slides, or outriggers, are made of good straight-grained oak, about 6 in. longer than the outside width of the canoe at the point used. Four of these pieces will be required, and they should be smoothed down to slide easily under the straps without binding. Holes to coincide with those in the center straps are drilled in each piece at intervals of 2 or 3 in., for holding the slides in either the extended or housed position. One end of each slide is mitered for fitting to the pontoon arms. The pontoon

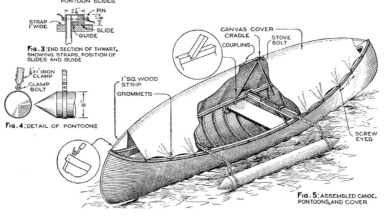

FIG. 1: PLAN

FIG. 2: MID-SECTION OF CANOE, SHOWING ARRANGEMENT OF PONTOON SLIDES

FIG. 3: END SECTION OF THWART, SHOWING STRAPS, POSITION OF SLIDES AND GUIDE

FIG. 4: DETAIL OF PONTOONS

FIG. 5: ASSEMBLED CANOE, PONTOONS, AND COVER

BY EQUIPPING AN ORDINARY CANOE WITH PONTOONS AND A CANVAS COVER, THE CANOEIST IS ABLE TO STAND UP WHEN "PLAYING" A GAMEY FISH OR MAKING A DIFFICULT LANDING; HE MAY ALSO SLEEP ABOARD IN SAFETY AND COMFORT.

arms are cut out and smoothed down to suit, and one end is mitered to fit the mitered ends of the slides, to which they are attached with iron angle plates, sunk flush with the wood, and fastened with countersunk screws. These plates must be flush so that they will not interfere with the operation of the slide in the straps. When the slides and pontoon arms are assembled, each will resemble a hockey stick in appearance, the pontoon arms being parallel with the sides of the canoe, as in *Fig. 2*. The pontoons are merely airtight cylinders made from fairly heavy galvanized iron, and provided with conical ends. The pontoons are held to the ends of the pontoon arms by means of iron clamps, as shown in *Fig. 4*. A hole is drilled in each clamp between the pontoon and the end of the arm to take a suitable clamping bolt, the tightening of which serves to hold the pontoons.

As a final touch for use when cruising, a canvas cover may be added as shown in *Fig. 5;* this drawing also shows the appearance of the canoe with the pontoons extended. A light, flexible wood strip is provided, a trifle longer than the distance between the bow and stern of the canoe, and a screw hook is turned into each end; a screw eye is inserted at each end of the boat to take the hooks on the end of the strip, as shown in the detail. For convenience in stowing, this strip is cut in two at the center, and the ends are rounded off for 2 or 3 in.; a coupling made from a short length of tubing is provided to slip over the rounded ends of the strip. A folding cradle, as shown in the drawing, supports the center of the strip and notches in the ends of the legs fit over the gunwales of the canoe, as in the detail. Light canvas is used for the cover, which fits over the whole canoe and buttons along the outside. This is accomplished by inserting grommets and small brass screw eyes at intervals in the edge of the canvas and the outside of the boat.

When under way and paddling along, the slides are pulled in and pinned in place so that the pontoons fit closely under the counter of the canoe. As they clear the water they will not impede progress. When it is desired to use them for any purpose, simply slide out a pair at a time to the distance required, and secure them in place with the pins. Only a slight tipping motion of the canoe will then bring one or the other of them into contact with the water, making the craft entirely stable and safe.

— Anchor for a Canoe or Small Boat —

Small craft, particularly those used for fishing or on streams where a current is encountered, should be provided with an anchor. The illustration gives details for making one that is simple in construction and inexpensive. It weighs about five pounds and is heavy enough for light craft up to 18 ft. long.

The main section was made of a piece of 1½-in. angle iron, 10 in. long. The flukes, or end pieces, were made of sheet iron, 2 in. wide and 8 in. long, bent at a right angle and riveted in place. The straps that hold the link, permitting it to swing freely, were made of band iron. The link was made of an old bicycle crank into which a ring was forged. It may be made of iron rod, forged into the desired shape and fitted with a ring. A convenient method of handling the anchor on a boat is to run the line through a pulley at the bow

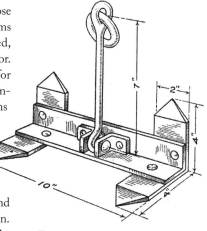

This homemade anchor is a practical addition to the equipment of a canoe or small boat, and weighs five pounds.

and fasten the end of it to a cleat, near the seat of the person handling the craft. Care must be taken, in a canoe or small boat, that sufficient line is provided to reach the bottom of the anchorage, as otherwise the craft may be overturned.

— A Simple Canoe Awning —

Canoeists are familiar with the disadvantages of their craft in the lack of protection from the burning effects of the sun. However,

a very neat and effective protection is afforded by an awning of the type shown in the drawing.

The awning consists of five pieces,

the canvas awning and four removable uprights. Naturally, no dimensions can be given, the awning being made according to the length and width of the canoe. The uprights are made of 1-in. square material, rounded at both ends to fit into ½-in. holes in the thwarts, or gunwales, and into the stretcher across the top. If it the owner prefers not to drill holes in the canoe to hold the awning supports, there are various types of sockets that can be bought or easily made. The canvas awning strip has a stretcher inserted through a hem at each end, and a light rope is tied to the awning as indicated. After the uprights are in position, the awning is stretched across them, and the ends of the ropes are made fast through conveniently located screw eyes. An awning of this or any other type positively should not be used in waters where danger of a sudden wind exists.

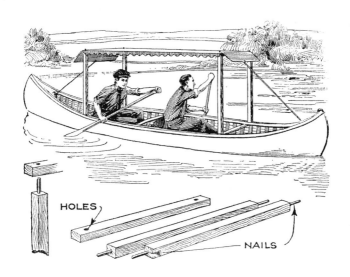

A NEAT AWNING FOR THE CANOE ADDS GREATLY
TO THE PLEASURES OF SUCH A BOAT. THIS AWNING CAN BE STOWED
AWAY COMPACTLY AND SET UP IN A FEW MINUTES.

— HOW TO MAKE A MOTORIZED CANOE —

A staunchly built canoe of sufficient length and beam may be converted into a light, serviceable, and convenient powerboat by the installation of a lightweight motor of about 2 horsepower. While the craft thus becomes less available for shallow waters and cannot be used on trips where portages are necessary, a power canoe has advantages in that longer trips may be undertaken with less regard for weather conditions. Greater speed and the fact that physical power need not be expended also increase the value and range of operations of such a craft.

Unless a motor of extremely light weight is procured, a canoe of frail construction and less than 16 ft. long is not likely to stand the jar of the driving mechanism. The canoe illustrated in the page plate is 18 ft. long, with a 36-in. beam, and strongly planked, decked, and braced. A canoe of even broader beam would tend to give more stability in rough water, and if heavy camping packs or other material must be transported, this factor should be observed particularly. Likewise, the depth and draft must be considered, because the carrying capacity and seaworthiness

of a canoe depend in part on these factors. The fitting of the various parts of the mechanism and accessories must be done with the aim of balancing the load evenly. If properly disposed, the weight of these parts should tend to lower the center or gravity of the canoe, thus rendering it more stable.

The actual work of installing the motor and fittings should be preceded by careful planning and the making of a full-size diagram of the stern portion of the canoe as rebuilt. Too much care cannot be taken in this work because, if it is neglected, the craft may be rendered unsafe, or the motor and fittings may not operate correctly. The motor should be set in the stern, as shown in the illustration, because this will permit the use of a minimum of shafting and other fittings that must be accommodated. The exact location of the motor may vary with canoes and engines of different types. This should be tested by placing the motor in the canoe and noting the effect on its balance in the water. For a canoe of the dimensions indicated, and a lightweight motor, 5 ft. from the stern is a satisfactory position.

The motor should be placed as low in the canoe as possible, allowing the flywheel and crank case sufficient clearance below.

A convenient method of operation is as follows: Place the canoe on boxes or sawhorses, taking care that it its properly supported about 2 ft. from the ground, or floor. Take measurements directly from the canoe, or part to be fitted, whenever convenient. Procure two sheets of paper, 30 in. wide and 7 ft. long; mark one "diagram" and the other "templates," and use the former for the full-size detail and the other for the making of templates for curved or irregular parts.

Begin the diagram by drawing the base line *AB, Fig. 3*. This is the lower line of the engine bed and the upper surface of the ribs. Draw the line *CD* perpendicular to the baseline, and 18 in. from the left end of the sheet. The point *C* is the center of the stern end of the driving shaft. The dimensions of parts are not given, except in special instances, because they must be obtained from the particular canoe and other parts entering into the construction. Indicate the layer of ribs *E*, the planking *F*, and the keel *G*. Using the template sheet, cut a template or

pattern for the curved stern. This may be readily and accurately done by fusing a straightedge to the keel and permitting it to extend to *A*. Rest the long edge of the sheet on the straightedge when fitting the template to the curve. Use the template as a guide in marking the curve on the diagram, as in *HJ*. The curve *K*, of the stern decking, may be indicated similarly.

Determine the distance the motor is to be set from the stern and indicate it by the perpendicular line *L*. Measuring from the baseline, indicate the height of the center of the motor shaft from the floor, as in *M*. This should be made as low as possible, permitting sufficient clearance for the flywheel and the crank case. Draw a straight line from *C* to *M*, which will thus indicate the center line of the driving shaft. This line is fundamental in determining the dimensions and placing of certain parts and fittings and should be established with extreme care. The size and exact position of the engine bed *N* may now be indicated. Its dimensions, given in detail in the perspective sketch, *Fig. 5*, are suggestive only. They may be varied in order to provide proper bearing on the floor, and so that the bolts holding

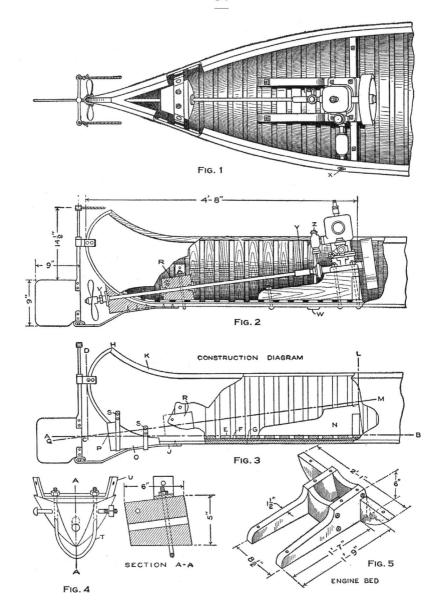

FIG. 1

FIG. 2

CONSTRUCTION DIAGRAM

FIG. 3

SECTION A-A

FIG. 4

FIG. 5

ENGINE BED

the bed may pass through ribs. The cross brace at the forward end is important and should be fitted carefully over a rib. The upper line of the engine bed must not be confounded with the centerline of the shaft, for in many engines they are on a horizontal line when viewed from the forward end, yet not necessarily so. The slant of the engine bed must be made accurately, as any deflection from the angle of the centerline of the shaft will disarrange the installation.

The shaft log O may next be indicated and a template made for use in guiding the bit when boring the hole for the shaft through it. The template used for the curve HJ may be altered by drawing the shaft log on it at the proper place. The point P, from which the bit is to be started when the shaft log is fixed into place, should be indicated and the centerline of the shaft, extended to Q, may then be used as a guide for the bit. If

the homemade type of bearing R is used, it should be indicated on the diagram. A metal bearing may be made, or a suitable one obtained from dealers in marine hardware. In the latter case it will probably be necessary to block up the bottom of the canoe in order to provide a flat, horizontal bearing surface for the bearing flange.

The rudder and other parts, which are not directly connected with the motive-power unit, may be indicated in detail on the diagram or be made from sketches of a smaller scale.

Paper patterns, made full size, offer a convenient method of outlining the parts of the engine, the rudder, and other irregular pieces. When the diagram is complete, measurements may be transferred directly from it without reducing them to figures. And, wherever possible, parts should be fitted to it.

A LIGHTWEIGHT, TWO-HORSEPOWER MOTOR INSTALLED IN A STAUNCH 18-FOOT CANOE WILL INCREASE THE RANGE AND UTILITY OF SUCH A CRAFT; THE CONSTRUCTION SHOWN IS SIMPLE AND WITHIN THE CAPABILITIES OF A CAREFUL NOVICE OF FAIR MECHANICAL SKILL. A VIEW OF THE STERN FROM ABOVE IS SHOWN IN FIG. 1. THE ENGINE IS SHOWN MOUNTED ON THE ENGINE BED, AND THE SHAFT BLOCK IS SHOWN NEAR THE STERN. A PARTIAL SECTIONAL VIEW IS SHOWN IN FIG. 2. THE RELATION OF THE ENGINE AND BED, SHAFT AND FITTINGS, SHAFT BLOCK, SHAFT LOG, AND RUDDER ARE SHOWN. THE CONSTRUCTION DIAGRAM, FIG. 3, IS DESCRIBED IN DETAIL IN THE TEXT. A LARGER-SCALE VIEW AND A SECTION OF THE SHAFT BLOCK ARE INDICATED IN FIG. 4, AND FIG. 5 ILLUSTRATES THE ENGINE BED WITH DIMENSIONS AND FASTENING HOLES.

The shaft log, shaft bearing, and engine bed may be made of oak or other strong hardwood. It's desirable to have the engine bed complete before an attempt is made to fit the shaft and its connections. It is made of 1½-in. stock, bolted together with lag screws and fixed firmly into the canoe with bolts. The heads of the bolts should be provided with cotton and red-lead packing, and care should be taken that the bolts pass through the ribs.

The shaft log should be fixed into place before it is bored. Bolts may be passed through it and fastened on the inside if there is room for drawing up the nuts in the stern. Large screws may be used to aid in the fastening and smaller screws may be used from the inside. The lower rudder support will also aid in holding the log in place, and the iron straps *S, Fig. 3,* will ensure its rigidity. This is an important point in the construction, because if the log is not fixed positively, the thrashing of the propeller will soon loosen it.

A detail of the shaft bearing *R* is shown in *Fig. 4.* The hole to receive the shaft must be bored accurately and the use of the template, as with the boring of the shaft log, is advisable. Flanged metal bearings are provided to take up the wear in the bearing block. The method of fastening the block, as shown in the detail view, ensures a rigid bearing with a minimum of holes through the bottom of the canoe. A U-bolt, *T,* binds the double angle brace *U* and the block firmly to the keel. The angles of the brace are fixed into the sides of the canoe with bolts, and a bolt at the stern end of the block supports it further. Place the block so that it will bear on the three ribs and fits to the curve of the canoe.

The rudder is made of sheet metal supported on a rod or pipe. Its general dimensions are shown in *Fig. 2.* The fan of the rudder is riveted to its supports and rests in a bearing strip of ¼- by 1-in. strap iron, which is shaped as a guard for the propeller. The upper bearing of the rudder post is formed from a strip of iron, bolted to the stern, and the upper guide bar, to which the ropes are attached, is cut from an iron strip.

The propeller is 8 in. in diameter, but may be installed of a size suitable to the power, speed, and type of the motor used. The stuffing box *V, Fig. 2,* the bearings for the bearing block *R,* the intake strainer W, the exhaust outlet *X, Fig. 1,* and the shaft coupling *Y* are all of manufactured types that may be purchased from marine-supply houses.

The intake strainer *W* is placed in the bottom directly below the pump *Z*. The exhaust outlet *X* is placed above the waterline, and a muffler should be installed to avoid noise from the exhaust explosions. The exhaust may be conducted under water or to a point near the stern. No indication is given for the placing of the gasoline tank, the supply pipes, electrical-energy source, and wiring. The tank may be placed in the stern of the canoe high enough to provide a good flow. A magneto may be used to give current for the sparking circuit, or batteries may be provided. They may be placed at any point convenient and should be encased in a waterproof container.

In assembling the parts care must be taken not to wrench the shaft or other pieces out of line. In general, it is wise to fix nonadjustable parts solidly when they are fitted into place. This applies particularly to the engine bed and the shaft log. The bearing block may be adjusted vertically by adding packing or by reducing the lower surface. The rudder and its fittings may be made in regular course but should not be fitted until the power unit and driving mechanism are finally in place. The propeller may be protected from possible injury by laying it aside until needed. All the openings in the hull through which bolts or other fastenings are placed should be packed with red lead or other waterproof packing. The working parts and finished metal surfaces should be oiled or greased thoroughly as the parts are assembled, and the unfinished metal parts painted with red lead. [Editor's note: Today we use alkyd or acrylic metal primer.] This will protect them from moisture and aid in the smooth operation of the mechanism.

Project Camp

— How to Make a Twine Hammock —

Cord hammocks may be made in two or more different ways, the knots being formed by the simple overhand tie, *Fig. 1*, the flat reef knot, *Fig. 2*, the Solomon's knot, *Fig. 3*, or by the triple throw-over, *Fig. 4*. Or they can be knotted by the process known as netting, *Fig. 5*, in which a special needle, or shuttle, is used.

In using any one of the first three methods of making the knots it is necessary to have cords arranged in pairs and long enough to reach from one end of the hammock to the other, allowing only sufficient length for the take-up in tying the knots and the spread of the meshes. The overhand knot is large and the Solomon's knot a little unwieldy, but is considered more beautiful when tied. The flat reef knot is small, is easily tied, and will not slip. The netting process has a good knot and has the advantage of a short single cord, because the meshes are made independently and the cord is carried on the netting needle.

It is a great advantage, when making a hammock with the simple overhand, the flat reef, or the Solomon's knot, to loop all the pairs of cords at the center about a rod, *Fig. 6*— which may handle— knotting from the center toward each end, one side

being tied and then the other. When the first pairs are being tied the opposite ends should be looped up together out of the way. Even half the length of a hammock makes a long cord to be drawn through each time a knot is tied. Each string can be wound about the fingers into a little bundle and secured with a half hitch, using the same cord, and left hanging, as shown in *Fig. 7*. Allow sufficient cord free to throw large

WHEN MAKING A HAMMOCK WITH THE SIMPLE OVERHAND, FLAT REEF, OR SOLOMON'S KNOT, LOOP ALL THE PAIRS OF CORDS AT THE CENTER ABOUT A ROD.

loops in the tying and to make about 10 additional meshes. About 3 ft. would be a good length to be left free.

It will be necessary to have 24 pairs of cords— 48 cords in all, each 18 ft. long—to make a hammock by the first two methods of tying the knots. Seine twine of medium-hard twist and 24-ply can be obtained from a store carrying sporting goods and is about the best material to use for this purpose. These pairs of cords are looped on the center rod, and the rod is anchored to a wall as shown in *Fig. 8*. Then begin by placing the mesh stick, or rather the mesh post, *Fig. 9*, between the first pair of cords, *A* and *B*, at the left end of the center rod, as

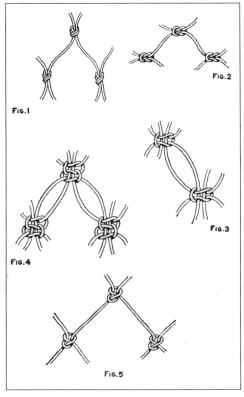

THE SIMPLE OVERHAND, FLAT REEF, SOLOMON'S KNOT, TRIPLE THROW-OVER, AND NETTING TIES.

in *Fig. 8* and *Fig. 6*. The simple device illustrated in *Fig. 9* is very useful for tying any one of the first three knots. The device needs no explanation other than the illustration. It will be seen that there are

two sizes on the top of the post; the smaller is for the first time across only. The mesh post should be of convenient height for a person when sitting on an ordinary chair. One foot rests on the base as the tying

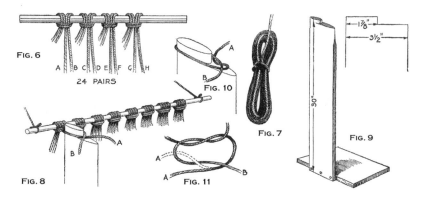

FIG. 6

A B C D E F G H

24 PAIRS

FIG. 10

FIG. 7

FIG. 8

FIG. 11

FIG. 9

THE MESH POST HAS TWO SIZES ON ITS UPPER END,
THE SMALLER FOR KNOTTING THE FIRST ROW OF MESHES AND
THE OTHER FOR THE REMAINING ROWS. THIS ILLUSTRATION
ALSO SHOWS THE MANNER OF TYING THE KNOTS.

proceeds, but there is no pulling over, as the tie draws both ways on the post. This also does away with the pull on the center rod.

The cord to the right, *B*, is taken in the right hand and thrown over the left cord *A, Fig. 8,* and is held by the left hand. The left cord *A* is then tucked down behind the right, as shown in *Fig. 10.* If the right cord goes over in making the first loop, the same cord *B* must also go over in the second throw, as in *Fig. 11,* in order to have a proper square knot that will not slip. The end of *A* is then tucked under *B,* as shown by the dotted lines. This makes a very serviceable knot for the hammock

but can be also used for other purposes. The knot is shown in *Fig. 2.* Draw it up tightly, very hard, for knotting is not worth much if it is not tied well.

In case the simple overhand knot is preferred, the mesh post is placed between the first pair as before, and cords *A* and *B* are brought to the front as in *Fig. 12.* But with this knot they are carried parallel into a large loop that is thrown over as illustrated, then tucked up through as indicated by the dotted lines. The thumb and first finger of the left hand now slide up to the point *P,* while the right hand pulls up the loop as it nears the finish. The thumb and first finger crowd the loop down hard against the mesh post. The small part is used for the first row across. The knot formed is shown in *Fig. 1.*

After tying the first pair of cords using the knot preferred, slip the first mesh so made off the tying post and place the post between *C* and *D,* which is the next, or second, pair. Tie the second pair and pass on to the third pair, which is *E* and *F.* Continue moving and tying until all the 24 pairs of cords have been similarly knotted in their first mesh. The last knotting will be the twenty-fourth pair, which is represented by the cords marked *Y* and *Z.* Instead of tying cords of the same pairs on the return trip across, one cord *Y* of the twenty-fourth pair is tied with one cord *X* of the twenty-third pair. The other cord *W* of the twenty-third pair is tied with the cord *V* of the twenty-second pair, and so on across the series.

On the second row of tying, the post is first placed between cords *Y*

and *X* and they are knotted together. But instead of tying about the small part of the post, the larger size is used. After cords *Y* and *X* have been tied, cords *W* and *V* are combined. It will be seen that this is tying the pairs together instead of combining the two cords of the same pair. The third time across the combinations are the same as in the first row. The large mesh is used on all but the first row. The alternations of rows is continued until the cords are tied to within 2½ ft. of the end.

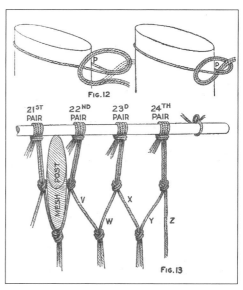

TYING THE OVERHAND KNOT AND HOW TO RUN THE FIRST AND SECOND ROWS ACROSS.

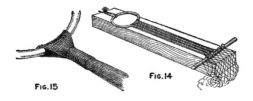

ATTACHING THE RINGS TO THE ENDS OF THE
CORDS AND THE BINDING NEAR THE RINGS:
ALL THE PAIRS OF CORDS ARE LOOPED
ABOUT A ROD IN THE CENTER, AND
THE KNOTS ARE MADE TOWARD THE ENDS.

Pull out the center rod, insert it in the second row of meshes, loosen the ends that were looped up, and begin the knotting of the opposite ends of the cords. When both sides are completed to within 2½ ft. of the ends, the center rod is removed and inserted in the last row of meshes. Another simple device will be found efficient, which consists of a 30-in. long board, three or more inches wide and 1 in. thick. Three nails are driven into the board at a slant, as shown in *Fig. 14,* to prevent the ring and rod from slipping off as the tying proceeds. One 1½-in. galvanized ring will be required for each end. The ring is attached to the single nail at the end with a string. This is better than just slipping the ring over the nail, because it is necessary to have a little more play in putting the cords through for the tying. The

distance from the rod to the ring should be 2 ft. The tie is made in pairs as before, one cord going under and the other over the side of the ring, using the flat reef knot. There will be a few inches of ends remaining after the tie is made and these are brought back to the main body of the cord and wound with an extra cord used for that purpose. The winding is started by looping the end of the extra cord or string about the whole bundle of cord together with the ends, pulling tightly and tying securely with flat reef knot. This is illustrated in *Fig. 15*. The winding should be about 1½ in. long where the turned-back ends are cut off. Each time the cord is wound about the bundle it should be looped through its own winding and drawn tightly. This is practically the buttonhole loop. Finish the winding the cord should be given a double looping through its own winding; then with an awl or other pointed tool, work a way through the under side of the other windings so that the end may be brought out farther back and pulled tightly to prevent unwinding when the pull comes on the hammock. Attach the ring to the opposite end in the same manner and the hammock is complete.

The edge can be bound the same as a tennis net, or a rope can be run through the outside meshes lengthwise, as desired. A very pretty effect can be obtained by knotting, in a similar manner to the body of the hammock, an apron fringe for the sides.

— HOW TO MAKE A NETTED HAMMOCK —

A good hammock should be about 12 ft. long, which includes 8 ft. of network and 2 ft. at each end of long cords that are attached to rings. Seine twine, of 24-ply, is the best material and it will take 1½ lb. to make a hammock. The twine comes in ½-lb. skeins and should be wound into balls to keep it from knotting before the right time. Two galvanized rings, about 2½ in. in diameter, are required.

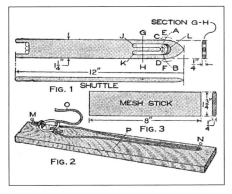

THE TOOLS NECESSARY CONSIST OF A NEEDLE, OR SHUTTLE, A GAUGE BOARD, AND A MESH STICK.

The equipment for netting a hammock consists of a wood needle, or shuttle, a gauge board for the long meshes at the ends, and a mesh stick for the regular netting of the main body of the hammock, all of which will be described in detail.

The shuttle is made of wood and is 12 in. long, 1¼ in. wide, and ¼ in. thick. The best material to use is maple or other hardwood, but very satisfactory ones can be cut from good grained pine. The sketch, *Fig. 1,* shows the general shape of the shuttle, one end being pointed and the other forked. Lay out the pointed end before beginning to cut down to size. Place a compass at the center of the end, and with a radius of 1½ in. describe the arc *AB*. With the intersections of this arc and the side lines of the needle, *C* and *D,* as centers, and the same radius, 1½ in., cut the arc *AB* at *E* and *F.* With *E* and *F* as centers draw the curves of the end of the shuttle. The reason for placing the centers outside the shuttle lines is to obtain a longer curve to the end. The curves can be drawn freehand, but will then not be so good.

The space across the needle at *GH* is divided into five ½-in. divisions. The centers of the holes J and *K* at the base of the tongue are 3½ in. from the pointed end. The opening is 2¾ in. long. Bore a ¼-in. hole at the right end of the opening, and three holes just to the left, as shown by the dotted lines. Cut out along the lines with a coping saw and finish with a knife, file, and sandpaper. Round off the edges as shown by the sectional detail. It is smart to bevel the curve at *L* so that the shuttle will wind easily. The fork is ¾ in. deep, each prong being ¼ in. wide. Slant the point of the shuttle and round off all edges throughout and sandpaper smooth.

The gauge board, *Fig. 2,* is used for making the long meshes at both ends of the hammock. It is a board about 3 ft. long, 4 in. wide, and 1 in. thick. An eightpenny nail is driven into the board 1 in. from the right edge and 2 in. from the end, as shown by *M,* allowing it to project about 1 in. and slanting a little toward the end; the other nail *N* will be located later.

The mesh stick, *Fig. 3,* should be made of maple, 8 in. long, 1¾ in. wide, and ¼ in. thick. Round off the edges and sandpaper them very smooth.

The making of the net by a specially devised shuttle is called "natting," or netting, when done with a fine thread and a suitably fine shuttle. Much may be done in unique lacework designs, and when coarser material and larger shuttles are used, such articles as fish nets, tennis nets, and hammocks may be made. The old knot used in natting was difficult to learn and there was a knack to it that was easily forgotten, but there is a slight modification of this knot that is quite easy to learn and to make. The modified knot will be the one described.

The shuttle is first wound by looping the cord over the tongue, as shown in *Fig. 4,* then bringing it down to the forked end and up to the opening on the opposite side. Then the cord is again looped over the tongue and returned to the fork or place of starting. Continue winding back and forth until the shuttle is full. The shuttle will accommodate from 20 to 35 complete rounds. If the shuttle is too full it crowds in passing through the meshes and delays the work.

Attach one of the galvanized rings by means of a short cord to the nail in the gauge board, as shown in *Fig. 2.* At a point 2 ft. from the lower edge of the ring, drive an eightpenny finishing nail, *N.* Tie the cord end of the shuttle to the ring, bring the shuttle down and around the nail *N.* Then bring it back and pass it through the ring from the underside. The cord will then appear as shown. A part of the ring projects over the edge of the board to make it easier to pass the shuttle through. Draw the cord up tightly and put the thumb on top of the cord *O, Fig. 5,* to prevent it from slipping back, then throw a loop of the cord to the left over the thumb and up over a portion of the ring and pass the shuttle

under the two taut cords and bring it up between the thumb and the two cords, as shown. Draw the looped knot tight under the thumb. Slip the long loop off the nail *N* and tie a simple knot at the mark *P.* This last knot is tied in the long loop to prevent looseness. Proceed with the next loop as with the first and repeat until there are 30 long meshes.

After completing these meshes, anchor the ring by its short cord to a hook or other stationary object. The anchorage should be a little above the level for tying the knots of the

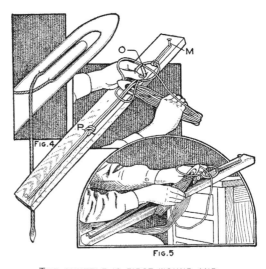

FIG.5

THE SHUTTLE IS FIRST WOUND AND THE LONG LOOPS AT ONE END FORMED OVER THE GAUGE STICK.

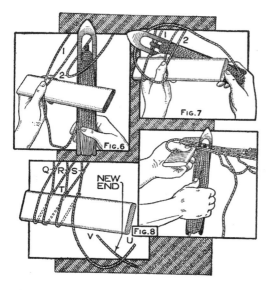

AFTER THE COMPLETION OF THE LONG MESHES, THE RING IS ANCHORED AND THE MESH STICK BROUGHT INTO USE.

the thumb down upon it in this position to prevent slipping. Pass the shuttle up through the loop 2 and draw that down to the mesh stick. Shift the thumb from the first position to the second. Throw the cord to the left over the thumb and about the loop 2, as shown in *Fig. 7*. Bring the shuttle under both of the cords of mesh 2 and up between the large backward loop and the cords of the mesh 2. Without removing the thumb, draw the knot up very tight. This makes the first netting knot. Continue the cord around the mesh stick, pass it up through mesh 3, throw the backward loop, put the shuttle under and up to the left of the mesh 3 and draw very tight. Do not allow a mesh to be drawn down below the upper side of the mesh stick. Some of these cautions are too often repeated, but if a mesh is allowed to get irregular, it will cause trouble in future operations.

net. Tie the cord of the shuttle to the left outside loop and always work from the left to the right. The first time across see that the long meshes do not cross over each other but are kept in the order in which they are attached to the ring.

After tying the cord to the mesh 1, *Fig. 6*, bring the mesh stick into use. Pass the cord down over the mesh stick, drawing the lower end of the loop down until it comes against the upper side of the mesh stick and put

Continue across the series until all of the long loops have been used; this will bring the work to the right side. Flip the whole thing over, and the cord will be at the left, ready to begin again. Slip all the meshes off the mesh stick. It makes no difference when the meshes are taken off the stick, but they must all come off before a new row is begun. Having the ring attached to the anchorage by a cord makes it easy to flip the work over. Be sure to flip to the right and then to the left alternately to prevent the twisting, which would result if turned one way all the time.

The first mesh each time across is just a little different problem from all the others, which may be better understood by reference to *Fig. 8.* The knots *Q, R,* and *S* are of the next previous series. The cord is brought down over the mesh stick and up through mesh 1, and when the loop is brought down it may not draw to the mesh stick at its center; it is apt to do otherwise and a sideways pull is necessary, which is pulled so that the knots *Q* and *R* are side by side, then the

knot at *T* may be tied. When the mesh 2 is drawn down it should pull to place without shifting, as should all the others of that row.

Continue the use of the mesh stick until a net 8 ft. long is made. When the cord gives out rewind the shuttle and tie with a small knot that will not slip. The weavers knot is good if known, or the simple square knot shown in *Fig. 9* is very good. It is too easy to make to need direction, but unless it is thrown over just right it will slip. Let *U, Fig. 8,* represent the short cord and *V* the new piece to be added. Place the cord *V* back of *U* and give *U* a complete turn around *V, Fig. 9,* and bring them together at a point above *U,* then to the front. Repeat the complete turn of *U* about *V,* shown by the dotted line, and pull tightly. If analyzed, it consists of two loops that are just

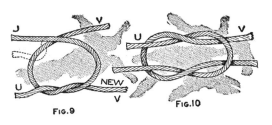

A SQUARE KNOT IS USED TO JOIN
THE ENDS OF THE CORD WHEN
REWINDING THE SHUTTLE.

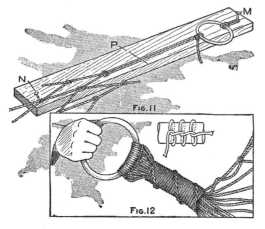

THE GAUGE BOARD IS AGAIN USED FOR THE LONG LOOPS AT THE FINISHING END, AND THEN THE CORDS ARE WOUND.

alike and linked together as shown in *Fig. 10.*

When the 8 ft. of netting has been completed, proceed to make the long loops as at the beginning. The same gauge board can be used, but the tying occurs at both ends. And because the pairs cannot be knotted in the center, two or three twists can be given by the second about the first of each pair. The long loops and the net are attached together as shown in *Fig. 11.* Slip on the meshes of the last run over the nail *N,* and when the cord comes down from the ring, the shuttle passes through the same mesh. When drawn up, the farthest point of the mesh comes against the nail. After this long loop has been secured at the ring, the first mesh is slipped off and the next put on. All of the long loops at this end will be about three inches shorter than at the other end, unless the finishing nail *N* is moved down. This will not be necessary.

With a piece of cord about 6 ft. long, start quite close to the ring and wind all the cords of the long loops together. The winding should be made very tight, and it is best to loop under with each coil. This is shown in *Fig. 12.*

The hammock is now ready for use. Some like a soft, small rope run through the outside edges lengthwise. Others prefer a fringe, and either can be added. The fringe can be attached about six meshes down from the upper edge of the sides. The hammock should have a stretcher at each end of the netted portion, but not as long as those required for web hammocks.

— DIVING TOWER
FOR THE SUMMER CAMP —

Aquatic pleasures and sports at a summer camp or lake may be considerably enlivened by the building of a diving tower like that shown in the sketch. It has proved very successful at a boys' summer camp at Crystal Lake, Illinois. The boys have made a practice for several years of building a tower early each swimming season on the opening of their camp in July and disposing of it at the close of camp some weeks later. Several resorts and cottages now boast towers made by the campers.

The tower is built largely of 2- by 4-in. stock. The longer pieces at the corners are 12 ft. in length, slanted so that the lower end of the tower is 7 ft. square and the platform at the top 3 ft. square. The handrail at the top is fixed to extensions of the rear uprights. A springboard is fastened on two horizontal braces near the middle of the tower and is reached by the ladder. The structure is built on the shore and towed out to its position. It is sunk and weighted by the box of stones supported on cross braces.

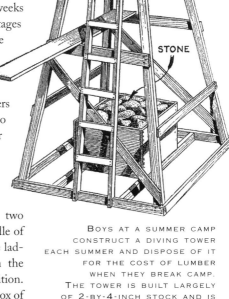

STONE

BOYS AT A SUMMER CAMP CONSTRUCT A DIVING TOWER EACH SUMMER AND DISPOSE OF IT FOR THE COST OF LUMBER WHEN THEY BREAK CAMP. THE TOWER IS BUILT LARGELY OF 2-BY-4-INCH STOCK AND IS WEIGHTED WITH A BOX OF STONES.

— WHISTLE WARNS OF FISH CATCH —

A toy railroad wheel, a piece of hollow can, and pieces of wire are the materials necessary for making the whistle shown in the illustration. The whistle warns a fisherman that a fish is attempting to make away with his bait. The wheel fitted into the end of the cane and wedged into place to form a tight joint. The wires are formed into loops at the ends of the cane and fixed to it. The whistle is attached to the fish line, as shown, with the open end down and slightly below the surface of the water. The fishing pole may be fixed so that the whistle will remain in this position while the fisherman is at ease

WHEN THE FISH STRIKES THE BAIT THE WATER IS FORCED UP INTO THE WHISTLE SUDDENLY, AND THE ESCAPING AIR WARNS THE FISHERMAN.

in the shade nearby. When the fish attempts to make away with the bait, as shown in the sketch, the water forces the air in the upper part of the cane out through the center hole of the wheel, and a whistling sound is the result.

— A FISH SCALER —

All kinds of devices, both simple and complex, have been made and patented for use in scaling fish. But for a novelty a fisherman found the following, which necessity compelled him to improvise on an outing trip, to be as efficient as any of them. As usual, the fisherman forgot the curry comb to clean the fish when packing up his gear. But, at the same time, he remembered to take a plentiful supply of bottled goods. Long before it became necessary to scale any fish, enough bottles had been opened to provide the basis of a tool for the purpose, which he constructed by using the small tin bottle caps, a few being nailed on a block of wood, about 3 in. wide by 4 in. long. This made a splendid fish scaler, as good and efficient at home as in the camp. It is both inexpensive

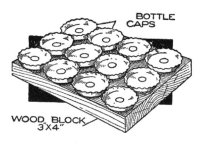

BOTTLE CAPS NAILED TO A WOOD BLOCK FOR REMOVING SCALES FROM A FISH.

and easily made. The sketch shows the general appearance.

— RAIN ALARM WITH DROP-OF-WATER CONTACT —

An annunciating device, which awakens a person sleeping in a room with the window open and warns him that it is raining so that he may close the window, is an interesting bit of electrical construction. On the outside of the house, as detailed, a funnel is fixed to the wall. Two separate wires have their terminals at the funnels small end. The wires enter the room at the frame of the window and connect to an electric bell and a dry cell. A drop of water entering the funnel flows down to the small end, falling on the terminals of the wires. The water acts as a

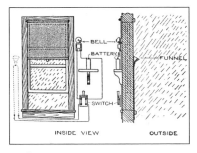

A DROP OF RAIN WATER COMPLETES THE BELL CIRCUIT, THUS GIVING WARNING OF THE RAIN.

conductor, completing the circuit and ringing the bell. A switch inside cuts out the circuit, stopping the bell's ringing.

— CORN POPPER MADE FROM COFFEE CAN AND BROOM HANDLE —

With an old coffee can or similar tin receptacle and a piece of a broom handle 2½ or 3 ft. long, it is easy to make a corn popper that is preferable in many ways to a wire one. Take a strip of wood a little shorter than the height of the can to be used and, after boring two holes in it to prevent its splitting, nail it to the end of the handle. The latter is then fastened to

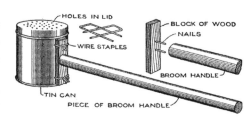

CORN POPPER MADE FROM A COFFEE CAN
OR SIMILAR TIN RECEPTACLE AND
A PIECE OF A BROOM HANDLE

the side of the can with two wire staples, as shown. Holes are made in the can top to admit air to the corn while it is popping.

— PRESERVING LEAVES IN A SPECIMEN BOOK —

The common method of preserving leaves by pressing them with an iron rubbed on beeswax may be improved by substituting the following process. Paint the underside of each leaf with linseed oil, ironing it immediately. Then paint and iron the upper side in the same way. This treatment gives the leaves sufficient gloss, while they remain quite pliable. It is not necessary to press and dry the leaves beforehand, but this may be done if desired. The tints may even be well preserved by painting only the upper side of the leaves with the oil and then placing them, without ironing, between newspapers and under weights to dry.

— HOMEMADE KITE REEL —

This kite reel is constructed from two old pulleys and few pipe fittings. The large pulley is about 14 in. in diameter, on the face of which are riveted flat strips of iron with extending arms. These arms are reinforced by riveting smaller pieces from one to the other, which connects all arms together on both sides of the wheel. Mounted on the shaft with the pulleys is a guide for the kite wire or string. This guide permits of being moved entirely over the top of the reel. The smaller pulley is attached to the shaft and used as a brake. The brake is used only when running out the wire or string, first removing the crank

SNOW DAY

— MAKING SNOWSHOES —

Shapes of Snowshoe

We owe the snowshoe to the inventive mind of the North American Indian, and its conception was doubtless brought about through that prolific source of invention—necessity. The first models were crude web-footed affairs, but improvements in model and manner of filling the frames were gradually added until the perfected and graceful shoe of the present day was finally reached. The first snowshoes were made by Native Americans, and tribes of Maine and Canada continue to fashion the finest handmade models today.

The snowshoe is a necessity for the sportsman and trapper whose pleasure or business leads him out in the open during the winter season, when roads and trails are heavily blanketed by a deep fall of powdery snow. But the use of the web shoe is by no means confined to the dweller in the wilderness. The charm of wintry wood and plain beckons many lovers of the outdoors to participate in this invigorating sport, and snowshoe tramps are fast growing in popularity in and about our cities and towns.

All the modern snowshoes are constructed upon practically the same general lines, although the types of frames differ considerably in size as well as in shape, and the filling of hide is often woven in many varied and intricate patterns. The frame or bow—usually made of ash in order to get strength with light weight—is bent in many shapes. But the one shown in the diagram is a typical general-purpose shoe and may

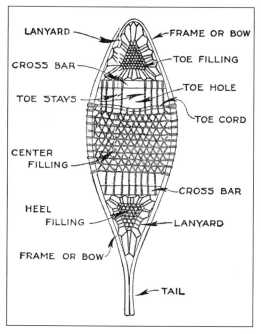

THE FRAME OF A SNOWSHOE IN ITS USUAL CONSTRUCTION, SHOWING THE CROSSPIECES WITH THEIR LACED FILLINGS OF HIDE AND DIFFERENT PARTS NAMED FOR READY REFERENCE.

frame through a double row of holes drilled in the wood. The center filling is woven of heavy strands of rawhide, in a fairly coarse mesh, because this part of the shoe must bear the weight of the body and the brunt of wear. The end fillers for toe and heel are woven of lighter strands of hide, and the mesh is, of course, smaller.

As may be noted by referring to the drawing, a center opening or "toe hole" is provided. And, because the greater strain on the filling lies directly under the ball of the foot, the shoe is reinforced at this point by the "toe cord" running across, and the "toe-cord stays" that are tied in on each side of the toe hole. One end of the stays is fastened to the toe cord and the other lashed over the wooden cross bar of the frame. These reinforcing cords are formed of several strands of hide, the stays being again wound with finer strands.

be called standard. The frame is held in shape by means of two wooden cross braces, neatly mortised into the frame. These braces are spaced some 15 or 16 in. apart, and so divide the shoe into three sections, known as the toe, center, and heel. The filling is woven into a lanyard, which is a light strip of hide firmly laced to the

The way the foot is attached to the shoe is important to prevent slipping and to secure a good foothold while walking. This is done with a toe strap, which will allow the toe to push down through the toe opening as the heel of the foot is lifted in the act of walking. A second strap, or thong, leading from the top around the foot and above the curve of the heel, is needed to lend additional support in lifting the snowshoe. This creates the easy shambling stride characteristic of the snowshoer.

There are, of course, a great number of models or styles. One style will be popular in one locality, while an altogether different style is preferred in another part of the country. The most representative types are well shown in the illustrations, and brief descriptions will point out their practical advantages. Each model possesses certain merits—one model being designed for fast traveling in the open, another better adapted for brush travel, while others are more convenient for use in hilly country where much climbing is done, and so on.

Style A is regarded by snowshoe experts as an extreme style, because it is long and narrow. It is designed for fast traveling over smooth and level country and over loose, powdery snow. This style is much used by the Cree Indian tribe, and is usually made 12 in. wide by 60 in. long, with a steeply upcurved toe. It is a good shoe for cross-country work, but is somewhat

SNOWSHOE EXPERTS CONSIDER THIS AN EXTREME STYLE BECAUSE IT IS LONG AND NARROW.

A

difficult to manage on broken trails, when the snow is packed, and also affords rather slippery footing when crossing ice. Owing to the stout construction of the frame and reinforcement needed to retain the high, curved toe, *Style A* is more difficult to manage than the more conservative models. Its frame is stiffer, making it more fatiguing to wear, while its use is a decided handicap in mountainous districts, because a curved toe always makes hill climbing more difficult.

THIS SNOWSHOE IS CONSIDERED THE ORDINARY EASTERN MODEL AND ONE BEST ADAPTED FOR ALL-AROUND USE.

Style B may be considered the ordinary eastern model, and a common style best adapted for all-around use. It is a neat and gracefully designed frame, about 12 in. wide and 42 in. long, and is usually made with a slightly upcurving toe, about 2 in. turn at the toe being correct. When made by the Native Americans of Maine, this model is fashioned with a rather heavy heel. This heel is an advantage for fast walking, but it increases the difficulty in quick turning.

Style C is a favorite model among the hunters and woodsmen of New England. This is a splendid style for general purposes in this section of the country, because the full, round toe keeps the toe up near the surface, and lets the heel cut down more than the narrow-toe models. *Style C* is an easy shoe to wear, and though it is not so fast as the long, narrow frame, its full shape is more convenient for use in the woods. It is usually made with about a 1- to 1½-in. turn at the toe.

Style D is the familiar "bear's paw," a model originating with the northeastern trapper. This model is well adapted for short tramps in the brush. Having a flat toe, it is likewise a good shoe for mountain climbing. For tramping about in thick brush, a short, full shoe enables one to take a shorter stride and turn more quickly, but it is a slow shoe for straight-ahead traveling.

When purchasing a pair of snowshoes, some few important considerations should be kept in mind. The size and model will depend upon the man to some extent, since a large heavy man will require a larger snowshoe than would suffice for a

C

THE STYLE ILLUSTRATED HERE IS SPLENDID FOR GENERAL PURPOSES AND IS A FAVORITE AMONG HUNTERS AND WOODSMEN.

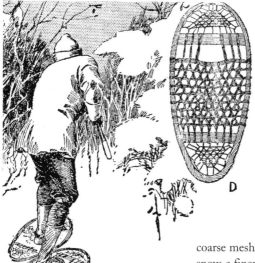

D

localities where the snow packs solidly and there is considerable ice, and in mountainous districts or for rough-country traveling, the smaller sizes will give more satisfaction and prove more durable also. For a wet-snow locality, the center filling should be strung in rather coarse mesh, while for soft, powdery snow, a finer mesh will be the logical choice.

There are snowshoes and snowshoes, and while there are fine models regularly stocked by a few of the better sporting-goods firms, there are likewise many poorly made snowshoes on the market. It is wise to pay a fair price and secure a dependable handmade article. Cheaper snowshoes—often filled with seine twine and the cheapest hide (commonly known in the trade as "gut")—will warp and twist in the frame, and the shoddy filling will soon become loosened up and "bag" after a little use. The best snowshoes are made by Native Americans, and

person of lighter weight. Height also enters into the choice, and while a small person can travel faster and with less fatigue when equipped with a proportionately small shoe, a tall man will naturally pick out a larger-sized snowshoe for his use. For a country where deep snows prevail, larger sizes are best. But in the filling is ordinarily made of neat's hide; cowhide for the center filling, and calfskin for the toe and heel. A first-class pair of snowshoes is a pleasure, and when possible to do so, it is best to have them made to order. This is necessary in case one wishes to incorporate any little wrinkles of his own into their making, or desires a flatter toe, lighter heel, or a different mesh from the usual stock models.

Where but one pair of snowshoes is purchased, *Style B* will probably prove the best selection. It should be ordered with the flat toe, or a turn not greater than 1 in. The frame may be in either one or two pieces, depending upon the size of the shoe and the ideas of the maker, but it is smart to specify white ash for the frames in the order. No quality maker would be guilty of using screws or other metal fastenings, but many of the cheap and poorly fashioned snowshoes are fastened at the heel with screws, thus making this a decidedly weak point. The wood is quite certain to split after a little rough service. In contrast to the poor workmanship of these low-priced snowshoes, the Native American-made article is fashioned from sound and properly seasoned wood. The

cross bars are snugly fitted by mortising to the frame and the filling is tightly woven. The heel will be properly fastened by lacing with a rawhide thong. However, Native American craftsmen are likely to make the toe small and leave the wood to form a rather heavy heel. Some few woodsmen and sportsmen may prefer this model, but the majority of users favor a fuller toe and a lighter heel for general use, because the regulation Native American model, cutting down at toe and heel equally deep, increases the difficulty of easy traveling over soft snow. It is, however, a good shoe when used over broken trails.

When buying snowshoes at the store, make sure the frames are stoutly and well made. For all-around use, it is a good idea to select a filling of good heavy weight and with a firmly woven and open mesh, say, about ¾ in. The toe and heel sections will, of course, be of finer-cut hide and smaller mesh. And it is wise to avoid those shoes employing seine twine for the end filling. Some factory-made snowshoes are given a coat or two of varnish, but this, while serving to make them partly waterproof, makes them rather slippery when crossing logs and ice. Most woodsmen prefer to leave both frame and filling in their natural condition.

The Native American-made snowshoe is always provided with a generously large toe hole, so that ample foot covering may be used. This point is generally overlooked in the machine-made products, and the toe cords are also frequently roughly formed, thus chafing the feet and making them sore. These details may or may not prove a handicap for short tramps near town, but for long trips through the woods, they are important considerations.

The Native American manner of tying the snowshoe to the foot by means of a single twisted and knotted thong is a good method of attachment. If the thong is properly adjusted to the requisite snugness in the first place, the shoes may be quickly removed by a simple twist of the ankle. A better fastening is secured by using a fairly wide (¾ in.) toe strap and a long thong. The toe strap is placed over the toes, immediately over the ball of the foot, and secured against slipping by weaving the ends in and out between the meshes of the filling until it reaches the frame on either side. This grips the toe strap firmly and does away with the necessity of tying a knot. A narrow thong, about 4 ft. long, is now doubled, the center placed just above the heel of the foot, and the ends passed under the toe cord, just outside of the toe-cord stays on each side. The thong is then brought up and across the toes, one end passing over and the other under the toe strap. Each end of the thong is now looped around the crossed thong on either side, and then carried back over the back of the heel and knotted with a common square are reef knot. Calfskin makes a good flexible foot binding, or a suitable strip of folded cloth or canvas may be used.

The regulation snowshoe harness, consisting of a leather stirrup for the toe and an instep and heel strap, will be found more comfortable than the thong. When once adjusted snugly to the foot, the shoes may be quickly taken off and put on again by pushing the heel strap down, when the foot may be slipped out of the toe stirrup.

The use of heavy leather shoes is, of course, undesirable. The only correct footwear for snowshoeing is a pair of high-cut moccasins, cut roomy enough to allow one or more pairs of heavy woolen stockings to be worn. The heavy and long German socks, extending halfway to the knee and drawn on over the trouser legs, are by far the most comfortable for cold-weather wear. The feet, thus shod, will not only be warm in the coldest weather, but the free use of the toes will not be interfered with. Leather shoes are cold and stiff, and the heavy soles and heels, chafing against the snowshoes, will soon ruin the filling.

Making the Shoe

Snowshoe making is an art, and while few craftsmen can equal the Native American in weaving the intricate patterns they prefer to employ for filling the frames it is not difficult to fashion a good solid frame and then fill it by making use of a simple and open system of meshing. For the frames, white ash is much the best wood, but hickory and white birch are dependable substitutes, if the former cannot be obtained. Birch is perhaps the best wood to use when the sportsman wishes to cut and split up his own wood. But as suitable material for the frames may be readily purchased for a small sum, probably the majority of

the readers will elect to buy the material. Any lumber dealer will be able to supply white ash, and it is a simple matter to saw out the frames

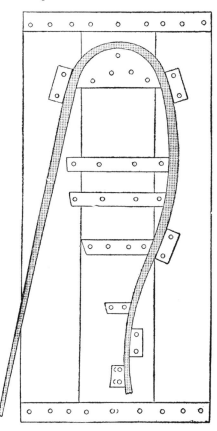

THE DESIGN OF THE SNOWSHOE IS TRACED ON A BOARD, AND BLOCKS ARE USED TO SHAPE THE FRAME OR BOW.

from the board. The sawed-out frame is inferior to the hand-split bow. But if good, selected material can be obtained, there will be little, if any, difference for ordinary use.

When dry and well-seasoned lumber is used, the frame may be made to the proper dimensions. But when green wood is selected, the frame must be made somewhat heavier, to allow for the usual shrinkage in seasoning. For a stout snowshoe frame, the width should be about 1 1/16 in.; thickness at the toe, 7/16 in., and thickness at heel, 9/16 in. The frame should be cut 2 in. longer than the finished length desired. In working the wood, remember that the toe of the finished frame will be the center of the stick; the heel, the end of the stick, and the center of the shoe will lie halfway between the heel and toe.

After the frames have been finished, the dry wood must be steamed before it can be safely bent to the required shape. Before doing this, a wooden bending form must be made. An easy way to make this form is to first draw a pattern of the model on a sheet of paper, cut out the pencil mark, and, placing this pattern on a board, carefully trace the design on the wooden form. A

LOCATE THE CROSSBARS BY BALANCING THE FRAME, THEN FIT THE ENDS IN SHALLOW MORTISES.

number of cleats, or blocks, of wood will now be needed. The inside blocks will be nailed in position, but the outside stay blocks will be simply provided with nails in the holes so they may be quickly fastened in position when the steamed frame is ready for the form.

To make the frame soft for bending to shape, it must be steamed. The easiest way of doing this is to provide boiling water in a wash boiler. Place the wood over the top and soak well by mopping with the boiling water, shifting the stick about until the fibers have become soft and pliable. After 10 or 15 minutes of the hot-water treatment, wrap the stick with a cloth and bend it back and forth to render it more and more pliable. Then repeat the hot-water treatment, and repeat the process until the wood is sufficiently soft to bend easily without splintering. The toe being the greatest curve, it must be well softened before putting on the form. Otherwise the fibers are likely to splinter off at this point. When the frame is well softened, place it on the bending form while hot and slowly bend it against the wooden inside blocks to hold it to the proper curve. Begin with the toe, and after fastening the outside blocks to hold this end, finish one side, then bend the other half to shape. The bent frame should be allowed to dry on the form for at least a week. If it is removed before the wood has become thoroughly dry and has taken a permanent set, the frame will not retain its shape. The same bending form may be used for both frames. But if you are in a hurry to finish the shoes, two forms should be made—but considerable pains must be taken to make them exactly alike in every way.

When the frames are dry, secure the tail end of the frame by boring three holes about 4 in. from the end, and fasten with rawhide. The work of fitting two crossbars may now be undertaken, and the balance of the snowshoe depends upon fitting these bars in their proper places. Before cutting the mortise, spring the two bars in the frame about 15 in. apart, and balance the shoe in the center by holding it in the hands. When the frame exactly balances, move the bars sufficiently to make the heel about 3 oz. heavier than the toe, and mark the place where the mortises are to be cut. The crossbars and mortise must be a good tight fit, and a small, sharp chisel will enable the

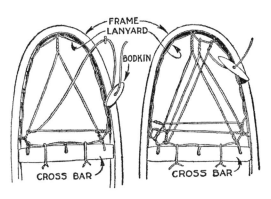

BEGIN WEAVING THE TOE FILLING AT THE CORNER OF CROSSBAR AND FRAME, CARRYING IT AROUND IN A TRIANGLE UNTIL COMPLETE.

AN ENDLESS THONG IS MADE WITH EYES CUT IN
THE ENDS OF THE LEATHER AND EACH PART IS
RUN THROUGH THE EYE OF THE OTHER.

builder to make a neat job. It is not necessary to cut the mortise very deep; ¼ in. is ample to afford a firm and snug mortised joint.

The lanyard to which the filling is woven is next put in by boring pairs of small holes in the toe and heel sections and lacing a narrow rawhide thong through the obliquely drilled holes. Three holes are then bored in the crossbar—one on each side about 1½ in. from the frame, and the third in the center of the bar. The lanyard is then carried through these holes in the cross bar.

Begin the toe filling first by making an eye in one end of the thong, put the end through the lanyard loop and then through the eye, thus making a slipknot. Start to weave at the corner where the bar and frame are mortised.

Carry the strand up and twist it around the lanyards in the middle of the toe, then carry it down and make a like twist around the lanyard loop in the opposite corner. The thong is now looped around the next lanyard (No. 2 from the crossbar lanyard) and fastened with the twisted loop knot illustrated. Continue the strand across the width of toe space and make a similar loop knot on No. 2 lanyard on the starting side. Twist it around the strand first made and loop it under the next crossbar lanyard loop. Then carry it up and twist it around the lanyard loop in the toe of the frame, continuing in the same

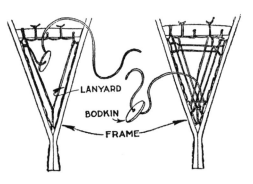

LANYARD

BODKIN

FRAME

THE HEEL FILLING IS WOVEN BY MAKING THE
CONNECTION WITH THE LANYARD IN THE SAME
MANNER AS FOR THE TOE FILLING.

manner until the last lanyard of the toe is reached, when the space is finished by making the twisted loop knot until the space is entirely filled. It is a difficult matter to describe by text, but the illustrations will point out the correct way and show the manner of making an endless thong by eye-

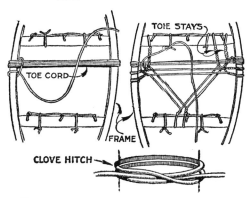

THE CENTER MUST BE WOVEN STRONG AND TIGHT, AND FOR THIS REASON A HEAVIER STRAND OF HIDE MUST BE USED.

splicing, as well as illustrating the wooden bodkin, or needle, used in pulling the woven strands taut. This bodkin is easily made from a small piece of wood about ¼ in. thick and about 2 in. long. To simplify matters, the heel may be filled in the same manner as the toe.

For the center, which must be woven strong and tight, a heavier strand of hide must be used. Begin with the toe cord first. To make this amply strong, carry the strand across the frame, five or six times, finishing with a half-hitch knot, as shown. Then carry it up and twist it around the crossbar to form the first toe-cord stay.

As may be noted, the center section is filled by looping back and twisting the strands as when filling the toe. However, the filling is looped around the frame instead of a lanyard, and a clove hitch is used. A toe hole, 4 in. wide, must be provided for. When enough of the filling has been woven in to make this opening, the thong is no longer looped around the crossbar but woven through the toe cord. As the filling ends in the toe cord, it should be woven in and out at this point several times, finishing the toe hole by looping a strand around the crossbar at the side of the toe hole, then passing it down the toe-cord stay by twisting around it. Then twist it around the toe cord along the filling to the other side of the toe hole, where it is twisted around the toe-cord stay on the opposite side, looped around the frame, and ended in a clove hitch.

At the first reading, it will doubtless appear difficult. But a careful examination of the illustrations will soon show how the trick is done, and indeed it is really a very simple matter. It is one of those things that are easier to do than to describe. The method of filling has been purposely made simple, but the majority of shoes are filled in practically the same manner—which does quite as well the more intricate Native American design.

The knack of using the snowshoe is quickly mastered, providing the shoes are properly attached to allow the toe ample freedom to work down through the toe hole as each foot is lifted. The shoe is, of course, not actually lifted in the air. Instead, it is slid along the surface, half the width of one shoe covering the other when it is lifted in the act of walking. At first the novice may be inclined to think snowshoes a bit cumbersome and unwieldy, and doubt his ability to penetrate the brush. However, as the snowshoer becomes accustomed to their use, he will experience little if any difficulty in traveling where he will. When making a trail in more or less open country, it is a good plan to blaze it thoroughly. This will enable you to return over the same trail, in case of a snowfall in the meantime, or drifting snow fills up and obliterates the trail first made. When the trail is first broken by traveling over it once by snowshoe, the snow is packed well and forms a solid foundation. Should even a heavy fall of snow cover it, the blaze marks on tree and bush will point out the trail. This will afford faster and easier traveling than breaking a new trail each time one journeys in the same direction.

A well-made pair of snowshoes will stand a couple of season's hard use, or last for a year or two longer for general wear. To keep them in good shape, they should be dried out after use, although it is never advisable to place them close to a hot fire or the hide filling will be injured. Jumping puts severe strain on the frame of the shoe. Though damage may not occur when so used in deep, soft snow, it is wise to avoid the possibility of breakage. Accidents will now and then happen, to be sure, and as a thong may snap at some unexpected moment, keep a strand or two of rawhide on hand to meet this emergency.

— A SNOWBALL THROWER —

The snow fort with its infantry is not complete without the artillery. A set of mortars, or cannon, placed in the fort to hurl snowballs at the entrenched enemy makes the battle more real. A device to substitute for the cannon or a mortar can be easily constructed by any boy, and a few of these devices set in a snow fort will add greatly to the interest of the conflict.

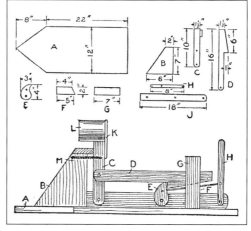

THE DIMENSIONED PARTS AND THE DETAIL OF THE COMPLETED SNOWBALL THROWER

The substitute—called a "snowball thrower"—consists of a base, *A*, with a standard, *B*, which stops the arm, *C*, controlled by the bar, *D*, when the trigger, *E*, is released. The tripping of the trigger is accomplished by the sloping end of *D* on the slanting end of the upright *F*, with their upper ends extending above the bar *D*, to prevent the latter from jumping out when it is released by the trigger.

CANNONADING A SNOW FORT WITH THE USE OF A SNOWBALL THROWER.

The trigger E is tripped with the handle, H, connected to the piece, J, on which all the working parts are mounted. The upper end of the arm C has a piece, K, to which is attached a tin can, L, for holding the snowball to be thrown. A set of door springs, M, furnishes the force to throw the snowball.

All the parts are given dimensions, and if cut properly, they will fit together to make the thrower as illustrated.

— BUILDING A SNOW LIGHTHOUSE —

This article describes a lighthouse made from snow that will be a big hit in the neighborhood when the candle placed inside is lit.

The lighthouse is made by rolling three large snowballs of different diameters and placing them on top of each other, the largest one at the bottom to form the base, and the smallest at the top for the light chamber. Snow is then packed tightly at the joints to make the tapered cylinder, which should be about 5 ft. high, 3 ft. in diameter at the base, and 20 in. in diameter at the top. A space is hollowed out for the light chamber, with four openings for windows, which are protected with glass. A candle is inserted in the center of the cavity. In order to make the candle burn, a hole is made in the top leading into the light chamber, and another hole from a point somewhat below the windows to conduct air to the candle. When the candle is lighted, the air supply through these openings allows it to burn perfectly.

— SIMPLY MADE COASTERS, SLEDS, AND SLEIGHS —

Make your own sled! There is no use in buying them, because your handmade sled is probably better than any purchased one and you can take so much more pride in it when you know it is of your own construction. There are so many different designs of sleds that can be made by hand that the matter can be left almost entirely to your own ingenuity. You can make one like the store-bought sleds and face

FIG. 1—BARREL-STAVE SLED.

the runners with pieces of an iron hoop that will answer every purpose. A good sled for coasting consists simply of two barrel staves and three pieces of board as shown in the picture, *Fig. 1*. No premade sled will equal it for coasting and it is also just the thing for carrying loads of snow for building snow houses. The method of its construction is so simple that no description other than the picture is needed. You can make a chair-sleigh out of this by fitting a

chair on the cross board instead of the long top board or it will be still stronger if the top board is allowed to remain, and then you will have a device that can readily again be transformed into a coasting sled. In making the chair-sleigh it is necessary to nail four L-shaped blocks on the cross boards, one for each leg of the chair, to hold the chair in place. Skating along over the ice and pushing the chair in front of him, the proud possessor of a chair-sleigh may take his mother, grown sister, or lady friend with him on his outings, and permit her to ride in the chair.

Folding-Chair Sleigh

A folding-chair sleigh is even more enjoyable and convenient than the device just described. If the ice pond is far from home this may be placed under your arm and carried where you like.

The illustrations *Figs. 2* and *3* show all the parts as they should look before being joined together. The seat may be made of a piece of canvas or carpet. The hinges are of leather. *Fig. 4* shows the folding-chair sleigh after it has been put together. Skates are used for the runners. The skates may be strapped on or taken off whenever desired. When

CHAIR SLEIGH

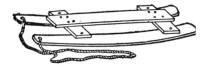

FIG. 2—
FOLDING-CHAIR SLEIGH BOTTOM

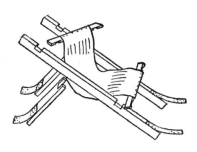

FIG. 3—
FOLDING-CHAIR SLEIGH WITH
TOP PARTS DISCONNECTED

FIG. 4—
FOLDING-CHAIR SLEIGH OPEN

the chair is lifted, the supports slip from the notches on the sidebars and fall on the runner bars. The chair is then folded up so that it can be carried by a small boy. With regular metal hinges and light timbers a very handsome chair can be constructed that will also afford an ornamental lawn chair for summer.

The Toboggan Sled

When the snow is very deep a toboggan sled is the thing for real sport. The runners of the ordinary sled break through the crust of the deep snow, blocking the progress and spoiling the fun. The toboggan sled, with its broad, smooth bottom, glides along over the soft surface with perfect ease.

To make the toboggan sled, secure two boards each 10 ft. long and 1 ft. wide and so thin that they can be easily bent. Place the boards beside each and join them together with cross sticks. Screw the boards to the cross stick from the bottom and

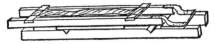

FIG. 5—
FOLDING-CHAIR SLEIGH CLOSED

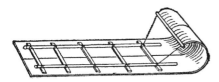

FIG. 6—THE TOBOGGAN

be sure that the heads of the screws are buried deep enough in the wood so as not to protrude. The bottom must present an absolutely smooth surface to the snow. Fasten two side bars to the top of the cross sticks and screw them firmly. In some instances the timbers are fastened together by strings, a groove being cut in the bottom of the boards so as to keep the strings from protruding and being ground to pieces. After the side bars are securely fastened, bend the ends of the boards over and tie them to the ends of the front crossbar to hold them in position. See *Fig. 6*. The strings for keeping the boards bent must be very strong. Pieces of stout wire, or a slender steel rod, are even better. The toboggan slide is the favored device of sport among the boys in Canada, where nearly every boy knows how to make them.

Norwegian Skis

You have often read of the ski, the snowshoe used by the Norwegians and other people living in the far north. With them the men and women glide down the snow-covered mountain sides, leap across ditches, run races, and have all kinds of sport.

They are just as amusing to American kids who have ever learned to manipulate them, and it is wonderful how much skill can be attained in their use. Any kid with a little mechanical ingenuity can make a pair of skis. They can be made from two barrel staves. Select staves of straight-grained wood. Sharpen the ends of each and score each end by cutting grooves in the wood, as shown in *Fig. 7*. A pocketknife or small gouge will suffice for this work. Then smear the end of the staves with oil and hold them close to a hot fire until they can be bent so as to tip the toes upward, as shown in the picture, *Fig. 7*. Then with a cord bind the staves as they are bent and permit them to remain thus tied until they retain the curved form of their own accord. Now screw on top of each ski a little block, just broad and high enough to fit in front of the heels of your shoe. Fasten a strap in front of each block through which to slip your toes, and the skis are made. The inside of the shoe heel should

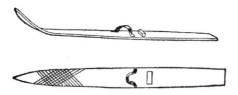

FIG. 7—HOMEMADE SKIS

feet. Now procure a stick with which to steer, and hunt for a snowbank. At first you will afford more amusement to onlookers than to yourself, for the skis have a way of trying to run in opposite directions, crosswise, and various ways. But with practice you will soon become expert in their manipulation.

press firmly against the block and the toe be held tightly under the strap. This will keep the skis on your

— MAKING SNOW BUILDING BLOCKS —

Forts, Eskimo igloos, and other buildings can be made quite elaborate architectural accomplishments if constructed of snow building blocks. The snow is compressed in a simple rectangular wooden mold, which produces a block about the same size as the standard concrete block, or 8 by 8 by 16 in., although any other size or shape may be produced by altering the mold. The mold is placed on a flat surface filled with snow that is tamped down hard, and the snow

struck off level with the mold top. After the snow has been sufficiently compacted, the mold is removed, and the block is set aside until a sufficient number have been made to

FORTS ERECTED WITH BUILDING BLOCKS MADE OF SNOW: THE BLOCKS ARE MOLDED IN A WOODEN FORM AND THEN LAID IN A MORTAR OF WET SNOW, WHICH, WHEN FROZEN, UNITES THE BUILDING INTO ONE SOLID MASS.

complete a fort or other structure. In building, the blocks are held together with a "mortar" of wet snow or slush, which, when frozen, unites the building into on solid mass. The trowel used for spreading the mortar can be made from a shingle or piece of board.

— FOUR-PASSENGER COASTING BOBSLED —

Coaster bobsleds usually have about the same form of construction, and only slight changes from the ordinary are made to satisfy the builder. The one shown has some distinctive features that make it a sled of luxury, and the builder will pride himself in the making. A list of the materials required is supplied. Any wood may be used for the sled, except for the runners, which should be made of ash.

Shape the runners all alike by cutting one out and using it as a pattern to make the others. After cutting them to the proper shape, a groove is formed on the under edge to admit the curve of a ⅝-in. round iron rod about ¼ in. deep. The iron rods are then shaped to fit over the runner in the groove and extend up the back part of the runner and over the top at the front end. The extensions should be flattened so that two holes can be drilled in them for two wood screws at each end. If the builder does not have the necessary equipment for flattening these ends, a local blacksmith can do it at a nominal price. After the irons are fitted, they are fastened in place.

The top edges of the runners are notched for the crosspieces so that the top surfaces of these pieces will come flush with the upper edges of the runners. The location of these pieces is not essential, but should be near the ends of the runners, and the notches of each pair of runners should coincide. When the notches are cut, fit the pieces in snugly, and fasten them with long, slim wood screws. Small metal braces are then fastened to the runners and crosspiece on the inside, to stiffen the joint.

As the rear sled must oscillate some, means must be provided for this tilting motion while at the same time preventing sidewise turning. The construction used for this purpose is a hinged joint. The heavy 2-by-5-in. crosspiece is cut sloping on the width so that it remains 2 in.

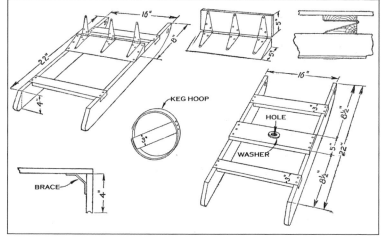

DETAILS SHOWING THE METHOD OF REAR-SLED OSCILLATION, THE BRACING AND THE STEERING WHEEL.

thick at one edge and tapers down to a feather edge at the opposite side. This makes a wedge-shaped piece, to which surface the three large hinges are attached. The piece is then solidly fastened to the upper edges of the runners that are to be used for the rear sled, and so located that the center of the piece will be 8 in. from the front end of the runners.

The supporting crosspiece on the font sled is fastened on top of the runners, at a place where its center will be 11 in. from the front end of the runners.

The top board is prepared by making both ends round and plan-ing the surfaces smooth. The two crosspieces are placed on the underside. Bore two ½-in. holes through the width of each cross-piece, near the ends, to receive the eyebolts. They are placed, one with its center 12 in. from the end to be used for the rear, and other with its center 8 in. from the front end, and securely fastened with screws. The shore is placed in the center of the board, and wires are run over it connecting the eyebolts. The eye-bolts are then drawn up tightly to make the wire taut over the shore. This will prevent the long board from sagging.

On the upper side of the board and beginning at the rear end, the backs are fastened at intervals of 18 in. They are first prepared by rounding the corners on the ends used for the tops, and the opposite ends are cut slightly on an angle to give the back a slant. They are then fastened with the small hinges to the top board. On the edges of the top board, 1-in. holes are bored about 1 in. deep, and pins driven for footrests. These are located 18 in. apart, beginning about 5 in. from the front end. The dowel

is used for the pins, which are made 4 in. long.

The steering device consists of a broom handle, cut 18 in. long, with one end fastened in a hole bored centrally in the 5-in. crosspiece of the front sled. A hole is bored in the top board through the center of the crosspiece fastened to the underside for the steering post. The broomstick is run through this hole after first placing two metal washers on it. After running the stick through, a hardwood collar is fastened to it just

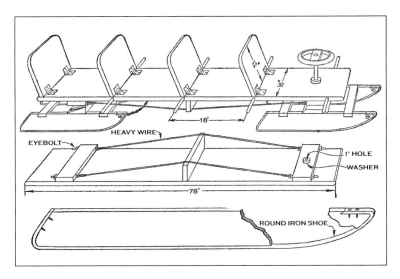

THE TOP BOARD IS WELL BRACED ON THE UNDERSIDE AND FITTED WITH FOUR BACKS ON TOP TO MAKE IT A LUXURIOUS RIDING SLED, AND THE RUNNERS ARE PROVIDED WITH METAL SHOES FOR SPEED.

above the top board, so that the top cannot be raised away from the sled. A steering wheel, made from a nail-keg hoop, is attached at the upper end of the broomstick. A piece of wood is fastened across its diameter, and the hoop is covered with a piece of garden hose and wrapped with twine. In the center of the crosspiece, a hole is bored to snugly fit on the broom handle, which is then fastened with screws.

The rear sled is fastened to the top board with screws through the extending wings of the hinges and into the crosspiece. Holes are bored in the front ends of all runners, and a chain or rope is attached in them. The loop end of the rear one is attached to the underside of the top board, and the one in the front used for drawing the sled.

Materials

1 top, 6 ½ ft. long, 16 in. wide, and 1¼ in. thick

4 runners, 22 in. long, 4 in. wide, and 1 in. thick

4 crosspieces, 16 in. long, 3 in. wide, and 1 in. thick

3 pieces, 16 in. long, 3 in. wide, and 1 in. thick

1 piece, 16 in. long, 5 in. wide, and 2 in. thick

1 shore, 16 in. long, 3 in. wide, and 1 in. thick

4 seat backs, 12 in. long, 16 in. wide, and 1 in. thick

1 dowel, 3 ft. long, and 1 in. in diameter

4 rods, ⅝ in. in diameter, and 30 in. long

4 eyebolts, ½ in. by 6 in. long

3 hinges, 5-in. strap

8 hinges, 3-in. strap

— HOW TO BUILD A TOBOGGAN SLED —

The first object of the builder of a sled should be to have a "winner," both in speed and appearance. The accompanying instructions for building a sled are designed to produce these results.

The sled completed should be 15 ft. 2 in. long by 22 in. wide, with the cushion about 15 in. above the ground. For the baseboard select a pine board 15 ft. long, 11 in. wide, and 2 in. thick, and plane it on all edges. Fit the baseboard with ten oak footrests, 22 in. long, 3 in. wide, and ¾ in. thick. Fasten them on the underside of the baseboard at right angles to its length and 16 in. apart, beginning at the rear. At the front

24 or 26 in. will be left without crossbars for fitting on the auto front. On the upper side of the crossbars at their ends on each side, screw a piece of oak 1 in. square by 14 ft. long. On the edges of the upper side of the baseboard screw an oak strip 3 in. wide by ¾ in. thick and the length of the sled from the back to the auto front. These are to keep the cushion from falling out. See *Fig. 1*. For the back of the sled use the upper part of a child's high chair, taking out the spindles and resetting them in the rear end of the baseboard. Cover the outside of the spindles with a piece of galvanized iron.

The construction of the runners is shown in *Figs. 2* and *3*. The stock required is oak, two pieces 30 in. by 5 in. by 1¼ in., two pieces 34 in. by 5 in. by 1¼ in., two pieces 14 in. by 6 in. by 2 in., and four pieces 14 in. by 2 in. by 1 in. They should be put together with large screws about 3 in. long. Do not use nails, because they

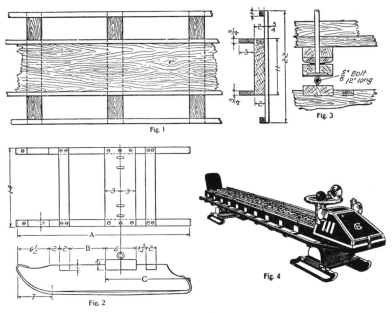

Fig. 1

Fig. 3

Fig. 2

Fig. 4

CONSTRUCTING A "WINNER" TOBOGGAN SLED.

are not substantial enough. In proportioning them, the points *A, B,* and *C, Fig. 2,* are important. For the front runners these measurements are: *A,* 30 in.; *B,* 4 in.; *C,* 15½ in. For the rear runners: *A,* 34 in.; *B,* 7 in.; *C,* 16½ in. The screw eyes indicated must be placed in a straight line and the holes for them carefully centered. A variation of ¹/₁₆ in. one way or another would cause a great deal of trouble. For the steel runners use ⅜-in. cold-rolled steel flattened at the ends for screw holes. Use no screws on the running surface, however, as they "snatch" the ice.

The mechanism of the front steering gear is shown at *Fig. 3.* A ¾-in. steel rod makes a good steering rod. Flatten the steering rod at one end and sink it into the wood. Hold it in place by means of an iron plate drilled to receive the rod and screwed to block *X.* An iron washer, *Z,* is used to reduce friction; bevel block *K* to give a rocker motion. Equip block *X* with screw eyes, making them clear those in the front runner, and bolt through. For the rear runner put a block with screw eyes on the baseboard and run a bolt through.

Construct the auto front (*Fig. 4*) of ¾-in. oak boards. The illustration shows how to shape it. Bevel it toward all sides and keep the edges sharp, as sharp edges are best suited for the brass trimmings that are to be added. When the auto front is in place, enamel the sled either a dark maroon or a creamy white. First sandpaper all the wood, and then apply a coat of thin enamel. Let stand for three days and apply another coat. Three coats of enamel and one of thin varnish will make a fine-looking sled. For the brass trimmings use No. 24 B. and S. sheet brass 1 in. wide on all the front edges and pieces 3 in. square on the crossbars to rest the feet against. On the door of the auto front put the monogram of the owner or owners of the sled, cutting it out of sheet brass.

For the steering wheel procure an old freight-car "brake" wheel, brass-plated. Fasten a horn, such as used on automobiles, to the wheel.

Make the cushion of leather and stuff it with hair. The best way is to get some strong, cheap material, such as burlap, sew up one end and make the form of an oblong bag. Stuff this as tightly as possible with hair. Then get some upholstery buttons, fasten a cord through the loop, bring the cord through to the underside of the cushion, and fasten the button by slipping a nail through the knot. Then put a leather covering over the burlap, sewing it to the burlap on the underside. Make the cushion for the back in the same way. On top of the cushion supports run a brass tube to serve the double purpose of holding the cushion down and affording something to hold on to.

If desired, bicycle lamps may be fastened to the front end, to improve the appearance. It is wise to have a light of some kind at the back to avoid the danger of rear-end collisions.

The door of the auto front should be hinged and provided with a lock so that skates, parcels, overshoes, lunch, etc., may be stowed within. A silk pennant with a monogram adds to the appearance.

If desired, a brake may be added to the sled. This can be a wrought-iron lever 1½ in. by ½ in. by 30 in. long, so pivoted that moving the handle will cause the end to scrape the ice. This sled can be made without lamps and horn at a reduced cost. If the expense is greater than one can afford, a number of boys may share in the ownership.

— Rudder for a Toboggan —

Learning to steer a toboggan by means of the foot dragged behind it is an interesting feature of the sport, but this method is dangerous at times and results in much wear on shoes and clothes. The device shown in the illustration makes this method of steering unnecessary and gives the rider accurate control over the sled. It consists of a strip of ¼ by 1-in. iron curved to form a rudder at one end and twisted at the middle to provide a flat piece

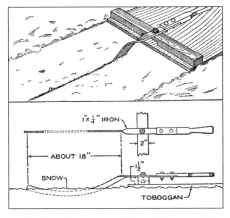

This rudder for a toboggan ensures positive control and prevents wear on the shoes and clothes of the rider.

for pivoting it on the rear cleat of the sled, as shown in the working drawing. A handle is fastened to the front end of the strip with bolts. The rudder should not be curved too deeply or it will cut through the snow and be damaged, or ruin the track.

— HOW TO MAKE A MONORAIL SLED —

AN EXHILARATING GLIDE ACCOMPANIED BY A BUOYANT SENSE OF FREEDOM OBTAINED ONLY ON THE MONORAIL TYPE.

A monorail sled, having a simple tandem arrangement of the runners, is very easily constructed as follows: The runners are cut from 1-in. plank of the size and shape given in the sketch, and are shod with strap iron, 1 in. wide and ¼ in. thick. Round iron or half-round iron should not be used, as these are liable to skid. The square, sharp edges of the strap iron prevent this and grip the surface just as a skate.

The top is a board 6 ft. long and 1 in. thick, securely fastened to the runners as follows: Blocks are nailed or bolted on either side of the upper edge of the rear runner, and the top is fastened to them with screws. The runner is also braced with strap iron, as shown. The same method applies to the front runner, except that only one pair of blocks is used at the center and a thin piece of wood fastened to their tops to serve as the fifth wheel.

The hole for the steering post should be 6 in. from the front end and a little larger in diameter than the steering post. The latter should be rounded where it passes through the hole, but square on the upper end to receive the steering bar, which must be tightly fitted in place.

In coasting, the rider lies full length on the board with his hands on the steering bar. This makes the

center of gravity
so low that there
is no necessity for
lateral steadying
runners. In addi-
tion to the exhila-
rating glide of the

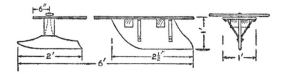

THE CONSTRUCTION IS MUCH MORE SIMPLE THAN
MAKING A DOUBLE-RUNNER BOBSLED.

ordinary sled, the rider experiences a buoyant sense off freedom and a zest peculiar to the monorail type. Then, too, the steering is affected much more easily. Instead of dragging the feet, a slight turn of the front runner with a corresponding movement of the body is sufficient to change the direction or to restore the balance. This latter is, of course, maintained quite mechanically, as everyone who rides a bicycle well knows.

— THE RUNNING SLEIGH —

Another winter sport very popular in Sweden, and one that has already reached America, is the "running sleigh," shown in the illustration. A light sleigh is equipped with long double runners and is propelled by foot power. The person using the sleigh stands with one foot upon a rest attached to one of the braces connecting the runners and propels the sleigh by pushing backward with the other foot. An upright support is attached to the runners to steady the body. The contrivance can be used upon hard frozen ground, thin ice, and snow-covered surfaces. Under favor-

RUNNING SLEIGH

able conditions it moves with remarkable speed. The running sleigh has a decided advantage over skis, because the two foot supports are braced so that they cannot come apart.

— A Ski Sled —

The sled is built low and wide so that it will not tip easily. The skis, or runners, are cut 10 ft. long and 6 in. wide, from 1-in. ash boards that are straight-grained. At the points where the curve is to be formed, plane off about ¼ in. on the upper side, but do not plane off any at the very tip end. This will allow the skis to be more easily bent. If it is not handy to steam the skis, put them in boiling water, and be sure that at least 1½ ft. of the points are covered. Provide a cover for the vessel, so that only very little steam may escape. Let them boil for at least one hour. A good method of bending the points is shown. When the skis are taken from the water, put them as quickly as possible in the bending blocks, side by side, and bend them with a slow, even pressure. Weight the extending ends and leave the skis in the blocks 8 or 10 hours to dry. Sharpen the points after they are bent.

The sled will run easier if the skis have slight rocker curve. To make this curve, have the center block 6 in. while the two end blocks are 5½ in. high. A ¼-in. flathead bolt is run through the ski, the block, and the cross strip. The holes are countersunk in the surface for the heads of the bolts. The top is made of three 6-in. boards, fastened to the cross-pieces. It is a good plan to brace the tips of the skis with a 2-in. strip.

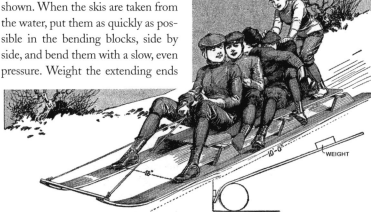

THE RUNNERS ARE SHAPED LIKE A SKI AND ARE JOINED TOGETHER WITH KNEES FOR THE TOP BOARD.

— A Motorcycle Bobsled —

Most motorcycle owners put their machines away when the snow begins to fly, and forego their use during the winter months. However, the photograph shows how one enthusiast constructed a bobsled that uses the motorcycle power plant to drive it along the frozen surface.

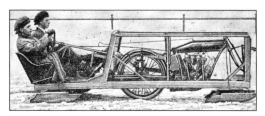

INSTEAD OF STORING THE MOTORCYCLE DURING THE COLD WINTER MONTHS, IT IS USED, IN THIS CASE, TO DRIVE A BOBSLED. THE FRONT WHEEL AND HANDLEBARS ARE REMOVED, AND THE MACHINE IS HELD UPRIGHT IN A WOODEN FRAMEWORK.

The front wheel and handlebars are removed from the machine, which is held vertically in a framework built as a part of the sled body. The front fork is firmly fastened and the rear wheel is placed between two guideboards, so arranged as to prevent the walls of the tire from rubbing against the sides. An old tire was used on the single wheel, and additional traction obtained by the use of a tire chain. The sled is steered by means of a steering wheel operating the front set of runners, which swivels on a pin at the center.

— Motor-Driven Sleds —

For those who wish to build a motor-driven sled but do not want to go to the trouble and expense of making or buying an aerial propeller and adapting the engine to this form of drive, the wheel-driven sleds described in this article will be of great value.

The first machine has a light steel frame supported on oak runners, shod with round steel. The sled is driven by a four-cylinder motorcycle engine, geared to the driving wheel in the same manner as in the motorcycle. The driving wheel, which is a standard motorcycle wheel, is mounted in a U-shaped angle-iron yoke. The ends of the yoke are attached to a crosspiece on the steel frame by means of stout hinges. A stiff spring is provided on each side of the yoke for holding the wheel to the surface, while at the same time permitting free vertical movement. Thus there is no loss of traction and the sled can travel over uneven ground. The wheel is covered by a sheet-metal hood, forward of which and a little above the top of the engine, the gasoline tank is mounted on a frame made of flat iron. The sled is steered by means of the front runners, which are controlled through sash-cord steering ropes running to the steering wheel. The steering wheel is located immediately behind the wheel hood, on the right-hand side of the sled. Footrests are provided on each side of the machine, and the brake lever is within easy reach of the driver's hand on the right-hand side. The brake is simply a pointed steel lever that digs into the ice when the hand lever is pulled back; the clutch-control lever is at the left of the driver's seat. The small tank seen on top of the engine, at the front, is a two-quart oilcan.

A somewhat similar sled, though less ambitious in design, is driven by a twin-cylinder motorcycle engine. This one is designed along the lines

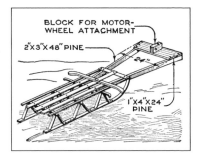

of a light automobile or cycle car. The builder has used it on both snow and ice, and found it to be an excellent hill climber. The machine is 9½ ft. long over all, and the frame is made of light angle iron, with front and rear runners of wood. The chain-driven drive wheel, which is mounted as described in the first type, has short sections of 2-in. angle iron riveted around its circumference. The sled is guided by the front runners, through a regulation automobile steering post and drag line connected to a steering knuckle fastened to the runners. The spark and throttle control are regulated from the levers on the steering wheel.

The simplest type of these kind of sleds consists merely of an ordinary "coaster," to which is attached a motor wheel. The small drawing shows the framework to which the motor wheel is fastened. To create this frame two pieces of pine, 2 by 3 by 48 in., and a crosspiece, 1 by 4 by 24 in., are required. Combined with a block attached to the crosspiece, the pieces of pine are drilled for attaching the motor wheel, which is mounted so as to permit steering. This sled has attained a speed of 20 miles an hour on a level surface.

These brief descriptions may stimulate interest in the fascinating winter sport of motor sleighing, and will also serve to crystallize the ideas of those who wish to build such a sled, and are wondering which type to select. All of these designs have been tried out and found to be successful, and it is merely a matter of the builder's choice which one to select.

WATER SPORTS

— HOW TO MAKE A WATER BICYCLE —

Water bicycles afford fine sport and, like many other devices boys make, can be made of material often cast off by their people as rubbish. The principal elements necessary for the construction of a

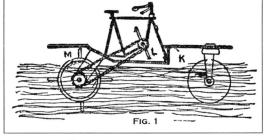

FIG. 1

WATER BICYCLE COMPLETE

water bicycle are oil barrels. Flour barrels will not do—they are not strong enough, nor can they be made perfectly airtight. The grocer can furnish you with oil barrels at a very small cost, and may even let you have them for making a few deliveries for him. Three barrels are required for the water bicycle, although it can be made with but two. *Fig. 1* shows the method of arranging the barrels after the manner of bicycle wheels.

Procure an old bicycle frame and make for it a board platform about 3 ft. wide at the rear end and tapering to about 2 ft. at the front. Use cleats to hold the board frame, as shown in the shaded portion *K.* The construction of the barrel part is shown in *Fig. 2.* Bore holes in the center of the heads of the two rear barrels and also in the heads of the first barrel and put a shaft of wood through the rear barrels and one through the front barrel, adjusting the side pieces to the shafts, as indicated.

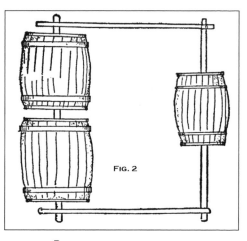

FIG. 2

BARREL FLOAT FOR BICYCLE

Next place the platform of the bicycle frame and connections thereon. Going back to *Fig. 1* we see that the driving chain passes from the sprocket driver, *L,* of the bicycle frame to the place downward between the slits in the platform to the driven sprocket on the shaft

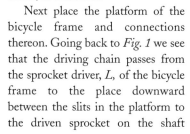

FIG. 3

ANOTHER TYPE OF FLOAT

between the two barrels. Thus a center drive is made. The rear barrels are fitted with paddles as in *M,* consisting of four pieces of board nailed and cleated about the circumference of the barrels, as shown in *Fig. 1.*

The new craft is now ready for a first voyage. To propel it, seat yourself on the bicycle seat, feet on the pedals, just as you would were you on a bicycle out in the street. The steering is affected by simply bending the body to the left or right, which causes the craft to dip to the inclined side and the whole affair turns in the dipped direction. The speed is slow at first, but increases as the force is generated and as one becomes familiar with the working of the bike. There is no danger, because the airtight barrels cannot possibly sink.

Another mode of putting together the set of barrels, using one large one in the rear and a small one in the front is presented in *Fig. 3*. These two barrels are empty oil barrels like the others. The head holes are bored and the proper wood shafts are inserted and the entrance to the bores closed tight by calking with hemp and putty or clay. The ends of the shafts turn in the wooden frame where the required bores are made to receive the same. If the journals thus made are well oiled, there will not be much friction. Such a frame can be fitted with a platform and a raft to suit one's individual fancy built upon it, which can be paddled about with ease and safety on any pond. A sail can be rigged up by using a mast and some sheeting. Or even a little houseboat, which will give any amount of pleasure, can be built.

— WATER-COASTING TOBOGGAN AND SLIDE —

Coasting down an incline and being projected through the air to plunge into the warm water of a summer lake, or other outdoor bathing spot, offers thrills and excitement to the person seeking a new aquatic diversion. The illustration shows a slide and the toboggan sled for use on it, which were built by a group of young men at a summer resort. Though the slide shown is perhaps more extensive than most boys would care to undertake, the principle involved may be adapted easily to a model one-fourth as long, less than 20 ft. The slide shown was strongly built of 2- by 4-in. material for the framework, 2- by 6-in. planks for the slide guides, and 2- by 12-in. planks for the roller bearing. Lighter material may be used for the guides and the roller bearing on a smaller slide, but the framework should be of 2- by 2-in. stock.

The high end of the slide illustrated is about 7 ft. from the ground, but a proportionately greater incline is provided because the beach slopes gradually to the water's edge. It is reached by a ladder fixed to a tree, which acts as an end brace for the slide. If no such natural support is available, the end of the slide must be strongly braced on three sides, to ensure safety. It is inadvisable to build the slide unduly high to provide the necessary incline, because this may result in accidents. A location where the ground is suitable should be selected rather than assume danger or risk.

The end of the slide nearest the water may be given a slight upward turn, so that when the toboggan leaves it the rider is carried upward before striking the water. The hold on the toboggan should be retained when entering the water, because injury may result by failure to clear it in the plunge. With experience a dive may be made as the toboggan leaves the slide.

The construction of the slide is shown in detail in the lower sketch. The framework of 2- by 4-in. material should be only slightly wider than the guides, and the supports should be spread toward the ground to give rigidity. The supports, *A*, should be nailed firmly, or bolted, to the horizontal members, *B*. If lighter stock is used, the pieces at *B* should be nailed in pairs, one on each side of the uprights. The guides *C* and *D*

should be of smooth lumber, and the edges of these pieces, as well as of the bearing plank *E*, should be rounded off to remove splinters. The joints in the sections of the guides should be made carefully and placed over the framework supports. They should be reinforced from the lower side by plates of wood.

The bearing plank, *E*, is of 2-in. stock and 12 in. wide. It may be made of lighter material in a smaller slide. The joints in it should likewise be made carefully, to ensure smooth riding over them. They should be set directly over the framework supports, but not on those over which joints have been made in the guides. The plank forming the bearing for the roller should not extend to the end of the slide at the lower end, but should be set back about 18 in. This permits the toboggan to slide off smoothly rather than to spring directly into the air from the bearing on the rollers. The bearing plank may be nailed into place, but care must be taken to set all nails below the surface. A better construction is to use screws or bolts. Bore holes for them through the plank, countersinking their heads.

The toboggan, as shown in the detail sketches, is built strongly. It is to be fitted over the 12-in. bearing

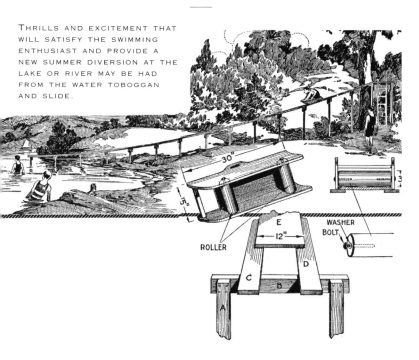

THRILLS AND EXCITEMENT THAT WILL SATISFY THE SWIMMING ENTHUSIAST AND PROVIDE A NEW SUMMER DIVERSION AT THE LAKE OR RIVER MAY BE HAD FROM THE WATER TOBOGGAN AND SLIDE.

plank, allowing ¼-in. play on each side. The sides are of 1¼-in. stock and high enough to accommodate the rollers, which should be about 3 in. in diameter. The dimensions of 15 in. in width and 30 in. in length, on the top surface, are suggestive only, and will vary with the materials used. The toboggan will not stand the necessarily hard wear unless good-quality oak or other hardwood is used. The top and foot brace should be fixed strongly with screws,

their heads countersunk.

The rollers are fixed in the sides by means of screws, or a bolt may be set through the length of the roller. In either case the bearing should be in holes bored through the side-pieces. Washers should be fitted at the sides of the bearings, and the latter must be kept greased. All the edges and corners of the toboggan should be rounded off so that there is a little possibility of injury from slivers or contact with the edges.

— Making a Catamaran Raft —

A simple raft that will meet the requirements for an inexpensive and simple boat can be made from two or three logs in the manner indicated in the drawing.

Two logs, about 12 ft. long, are used for the sides. These are connected with crosspieces, spikes or wooden pegs being used to secure the parts together. A piece of split log answers for a seat, and two forked branches inserted into the sidepieces make satisfactory oar-

A USEFUL BOAT, BUILT OF LOGS
AS A CATAMARAN RAFT, TAKES THE PLACE
OF A REGULATION ROWBOAT WHEN THE LATTER
IS NOT EASILY OBTAINED.

locks. In the absence of regulation oars, pieces of board can be cut to approximately the proper shape.

— How to Make a Sailomobile —

Having read of the beach automobiles used on the Florida coast an enthusiast noted that they were like an ice boat with a sail, except they had wheels instead of runners. So he set to work to make something to take him over the country roads.

He found and used seven fence pickets for the framework, and other things, as they were needed. He spliced two rake handles together for the mast, winding the ends where they came together with wire. (A single piece is superior if you can get one long enough.) The gaff, which is the stick to which the upper end of the sail is fastened, is a broomstick. The boom, the stick at the bottom of the sail, was made of a rake handle with a broomstick spliced to make it long enough. The innovative mechanic borrowed a sheet, which he put down on the floor and cut in the shape of a mainsail. The wind was the cheapest power to be found, thus it was utilized; the three wheels were cast-off bicycle wheels.

The rider steers with the front wheel, which is the front wheel of an old bicycle with the fork left on. The axle between the rear wheels is an iron bar, and the pulley that raises and lowers the sail.

A saw, hammer, brace, and bit were the tools used. Slats made a seat and a cushion from the house made it comfortable, and in a week everything was ready for sailing.

On *the* Ice

— Building an Ice Yacht —

Hull Construction

Although the northern part of this country is blessed with innumerable lakes and streams where that king of winter sports, ice yachting, should be enjoyed, comparatively little definite is known of the construction of fast, easily handled craft, except around such ice-yachting centers as the Hudson and Shrewsbury rivers, Orange Lake, and some Midwestern lakes.

From the number of crude makeshift affairs so often seen, it is obvious that many real yachts would be built to the lasting delight of the owners and their friends, if their design and construction were only better understood. It is for the purpose of providing this information that this article is written. The yacht herein described, while not too large to be used on a good sized pond or small lake, is of sufficient size and speed for the most exciting races. At the same time it is perfectly safe and easily handled, provided the given measurements are strictly adhered to.

The material used in the construction depends to a great extent on available supply. In purchasing the lumber, one should always buy the driest obtainable, and the better the quality the better looking the completed boat will be. There is no reason why one who can use carpenters'

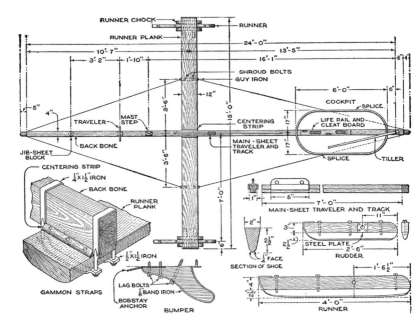

DETAILS OF THE BACKBONE, RUNNER PLANK, AND RUNNERS.
NOTE THE CURVE ON THE EDGE OF THE RUNNER, AND
THE POSITION OF THE SPLICES ON THE COCKPIT.

tools with ordinary skill should not be able to turn out a first-class job with a moderate outlay—if the instructions are closely followed.

For the backbone, butternut, white pine, and basswood are the most suitable woods, although cypress may also be used. The tendency of spruce to "wind" eliminates that wood from all consideration. Because it is hardly possible to obtain one stick long enough for this part, allowance must be made for a splice of not less than 8 ft., and longer than this if possible. This splice should be made with one long, straight cut, without notches of any sort, as the notches weaken the timber. Only the best grade of pot glue should be used, and the joint thoroughly fastened with ½-in. lag bolts, put in from the bottom, with large washers under the heads. When spliced, the stick should measure 4 in. by 8 in. by 25¼ ft. It is left straight on the underside throughout its entire length and of full width. But the top of the bowsprit is tapered in a curve, beginning at the mast, down to the shoulder where the eyebolt for the forestay goes through. Here it is made 4 in. thick, and from a point 2 ft. aft of the runner plank another curved taper should run to the stern shoulder, where it is 6 in. thick. All four corners on the bowsprit are rounded, and after the cockpit is in position, the afterpart of the backbone should be slightly rounded all the way to the stern. The tip of the bowsprit is rounded for a distance of 5 in., to receive the guys and bobstay, and the stern for a distance of 4 in., as shown in the deck plan. To ensure an accurate rudderpost hole, it is bored halfway through from the top and finished from the bottom. The whole backbone should then be planed smooth, and finished with cabinet scraper, sandpaper, and generous quantities of elbow grease. It should then be soused with boiled oil. This applies to every part made of wood, because the oil prevents it from turning black should the varnish be marred.

The cockpit is the only really difficult part of the whole boat to make. The rims are made of cherry and oak, and require steaming and bending over a form, with two splices where shown. The oak rim is 4 in. wide by 1 in. thick, is finished smooth and, after forming and splicing, is placed in position and accurately centered on the backbone. Marks are made on the under edge of the rim to correspond with the edges of the backbone, and notches ½ in. deep and as wide as the backbone are cut in the rim. These notches fit over the backbone, to which the cockpit is securely fastened by two large screws at each end. A heavy iron strap, bent in the shape of an "L," is screwed to both the backbone and the inside of the cockpit rim at each end.

The bottom can be made of either ½-in. whitewood, in one piece, or of oak strips 1 in. wide, with ¼-in. space left between them. Strips are better, because the spaces permit snow and water to pass through so that no ice can form. The bottom is screwed to the underside of the oak rim shaped to the form shown, and reinforced by three strips of flat iron. The cherry covering board extends just below the joint of the bottom and rim, and is spliced on the side opposite to the splice in the oak and thoroughly screwed to the rim. All screw heads are sunk in deeply and wood-plugged. The handrail is of oak, on apple or maple spindles. The life rail and cleat board are of 1-in. oak, the same width as the backbone, with the forward end screwed to the cockpit rim and the after end raised level on an oak block.

Butternut, white pine, basswood, and ash are the most suitable woods from which to make the runner plank, although cypress is also excellent. If ash is used, the finished plank should be ½ in. thinner than the softer woods. The rough plank should measure 16 ft. long by a full 4-by-12-in. section. As in the backbone, the underside is planed perfectly straight. The center is then marked with pencil, and from this all measurements are taken. A thickness of 2½ in. measured from the under edge is marked at each end. A long, thin batten is sprung from these marks to the top edge at the center, and a line drawn to mark the curve to which the plank is finished. The four runner chocks and four brackets are made in pairs from 2-in. oak, or maple, of best quality. Lay off and mark the position of the inner starboard (right-hand, looking forward) chock, referring to the deck plan.

Square the chock very accurately and bolt with four ½-in. carriage bolts, after sinking the chock into the runner plank ¼ in. This prevents the runners from becoming twisted out of true, and applies to all four chocks, because no other part of the boat is subject to such a terrific strain. All bolts should have washers under the heads as well as under the nuts. One pair of brackets is fastened to the chock using very large screws, then fastened to the plank. Assuming that the runners are finished, mark one with an "S," indicating that it is always to be used on the starboard side. Place it in position with built-up cardboard, 1 in. thick, between it and the chock. Put the outer chock in position, and then put the runner bolt through all three, tightening the nut with your fingers. This will give the position in which the outer chock is to be bolted, with sufficient allowance of space to ensure free play for the runner. Cut an "A" with a chisel on the rear edge of the plank at the center, corresponding with the heel of the runner, indicating that this is the after edge. Mark the position of the inner chock on the port (left-hand) side, and bolt with one bolt only, without sinking the chock into the plank. Place the runner, cardboard, and the outer chock in place, as on the starboard side. Cut a 2-in. notch in the edge of a board equal in length to the runner plank, place it over the heel of the starboard runner, and make a slight mark where it rests on the heel of the port runner. Shift the plank to the forward end of the runners to find if the running edges are parallel. Repeat this, shifting the port runner and chock until the running edges prove absolutely parallel. Upon their accuracy—more than on any other one thing—depend the sailing qualities of the boat. Sink in and secure the remaining chocks and brackets permanently, and remove the cardboard strips. Saw off and round the ends of the plank, as shown. From a point opposite the inner ends of the chock brackets, spring another curve parallel with the top of the plank. Chamfer off the under edge, giving the plank a curved appearance. Strips of quarter-round hardwood are then screwed across the center in such a position that the backbone will always rest across the center of the plank.

Cast iron of the best grade is the only material that may be used for the runner shoes of an ice yacht. Therefore a wooden pattern of the exact size and shape of the finished shoe must be made, from which to have the shoes cast, and one for the rudder also. Although the drawings show the runners in detail, a description of the shoe is necessary. The running edge is a true right angle, and must be kept so in order to the get the utmost speed out of the boat. The faces of the right angle are ¼ in. wide. The upper face must be trued in a planing machine and then drilled and tapped for cap screws. As a majority of foundries have a machine shop in connection with them, this should not be an expensive piece of work. The oak or maple top must be perfectly fitted and bedded to the shoe, and the joint made with a marine gasket. The cap screws are ⅜ in., with washers under the heads, and are drawn up very tight. The bolt just aft of the runner bolt hole is countersunk to clear the runner plank. The runners must be filed with the greatest possible accuracy by the following method: Place one in the vise and, using a wooden straightedge as a guide, file the running edge to the perfect curve. The point beneath the bolt hole should be left untouched and the toe and heel filed down 3/16 in. The straightedge should rock back and forth smoothly. File the faces back to a sharp right angle and finish with a carborundum stone. The runner bolt holes are bushed with brass pipe of sufficient diameter to take a ½-in. bolt freely. These bolts have square heads, sunk into the chock ¼ in. to prevent turning, and are 8 in. long, with cotter pins outside the washers and nuts. A box, or crate, should be made to hold and protect the runners when not in use. Any slight damage to the running edge may mean a long job of filing. In use, the runners should always remain on the ice overnight, to prevent rusting, and the edges kept in perfect and sharp condition for racing.

A hardwood bumper, made from 2-in. stuff and bound with flat iron, screwed on, is placed just forward of the rudder. It will be necessary to take measurements for this part with the rudder in position. The bobstay anchor is of ¼- by 1¼-in. flat iron, with holes drilled for lagscrews and for attaching a turnbuckle.

The track for the main sheet traveler is made of any close-grained hardwood, in two pieces. It is screwed to the backbone, as shown. The forward part should be removable, to allow the gammon straps too be placed in position. It should be well oiled, and only the top varnished. If it is varnished all over, the traveler will stick. The traveler must be made of brass or bronze.

As soon as the oil is thoroughly dried, go over the whole lightly with fine sandpaper and apply two or three coats of the best spar varnish obtainable, rubbing lightly between coats. All metal work not of brass should be painted with aluminum paint. This completes the hull woodwork.

Spars, Rigging, and Assembling

Only the best grade of spruce is suitable for spars. Unquestionably hollow ones are lighter and stronger, but they cost a lot more. If expense is no object, buy hollow spars. Otherwise proceed as follows: For the mast select the clearest 4-by-4-in. stick to be found. For the boom and gaff use a 3-by-3-in. stick, and for the jib boom a 2-by-2-in. piece. Plane the stick for the mast fairly smooth on all four sides, then layoff a taper from a point 6 ft. from the foot, reducing the diameter to 3 in. at the heel. Plane all four sides, still keeping the stick square. From a point 5 ft. from the masthead, taper to 2½ in. Plane off all four corners, making an octagonal stick. Then, with a small plane, round the spar, and finish with

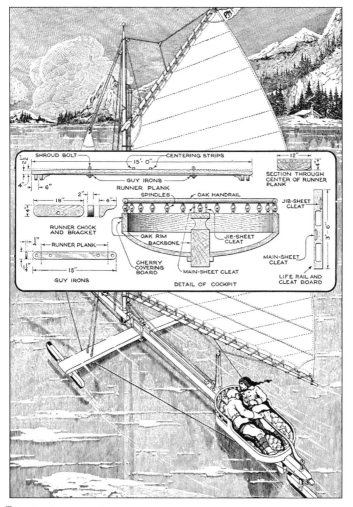

Labels in illustration:

SHROUD BOLT · CENTERING STRIPS · 15'- 0" · 12" · SECTION THROUGH CENTER OF RUNNER PLANK

GUY IRONS · 4" · 6" · RUNNER PLANK · SPINDLES · OAK HANDRAIL · JIB-SHEET CLEAT

18" · 2" · 6" · RUNNER CHOCK AND BRACKET · OAK RIM BACKBONE · JIB-SHEET CLEAT · 3'-6"

RUNNER PLANK · CHERRY COVERING BOARD · MAIN-SHEET CLEAT · MAIN-SHEET CLEAT

15" · GUY IRONS · DETAIL OF COCKPIT · LIFE RAIL AND CLEAT BOARD

THE GENERAL CONSTRUCTION OF AN ALL-AROUND ICE YACHT OF THE HUDSON-RIVER TYPE IS SHOWN IN THIS ILLUSTRATION. IF MADE ACCORDING TO THE INSTRUCTIONS GIVEN, THIS YACHT WILL PROVE NOT FAST ENOUGH FOR RACING, BUT VERY EASILY HANDLED AND SAFE.

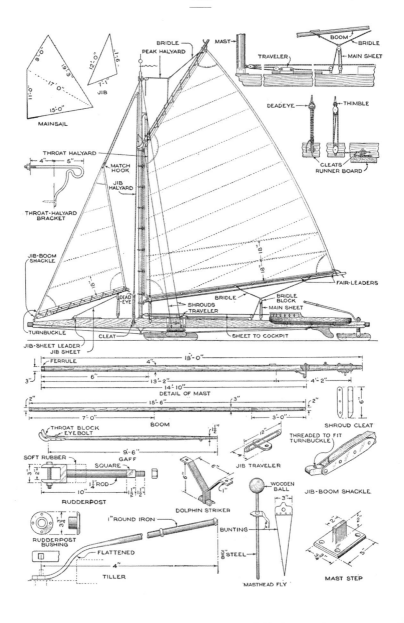

JIB

MAINSAIL

BRIDLE
PEAK HALYARD
MAST

BOOM
BRIDLE
TRAVELER
MAIN SHEET

THROAT HALYARD

MATCH HOOK

JIB HALYARD

THROAT-HALYARD BRACKET

DEADEYE
THIMBLE

CLEATS
RUNNER BOARD

JIB-BOOM SHACKLE

DEAD-EYE
SHROUDS
TRAVELER

BRIDLE
BRIDLE BLOCK
MAIN SHEET

FAIR-LEADERS

TURNBUCKLE
CLEAT
JIB-SHEET LEADER
JIB SHEET
SHEET TO COCKPIT

FERRULE
DETAIL OF MAST

BOOM

SHROUD CLEAT

THROAT BLOCK
EYE BOLT

GAFF

JIB TRAVELER

THREADED TO FIT TURNBUCKLE

SOFT RUBBER
SQUARE
ROD
RUDDERPOST

DOLPHIN STRIKER

JIB-BOOM SHACKLE

RUDDERPOST BUSHING

1" ROUND IRON

FLATTENED
TILLER

WOODEN BALL

BUNTING

STEEL

MASTHEAD FLY

MAST STEP

enough sandpaper and elbow grease—especially the elbow grease—to remove all plane marks. If any attempt is made to round the spar before tapering, it will be found impossible to keep it straight. A brass or iron ferrule, 2 in. wide, is fitted to the foot to prevent splitting, and a mortise cut to receive the mast step. Shroud cleats of apple wood or maple, of the form shown, are screwed at the points indicated, and the throat-halyard bracket and eyebolts put in place. The boom and gaff are identical in construction to the mast. The boom tapers to 2 in. at either end, with a large hole through the after end for the sail haul-out. The gaff tapers to 1½ in. at each end, with a haul-out hole at the peak. Oak jaws, fitted with a throat block, are riveted at the throat. It is best to buy the jaws from a ship chandler. The jib boom is not tapered, but is rounded, and the jaws of the jib-boom shackle are riveted in place. The bridle cleats for the boom and gaff are similar to the shroud cleats, but smaller.

Wherever possible, brass or bronze should be used for the fittings, although iron will do. The detail drawings show the masthead fly, throat-halyard bracket, and the two guy irons so plainly that no description is needed. The jib traveler is of ⅜-in. rod, riveted and brazed to a ¼ in. plate. Tenpenny nails make excellent cross pins for the traveler. The object of these is to prevent the sheet block from slipping around to the underside of the traveler. The two members of the mast step are also riveted and brazed. The dolphin striker is of ¼-by-1-in. stock, with a half section of pipe brazed in the lower end of the "V." The jib-boom shackle is all brass, with the end hole threaded to fit the forestay turnbuckle. The gammon-strap set cannot be made until the backbone and runner-plank parts are in place. It will probably be found advisable to cut strong paper patterns of the gammon straps for the blacksmith or machinist to work from. The bolts on the straps are riveted and brazed to the flat iron. Unless cast of bronze and turned,

DETAILS OF SAILS, RIGGING, AND HULL FITTINGS.
IN THE UPPER RIGHT-HAND CORNER IS A DETAIL DRAWING
OF THE METHOD OF RIGGING THE MAINSHEET; BELOW THIS IS
SHOWN THE METHOD OFF FASTENING THE JIB, PEAK, AND
THROAT HALYARDS TO THE PURCHASE BLOCKS.

the rudderpost must be forged by a first-class blacksmith, it being a somewhat difficult piece of work. It is fitted with a soft-rubber bumper, which greatly relieves the shock of sailing over rough ice. Of course, the tiller must be fitted to the post so that there is no lost motion. The handle is wound with cotton cord, filled with shellac, and varnished. Plates may be used in place of the rudderpost bushings. But they will soon wear, and will, in turn, wear a groove in the post. That's why bronze or cast-iron bushings, of the form shown, are well worth the extra expense. They will last forever.

Because there are a number of first-class sailmakers who specialize in ice-yacht sails, one should be selected, and the sail plan sent to him when placing the order. Yacht twill will make strong, durable sails at a low price, but the better grades of sailcloth are more satisfactory. In giving the order, the fact that the sails are for an ice yacht should be mentioned, together with the following specifications: jib to have snap hooks for forestay, and be made to lace to the boom, or the foot will be cut as for a sailing yacht. Mainsail to have thimbles in pairs on hoist for mast-hoop lacing, and single thimbles on

foot. Otherwise leave it to the sailmaker. He knows.

The cockpit cushions are made of good-quality ticking, covered with corduroy or plush on the edges and one side only. They are filled with upholsterer's moss or the contents of a discarded hair mattress, and are 2½ in. thick. In length, the covering should be 6 in. longer than the cockpit, because proper filling shortens the cushion considerably. If made long, the finished cushions will fit tightly enough to stay in place. The buttons for tacking should be covered with the same material as the cushion.

The shrouds, forestay, and guys are made of ¼-in. iron wire, and the bobstay of ⅜-in. wire. In making up each piece, the measurements must be taken from the boat itself to avoid mistakes. Loops to fit the masthead, and the ends of the backbone are first spliced. Then the opposite ends are spliced into ⅜-in. galvanized shackle-and-shackle pipe turnbuckles of the slot and cotter-pin pattern. (Never use hook turnbuckles.) All turnbuckles should be fitted with wire-rope thimbles, and all loops and splices tightly served with hard cable-laid cotton cord about ⅛ in. in diameter, filled with shellac, and varnished.

The bobstay has an eye splice formed to fit the backbone nose; from there it runs down under the dolphin striker and aft to the anchor iron screwed to the bumper. The bridles for the boom and gaff are ¼-in. wire, with loops finished as above. The halyards should be crucible cast steel, 3/16 in. in diameter, finished as follows: The jib halyard is spliced in a pair of match hooks with wire-rope thimble for attaching to the jib, and the lower end spliced around a lignum-vitae deadeye. The upper end of the peak halyard is spliced into a self-locking brass bridle fitted with a thimble, and the lower end around a thimble to receive the purchase block. The throat halyard has a thimble in each end, one for attaching to the eyebolt at the jaws of the gaff, and one for a purchase block at the lower end. The splices are finished in the same manner as for the shrouds and stays. All Manila rope is ⅜-in., spliced in, with free ends moused with sail thread. The mainsheet proper is spliced into the becket of the bridle block at one end, and around a thimble at the other, for attaching to the mainsheet traveler by a screw shackle. This traveler is hauled along the track by a purchase attached to the foot of the mast, giving ample power to trim sail easily during a race, without luffing and losing speed. The remaining ropes are so plainly shown in the illustration as to require no further description.

The halyard blocks are of the type designed for wire rope only, all others being any first-class make of bronze yacht block, with fitting suited to the work for which each block is used. Galvanized blocks will not do, nor should any have hook fittings.

Together with the rigging described above, eyebolts, mast hoops, gooseneck, cleats, lacing, and screw fair-leaders must be purchased from the ship chandler. The jib and mainsail lacing is 3/16-in. braided cotton, and the same material is used for the sail haul-outs. Fair-leaders are screwed into the top of the main boom, alternating with the thimbles on the foot of the sail, and through all is run a Manila stop, drawn very tight. Two fair-leaders are also used in the runner plank on each side of the backbone, for lashing the halyard-purchase ropes.

The whole boat, including the sails, but not the runners, should be set up complete outside the shop to prove that every part fits properly before putting it on the ice.

Always, when setting up, the gammon straps are first bolted tight. Then the runner plank and backbone are squared by measuring from the center of the rudderpost hole to a certain point on corresponding chocks at opposite ends of the plank, tightening the guys accordingly.

A combined sail and cockpit cover, preferably of waterproof duck and extending the full length of the boat, is necessary for protection from the elements. It should be made in one piece, with an opening to go around the mast, and have grommets along each edge for ties to bind it down tightly to the guys and bobstay. A horse set under the boom will hold the cover up, tent-fashion. Colors for a craft of this size should be 18 by 12 in. During snow, the runners should be removed, dried, greased, and carefully put away in their box.

In many things one finds that the pleasure of anticipation and preparation far exceeds the actuality. This, however, does not apply at all to ice-yachting. For though the construction of such a craft will give the builder many happy hours' employment, the sailing of it will prove the greatest imaginable joy after the tricks of the trade are mastered. And the only way properly to master them is racing with some old hand at the game. When that incurable disease, "ice-yachting fever," attacks one's blood, the only relief is ice-yachting.

— An Ice Glider —

The enthusiastic pushmobilist need not push aside his hobby during the winter. An amusement device for use on ice—one that will surpass the very best pushmobile—can be easily made as shown in the illustration.

Similar to an ice yacht only a great deal smaller, the ice glider will require three ordinary skates. Two of these are fastened

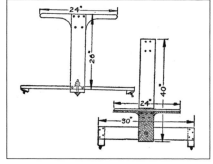

DETAIL OF THE PARTS FOR THE CONSTRUCTION OF THE ICE GLIDER.

to the ends of the front crosspiece so that their blades will stand at an angle of about 30 degrees with their edges outward. To get this angle, tapering blocks are fastened to the crosspiece ends, as shown. The skates are then fastened to these blocks.

The crosspiece is 30 in. long and about 8 in. wide. An upright is constructed, 26 in. high, in the center of this piece. The edges of the front crosspiece are cut on a slant so that a piece nailed to its front and back edges will stand sloping toward the rear. A handle, 24 in. long, is fastened between the two uprights at the upper end. The rear part is made of a board, 8 in. wide by 40 in. long. The remaining skate is fastened in a perfectly straight position on the rear rend. The skates may be attached with screws run through holes drilled in the top plates, or with straps. The front end of the rear board has a hole for a bolt to attach it to the center of the front crosspiece, so that the latter will turn to guide the glider.

A pusher is prepared from a block of wood, into which nails are driven with their ends projecting on the underside. The block is strapped to one shoe, as shown.

The glider is used in the same manner as a pushmobile.

THE GLIDER IS PUSHED OVER THE ICE SIMILARLY TO A PUSHMOBILE, AND THE SPEED THAT BE ATTAINED IS MUCH GREATER.

The pusher can be made in another way by using sole leather instead of the block. Small slots are cut in the sides for the straps. Nails are driven through the leather so that the points project. Either kind of pusher is especially adapted for the push-

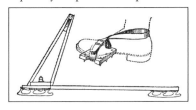

THE BLOCK OF WOOD WITH PROJECTING NAILS TO FASTEN ON THE SHOE THAT DOES THE PUSHING.

— Skates Made of Wood —

Skates that will take the place of the usual steel-runner kind and that will prevent spraining of the ankles can be made of a few pieces of ½-in. hardwood boards.

Four runners are cut out, 2 in. wide at the back and 1½ in. wide at the front. The length should be 2 in. longer than the shoe. The top edges of a pair of runners are then nailed to the underside of a board 4 in. wide, at its edges.

A piece of board, or block, 2 in. wide is fastened between the runners at the rear, and one 1 in. wide in front. Two bolts are run through holes bored in the runners, one just back of the front board, or block, and the other in front of the rear one.

Four triangular pieces are fastened,

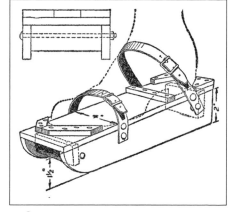

SKATES MADE OF WOOD TO TAKE THE PLACE OF THE STEEL-RUNNER KIND AND PREVENT SPRAINED ANKLES.

one on each corner, so that the heel and toe of the shoe will fit between them. If desired, a crosspiece can be nailed in front of the heel. Straps are attached to the sides for attaching the skate to the shoe. Both skates are made alike.

{ CHAPTER 4 }

FUN *for* LITTLE ONES

ANIMALS *at* PLAY

— A TOY HORSE THAT WALKS —

This toy, amusing for the young-sters and their elders as well, will repay in joy the effort taken in mak-ing it. Use a cigar box for the carriage, making it about 10 in. high, and shape it in the design shown. Nail a piece of wood, ⅛ by 2 by 4 in. wide, on each side of the carriage. Drill ⅛-in. holes in these pieces for the axle.

THE TOY IS PUSHED BY MEANS OF THE HANDLE, CAUSING THE HORSE TO WALK.

For the horse, take a piece of wood, ½ by 4 by 6 in. long, and draw an outline of the head, neck, and body.

Cut this out and drill ⅛-in. holes where the legs are attached.

Cut the legs as shown, about 3½ in. long. Attach them with small bolts, or rivets, allowing space enough for the parts to move freely. The wheels are made of pine, ½ in. thick and 3 in. in diameter. The axle is made of ³/₁₆-in. wire bent to the shape indicated, ½ in. at each offset. Fit the wheels on the axle tightly, so as not to turn on it, the axle turning in the pieces nailed to the sides of the carriage. The horse is attached to the top of the carriage by a strip of wood. A 3-ft. wooden handle is attached to the back of carriage to guide it. Wires are attached to the legs, connecting with the offsets in the axle.

— THE FIGHTING ROOSTERS —

The younger child will get a great deal of pleasure and may occupy long periods of time in playing with the toy shown in the photograph. The toy is simple to make and not apt to get out of order easily.

Two roosters are cut out of thin wood or heavy composition board and are painted in the manner illustrated. The feet of the roosters are fastened to a piece of thin spring steel by driving a tack or brad through a hole in the steel into the wood. The spring is then set into a base somewhat like the one shown, the ends being held so that the steel

TWO WOODEN ROOSTERS MOUNTED ON A PIECE OF SPRING STEEL AFFORD A COMICAL AND PERFECTLY SAFE TOY FOR THE AMUSEMENT OF A CHILD.

bends slightly upward in the middle. Finally, a wooden pin is fastened to the middle of the spring by the same method as described above. By pressing on the top of this wooden pin, the roosters are made to swing back and forth, thus giving a pretty good imitation of the belligerent barnyard fowls.

— Mechanical Toy Alligator of Wood —

A boy, using only a jackknife, can make a toy alligator that opens its mouth and wags its tail as it is pulled along. The various parts, as shown, are cut from soft wood, ½ in. thick. The method of fastening the parts is shown in the side sectional view. When the wheels turn, the cams, *A*, set on the crank portions of the wheel axles, raise and lower the jaw and tail. The upper jaw is 1 in. wide at the widest part, and 3 in. long. The lower jaw is smaller, and the same length. The body is

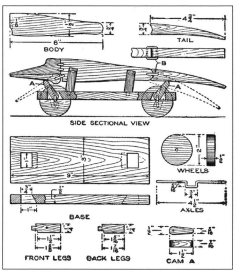

THE ALLIGATOR IS DRAWN ALONG WITH A STRING, AND THE JAWS AND TAIL FLIP UP AND DOWN.

6 in. long, and tapering in width from 1½ to ¾ in. The tail is 4¾ in. long, and ¾ in. wide. Holes are drilled in each piece near the edge, at joining points, through which wires are drawn and clamped, as in *B*. The legs are shown in detail. They are attached to the body by drilling a 1/16-in. hole in each, and a hole though the body, through which the fastenings are passed. The lower ends of the legs are fastened to

the base, which is 3 by 9 in. long. Square holes, 1 in. wide, near each end, are provided for the cams *A*. The axles and wheels are made as shown. The axles fit tightly in the wheels so that the latter can move the axles around with each turn. The axles are made from ⅛-in. wire, bent as shown. They should be long enough, after passing through the bottom, to extend through the wheels on each side.

— TOY DONKEY NODS AND WAGS ITS TAIL —

The most popular toys are those that move in imitation of some well-known object. The donkey, shown in the drawing is a good example of this. The outline is drawn on a ¾-in. block and sawed out with a scroll, band, or coping saw. The head is sawed off, as indicated. A slot is then sawed up through the legs and partway into the body. A similar, but narrower, slot is cut in the back of the head, and a strip of tin is used to connect the head to the body, as shown. A piece of tin, cut to the shape of a tail, is similarly attached in the slot behind. Both the tail and the tin strip that connects the head to the body are pivoted to the latter with small brads. Motion is imparted to the head and tail by wires that connect the parts to a screw eye underneath the wheeled

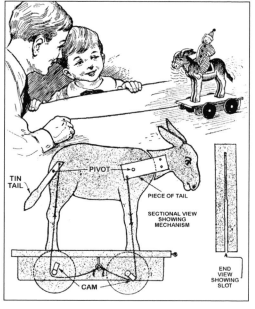

A TOY DONKEY THAT WAGS ITS TAIL AND NODS ITS HEAD WHEN DRAWN ACROSS A TABLE HAS A SIMPLE MECHANISM THAT MAKES IT EASY TO CONSTRUCT.

base on which the figure is mounted. Flat strips of wood with rounded edges, attached to the revolving axles, strike the wires as the toy is pulled across a table and cause both head and tail to move up and down. The animal may be decorated as desired.

— A JUMPING-FROG TOY —

An entertaining little toy can be made from the wishbone of a fowl after it has been well cleaned and freed from flesh.

Take a piece of strong thin string and double it, tying it securely to opposite sides of the wishbone about 1 in. from the ends, as in the drawing. Cut a strip of wood a little shorter than the bone, and make a

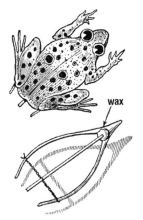

circular notch about ½ in. from one end. Push the stick through the doubled string for about half its length, twist the string tightly by means of the stick, then pull the stick through until the notch is reached. From a piece of paper or thin cardboard cut out the outline of a frog. Paint it to resemble the animal as nearly as possible, and paste this to one side of the wishbone. The only material now required is a piece of shoemaker's wax, which is placed on the underside of the bone, just where the free end of the stick will rest. When a child wants to make the frog jump, he only needs to push the stick down and press the end into the wax. Place the frog on the table, and after a short while the toy will, all of a sudden, make a very lifelike leap as the end of the stick pulls away from wax.

INCREDIBLE FLYING MACHINES

— HOW TO BUILD MODEL AIRPLANES —

The model airplanes illustrated, while they do not exemplify the very best performance or design, nevertheless have proved to be very satisfactory in flight. They also include structural features that make them easy to build. Because of this simplicity of design, they will appeal to the person who likes to build, whether he has the experience in this line or not. He will be able to complete the style of his choice, provided he has the necessary patience and consideration for detail.

Because the "race," *Fig. 1,* the "fly-about," *Fig. 2,* and the "rise-off-ground," *Fig. 9,* are nearly alike, they will be described first. The wings of all three are built up in the same manner, using materials of the same kind, but differing in their dimensions. To build the wings for any of these, two strips of white pine, basswood, or spruce are selected. They should be a trifle over the required length, and planed down to measure exactly ⅛ by ¼ in., and then cut to length. Mark the middle of the strips and drill a 1/16-in. hole through each. In the center of each end of the strips drill a 1/16-in. hole ½ in. deep. Next, cut several strips of tough paper 1 in. wide, coat them with glue, and bind each end and the middle of the spars, wrapping two or three thicknesses of paper around them. This is to prevent splitting.

From a piece of soft wire, 1/16 in. in diameter, cut a piece 1 in. longer than the distance between the centers of the spars and bend right angles ½ in. from each end. Flatten the ends of the wires on an anvil or vise, lay the spars flat on a smooth surface, and insert the short ends of the wires into the holes in the ends of the strips. Force them in as far as they will go, as indicated in *Fig. 5.* When these wires are bent to control the direction of flight they will stay so, because they are soft and because the flattened ends prevent them from moving up and down. This method bends the rear spar a little, but it has proved satisfactory on many models. After the wing frame has been assembled, lay it on a piece of tough paper, mark the outline, and then cut it out. Leaving a ½-in. margin on all sides. Now coat the underside of the frame with glue, place it on the paper, with the margin even all around. Work out the wrinkles, being careful not to bow in the spars. Cut the ends of the paper to fit between the spars, coat them with

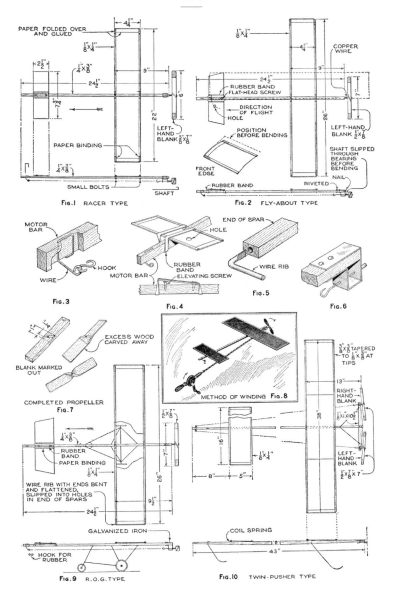

PAPER FOLDED OVER AND GLUED

$\frac{1}{8}"\times\frac{1}{4}"$

$\frac{1}{4}"\times\frac{3}{8}"$

$2\frac{1}{2}"$

9"

$24\frac{1}{2}"$

$\frac{3}{4}"$

22"

PAPER BINDING

LEFT-HAND BLANK $\frac{5}{8}"\times7"$

$\frac{1}{4}"\times\frac{3}{8}"$

SMALL BOLTS

SHAFT

FIG. 1 RACER TYPE

$\frac{1}{8}"\times\frac{1}{4}"$

$4\frac{1}{4}"$

COPPER WIRE

RUBBER BAND FLAT-HEAD SCREW

$24\frac{1}{2}"$

DIRECTION OF FLIGHT

HOLE

26"

7"

LEFT-HAND BLANK $\frac{1}{2}"\times\frac{7}{8}"$

POSITION BEFORE BENDING

FRONT EDGE

SHAFT SLIPPED THROUGH BEARING BEFORE BENDING

RUBBER BAND

NAIL

RIVETED

FIG. 2 FLY-ABOUT TYPE

MOTOR BAR

HOOK

WIRE

FIG. 3

HOLE

RUBBER BAND

MOTOR BAR

ELEVATING SCREW

FIG. 4

END OF SPAR

WIRE RIB

FIG. 5

FIG. 6

BLANK MARKED OUT

EXCESS WOOD CARVED AWAY

COMPLETED PROPELLER

FIG. 7

METHOD OF WINDING FIG. 8

$\frac{1}{2}"\times\frac{7}{8}"$

7"

$\frac{1}{4}"\times\frac{3}{8}"$

RUBBER BAND

PAPER BINDING

$\frac{1}{8}"\times\frac{1}{4}"$

26"

$9\frac{1}{2}"$

$24\frac{1}{2}"$

WIRE RIB WITH ENDS BENT AND FLATTENED, SLIPPED INTO HOLES IN END OF SPARS

GALVANIZED IRON

HOOK FOR RUBBER

FIG. 9 R.O.G. TYPE

$\frac{1}{2}"\times\frac{7}{8}"$

6"

$\frac{1}{8}"\times\frac{1}{4}"$

8"

5"

$\frac{3}{8}"\times\frac{3}{8}"$ TAPERED TO $\frac{1}{8}"\times\frac{1}{8}"$ AT TIPS

13"

RIGHT-HAND BLANK

$\frac{1}{2}"\times1"\times10\frac{1}{2}"$

36"

LEFT-HAND BLANK

$\frac{1}{2}"\times\frac{7}{8}"\times7"$

COIL SPRING

43"

FIG. 10 TWIN-PUSHER TYPE

ABOVE, LEFT: THE "FLY-ABOUT" MODEL SHOWN WITH TWO EXTRA WING RIBS. CENTER: THE "TWIN-PUSHER" TYPE WITH A CRUISING RADIUS OF FROM 600 TO 800 FEET. BELOW, LEFT: THIS VIEW OF THE FLY-ABOUT MODEL SHOWS HOW THE MOTOR IS ASSEMBLED. CENTER: A TINY MODEL COMPARED WITH THE 12-INCH RULE; IT IS DRIVEN BY A TWO-INCH PROPELLER. RIGHT: ONE OF THE MODEL PLANES IN FLIGHT.

glue, fold over the wires, and stick to the top side of the paper. After the glue has dried thoroughly, lay the wing on a smooth board and trim off the surplus paper. Punch a hole through the paper binding over the holes in the spars, and give the whole a coat of waterproof varnish to make an exceedingly tough and durable unit.

For the motor bar, cut a piece of pine or spruce, ¼ by ⅜ by 24½ in. Lay it flat, drill a ¹⁄₁₆-in. hole about ¾ in. from one end, and another ½ in. from the first. Bend a piece of soft wire as in *Fig. 3,* slip it through the holes, and bend the ends as shown. The propeller bearing on the

racer is made from a piece of sheet metal, drilled for the ¹⁄₁₆-in. diameter shaft, and fastened to the bar as shown in *Fig. 6.* It can be bound to the shaft with glued paper, which will, perhaps, be the better way for the beginner. *Fig. 7* shows how to make the propeller. The shaft should be made of wire, bent as shown in *Fig. 1,* and slipped through the hole drilled in the center of the propeller. By indenting the hub a little with the short end of the shaft, the exact position for the extra hole can be found. When this is drilled, slip the shaft through the hub again, pressing the short end into the extra hole. This prevents any chance of the propeller turning on its shaft. Another way is to flatten the end of the shaft and force the widened part into the wood, parallel with the grain.

The elevator, *Fig. 4,* is made of pine or basswood. It is bound in the middle with glued paper, as described for the wing spars and indicated by the shaded section in *Fig. 1.* Plane down the wood to ¹/₁₆ in. in thickness, and cut a piece of the proper size; for the racer, it should measure 2½ by 8 in., for the fly-about 2½ by 8½ in., and for the rise-off-ground model 3 by 9 in. Bind the edges with a strip of paper and varnish. The elevator of the racer is not movable but is attached with two roundhead screws to the motor bar. This makes it impossible to alter the angle of the elevator on this model without removing it from the bar. Two or three small washers underneath the forward edge serve to place it at the correct angle. On the fly-about and rise-off-ground models, however, the elevator is adjustable, and is fastened with but one screw near the rear edge. This serves as a pivot. Use a rubber band to hold the elevator down against a flat-headed screw located under the front edge, and keep it straight. To increase or decrease the angle of the

elevator, merely turn it to one side, so that the hole shown in the drawing will come over the screw head. Then, with a small screwdriver, turn the screw in or out as needed, and allow the elevator to return to its normal position. The rubber band also prevents the elevator from breaking by absorbing some of the landing shock.

The rise-off-ground model, *Fig. 9,* is just like the fly-about, except that it has a little more surface than the latter, and the wing is set at an angle large enough to give it a good lift. This is done with small washers or coiled wire of sufficient thickness to raise the front wing spar about ⅛ in. The drawing shows how the landing gear, which consists of three wheels mounted on hard wire, is attached. Make the wheels of cigar-box wood, drill the centers, and use the same size of wire for the axles as for the wire supports. The ends should be looped around the axles. The small front wheel must be a little lower than the others so that the forward end of the motor bar will be higher than the rear when the model is resting on the ground. The diameter of the front wheel is 1½ in., and the larger ones are 2 in. in diameter.

The "twin pusher," *Fig. 10,* is

more elaborate than the other three but is not beyond the amateur's ability. Its elevator does not swing, but it is made in exactly the same manner as the other models. This is also true of the wing, except that in this case the spars are ⅜ in. square in the middle, tapered down to ⅛ by ⅜ in. at their tips. Two extra wire ribs are placed 6 in. from the center between the spars. The holes are drilled and the ribs inserted before the paper wing covering is applied. The motor bar is of pine or spruce, ½ by 1 by 43 in., shaped as shown in the drawing. Make the front hook from a 4-in. length of wire, insert it in a small hole drilled near the front of the bar, and bend the loops. The crossbar that takes the bearings should be of ash or other hardwood, and be braced with ¹⁄₁₆-in. hard wire. The bearings are strips of sheet metal, bent to U-shape and riveted to the crossbar. Hard wire is used for the landing skids. The front edge of the wing should be raised about ¹⁄₁₆ in. The elevator is adjustable and is attached to the motor bar by two screws. The front one runs through a small coil spring between the spar and motor bar, and furnishes a means of changing the angle of the elevator.

The power on all these models is furnished by rubber bands, about ³⁄₆₄ in. thick, ³⁄₁₆ in. wide, and 4 in. long. They should be linked together chain fashion, so that three of the bands will only make a length of 6 in. instead of 12 in. This method allows broken bands to be replaced with new ones quickly and easily.

A wire hook, inserted in the chuck of a hand drill, as shown in *Fig. 8*, will serve as a winder. After linking the bands together on the mold, release the front end of the "motor," and hook it to the drill. Stretch the rubber to about twice its length and turn until about half wound. Then keep turning, but gradually release the tension so that the rubber will be straight when fully wound, and hook on again. The number of turns needed will be found through experience; the twin model will stand more than 1,000 turns to each propeller, which means that with a gear ratio of 4 to 1 on the drill, the handle will have to be turned 250 times. The two propellers on this model must revolve in opposite directions.

To launch, hold the motor bar with the right hand, just ahead of the wing, and the propeller with the left. Then, with a quick upward push, send the airplane into the air. If it has a tendency to climb too steeply, the elevator should be lowered a little; if it loses altitude, the elevator should be raised enough to correct this fault. With both wingtips flat, the planes will have a tendency to turn to the right. Curving the right wingtip down a little will give a straightaway flight; a left turn can be made by curving the right tip down still more. Several trial flights will probably be necessary before the proper adjustment is obtained.

— A TOY WATER PLANE —

The toy water plane shown in the drawing is something of a novelty in the way of model water craft, as the hull only rests upon the water when the propeller is not revolving. In traveling at full speed, the hull leaves the water quickly and rides with the fins on the surface of the water, as illustrated.

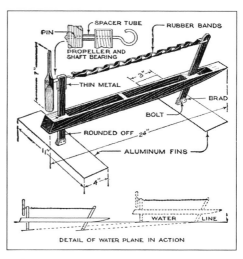

A TOY WATER PLANE THAT RIDES ON THE SURFACE OF THE WATER WHEN ITS PROPELLER IS REVOLVING.

The sides and bottom of the hull are built up from strips of pine, about ⅛ in. thick. Blocks are used to space the sides the proper distance apart and for the attachment of the wooden supports for the propelling mechanism and fins. The sheet-aluminum planes, or fins, are mounted as shown, so that each is tilted at the same angle. The plane is driven by a model-airplane propeller. For a 24-in. water plane, the propeller should be about 7 in. long. The power is derived from a motor made of a number of rubber bands linked together.

— A Simple Aerial Toy —

An interesting little toy that involves no more than a small piece of tin and an empty thread spool can be made in a few minutes. Two small wire brads are driven into one end of the spool, at diametrically opposite points. The heads are clipped off, leaving studs, ¾ in. long. A "whirler" is made from a piece of tin in the form of an airplane propeller, the blades being bent in opposite directions, as indicated. Holes to permit the propeller to make an easy fit on the studs are provided at the proper points. In use, the spool is placed on a shouldered stick, slightly smaller than the hole of the spool.

Then about 4 ft. of strong twine is wrapped around the spool and the propeller is placed on the studs. Holding the spool by its shaft in one hand, the string is given a sharp pull with the other hand, and the propeller flies off into space.

— A Feather Airplane Dart —

Four feathers, a nail, and some string are all the materials needed for making a glider that will fly gracefully through the air for considerable distances.

The feathers are cut and fitted together as shown in the drawing, the nail being placed horizontally in front of the wings, to keep the glider "trimmed."

The feather dart is shot in the same manner as a paper dart, and

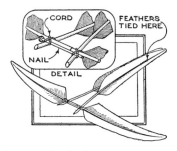

because the feathers are stronger, it will last much longer then a paper version.

— How to Make a Model Old-Four Monoplane —

The old-four monoplane model, made famous by its wonderful flights, is one of the most graceful that has been built. Its large size and slow, even glide make it a much more desirable flier than the ordinary dart-like model. It gives one a true insight into the phenomena of heavier-than-air flight. This machine, when complete, should weigh 9 oz. and fly 1,200 ft., rising from the ground under its own power and landing lightly. Its construction is simple, and with careful reference to the sketches, an exact reproduction may be made.

THE MECHANICAL BIRD WILL RUN ABOUT FIVE FEET ON THE GROUND AND THEN RISE AND FLY.

For the motor bases, *A, Fig. 1,* secure two spruce sticks, each 48 in. long, ⅜ in. wide, and ¼ in. thick. Fasten a wire hook on one end of each stick with thread wound around after giving it a coat of glue. These hooks are to hold one end of the rubber bands that act as the motive power, and are designated by the letter *B.* At the opposite ends of the sticks, at *C,* bearings are provided. These consist of blocks of wood, each 1 in long, 1 in. wide, and ⅜ in. thick. These are also bound in place with thread after gluing them. Holes are drilled through the blocks lengthwise and then lined with bushings made of brass tubing, ¹⁄₁₆ in. in inside diameter. The two motor bases *A* are connected with four cross sticks, *D,* each 9 in. long and ³⁄₁₆ in. square. These are bound and glued on the underside, one near each end and the others equidistant each from the other and from the nearest end stick. The front bumper, *E*, is made of round rattan, ⅛ in. in diameter.

The alighting gear is next in order of construction. This is made, as shown, entirely of bamboo 3/16 in. square. The pieces marked *F* are 11 in. long; *G*, 9½ in. long, and the crossbar *H*, 11 in. long. At the rear, the pieces *J* are 13 in. long; *K*, 4½ in. long, and the crosspiece *L*, 11 in. long. The distance between the points *M* and *N*, *Fig. 2*, is 6 in., and between *O* and *P*, 9 in. The bamboo is easily curved by wetting and holding it for an instant in the flame of a candle. It will hold its shape just as soon as it becomes cold. The wheels

are made of tin, 1½ in. in diameter, borrowed from a toy automobile. The axles are made from wire, 1/16 in. in diameter.

The wing spars *Q* are made of spruce, 3/16 in. wide and ¼ in. thick. Those for the front are 30 in. long, and for the rear, 36 in. long. The ribs *R* are made of bamboo pieces, 1/16 in. square, 5 in. long for the front plane, and 6 in. for the rear. These are bound and glued on top off the spars, 3 in. apart. They are given a slight upward curve. The round ends are made of 1/16-in. rattan.

It is rather difficult to make good propellers, but with a little time and patience they can be shaped and formed into good proportions.

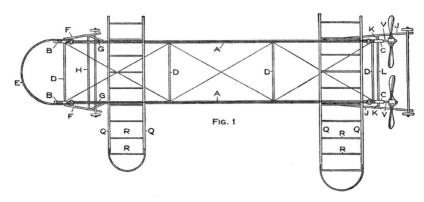

FIG. 1

THE MOTOR BASE IS MADE OF TWO SPRUCE STICKS JOINED TOGETHER WITH FOUR CROSS STICKS, BOUND AND GLUED TO THE UNDERSIDE.

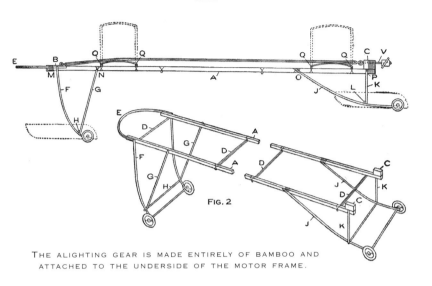

THE ALIGHTING GEAR IS MADE ENTIRELY OF BAMBOO AND ATTACHED TO THE UNDERSIDE OF THE MOTOR FRAME.

Procure two clear, straight-grained blocks of white pine, 8 in. long, 1½ in. wide, and ¾ in. thick. Draw a diagonal line on one block from opposite corners as shown in S, Fig. 3, then on the other block T, draw the line in an opposite direction. Turn the blocks over and draw opposite diagonals, as shown by the dotted lines. Draw a circle on each side exactly on the center, ½ in. in diameter. Drill ¹/₁₆-in. holes through the centers of the circles for the propeller shafts. The wood is then cut down to the lines drawn, leaving only enough materials that they will not break easily. The face of the blades should be flat and the back rounded. Leave plenty of stock near the hub. After the faces have been finished, the blades are shaped as shown at U. The propellers should be finished with sandpaper to make them perfectly smooth, as much of the success of the model will depend upon them. It is wise to shellac them and also the frame and the alighting gear. Aluminum paint costs but little, and it makes a fine finish for a model aeroplane.

The propeller shafts, V, Fig. 1, 2, and 4, are cut from bicycle spokes. An eye for the rubber band is bent in the spoke, about 2 in. from the threaded end. The end having the threads is run through the bearing block, *C, Fig. 4,* and the propeller fastened on with a small washer on each side of it by means of two nuts, *W,* cut from a bicycle nipple. These nuts may be turned up tightly with pliers.

The planes are covered with tissue paper put on tightly over the tops of the ribs, using a flour paste. The planes are movably fixed on the motor bases *A* by tying at the four points of contact with rubber bands. This makes it possible to adjust the fore-and-aft balance of the machine by changing the position of the planes.

The motive power, which is the most important part of the entire machine, consists of rubber bands. There are three ways of obtaining these bands. It is best, if possible, to purchase them from an aeroplane supply house. In this case, procure about 100 ft. of 1/16-in. square rubber, 50 ft. for each side. These are wound closely between the hooks *X.* This rubber can be taken from a golf ball. It will require

about 40 strands of this rubber on each propeller. The rubber is removed by cutting into the ball. Another way of obtaining the bands is to purchase No. 19 rubber bands and loop them together, chain-fashion, to make them long enough to reach between the hooks without stretching. About 30 strands on each propeller will be sufficient. The hooks *X* are made in the shape of the letter "S," to provide a way for taking out the rubber bands quickly. To prevent the hooks from cutting the rubber, slip some 1/16-in. rubber tubing over them. The rubber bands, or motor, when not in use, should be kept in a cool, dark place and powdered with

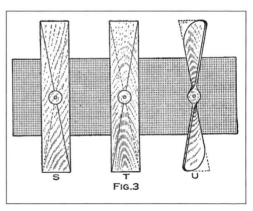

S   T   U

FIG.3

THE MOST DIFFICULT PART OF MAKING THE PROPELLERS CAN BE OVERCOME WITH A LITTLE PATIENCE.

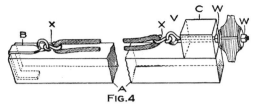

Fig.4

THE MOTIVE POWER, WHICH IS THE MOST
IMPORTANT PART OF THE MACHINE,
CONSISTS OF RUBBER BANDS.

French chalk to prevent the parts from sticking together.

With the model complete, flying is the next thing in order. With a machine as large as this one, quite a field will be necessary to give it a good flight. Test the plane by gliding it, that is, holding it up by the propellers and bearing blocks on a level with your head and throwing it forward on an even keel. Shift the planes forward or back until it balances and comes to the ground lightly.

Winding up the propellers is accomplished by means of an eye inserted in the chuck of an ordinary hand drill. While an assistant grasps the propellers and motor bearings, the rubber is unhooked from the front of the machine and hooked into the eye in the drill. Stretch the rubber out for about 10 ft., and as it is wound up, let it draw back gradually. Wind up the propellers in opposite directions, turning them from 4,000 to 800 revolutions. Be sure to wind both propellers the same number of turns, as this will assure a straight flight.

Set the machine on the ground and release both propellers at once, and at the same time push it forward. If everything is properly constructed and well balanced, the mechanical bird will run about 5 ft. on the ground and then rise to 15 or

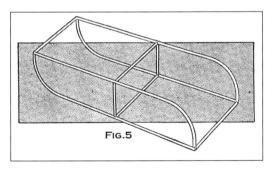

Fig.5

FRAMEWORK FOR CONSTRUCTING PONTOONS
BY COVERING THEM WITH WRITING PAPER
SOAKED IN PARAFFIN.

20 ft. and fly from 800 to 1,200 ft., descending in a long glide and alighting gracefully.

If the machine fails to rise, move the forward plane toward the front. If it climbs up suddenly and hangs in the air and falls back on its tail, move it toward the back.

After the novelty of overland flights has worn off, try flights over the water. To do this the wheels must be removed and four pontoons put in their place as shown by the dotted lines in *Fig. 2*.

Patience is the one thing necessary in model building. Sometimes a machine carefully made will not fly, and no one can make it do so until some seemingly unimportant alteration is made.

TRACTOR PULL

— A TOY FARM TRACTOR —

Driven by rubber bands—but in a manner entirely different from that in which model airplanes are operated—the toy tractor illustrated will furnish interesting work for the amateur maker. Most of the wooden parts are of ½-in. whitewood, with the exception of the rear wheels, which are made of ½-in. stuff. The front wheels are made from slices sawed from a curtain pole. Tin disks are fastened on both sides at the center of all wheels, for bearings. The axles are lengths of soft-iron wire, the ends of which are

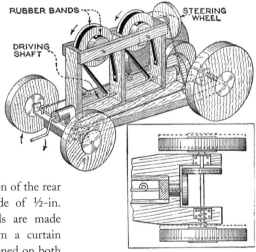

DRIVEN BY RUBBER BANDS, THIS MODEL TRACTOR WILL FURNISH AN INTERESTING OBJECT FOR THE AMATEUR TOYMAKER'S SKILL.

flattened; the rear axle is also flattened near one end for a part of its length, to prevent the drive disk from turning. Heavy tin is used for the axle bearings. The power from the rubber-band motor is transmitted to the rear wheels by means of friction disks. A small compression-coil spring is placed between the wheel and axle bearing on the side opposite the drive disk, to keep the friction disks in contact. This arrangement also serves as a clutch, allowing the drive disk to run free while the motor is being wound. This is done by pushing the rear axle to the position indicated by the dotted lines in the lower detail. A steering wheel is mounted at the rear of the engine frame, and turns the front wheels by means of cord fastened to the ends of the pivoted

front-axle bearing. In building up the motor, two small disks are fastened to larger ones with small nails, and a short rubber band attached to each small disk and to the frame upright, as shown. A longer rubber band has one end fastened to each of the larger disks, and the other end is fastened to eyes formed on the drive shaft. The disks are then mounted in the motor frame, as shown. After bending the eye in the driving shaft, it is important that the wire on either side be straightened accurately. The winding band should be nearly $1/16$ in. thick, $1/8$ in. wide, and long enough to reach once around the large pulley, and should be used single. The short band should be twice as strong as the former, or it may be of the same size and doubled.

— TOY TRACTOR PROPELLED BY CLOCKWORK —

A powerful toy tractor can be made by mounting the works of an old alarm clock on a small truck. Remove the balance wheel, which leaves four gears besides the mainspring gear. Cut a spool in half and secure it tightly to the shaft from which the hands

were removed, to form the driving pulley. The front-axle support is a block of wood, tightly fitted between the spacing rods that hold the side plates together. The front axle is made from a round stick, and the front wheels are two checkers. The axle is held to the support by a small tin scrap. The rear-axle support is a wood block, cut to fit between the side plates and held by small brads through openings in the plate. The block rests against the bottom of one of the spacing rods and no other fastening is required. Tin straps are used for securing the rear axle, which is ⅜ in. in diameter, to the block. An old spool, cut in half, forms the rear wheels, which are tightly fitted to the axle. To secure traction, small brads are driven into the rim of the wheels and cut off about ⅛ in. from it. The rear wheel on the same side as the drive pulley is grooved to take a string belt, which transmits the energy of the clock mechanism to the wheels.

— A Toy Tractor Built with Dry Cell and Motor —

An ordinary two-volt dry cell, a small motor, and the necessary wooden parts, as shown in the illustration, are all that is needed to make a toy tractor that will give its builder a great deal of fun. A good feature is that the parts can be taken down quickly and use for other purposes when desired. A base, ½ by 3 by 9 in. long, is made of wood, and two axles of the same thickness are set under it as shown. The wheels are disks cut from spools, or cut out of thin wood for the rear wheels and heavier wood for the front ones. They are fastened with screws and washers, or with nails. The dry cell is mounted on small

A BOY CAN MAKE THIS SIMPLE ELECTRIC TRACTOR IN A SHORT TIME, AND WILL GET MUCH FUN OUT OF IT.

strips and held by wires. The motor is fastened with screws and wired to the dry cell in the usual manner. One of the front wheels serves as the driver, and is grooved to receive the cord belt.

MAKING WAVES

— MAKING A TOY WATER "SCOOTER" —

The drawing shows a water "scooter" that can easily be made by the average boy from a few bits of light board, some stiff wire, and a handful of rubber bands. The pontoons are tapered at the stem of the craft and are held the right distance apart by cross strips. The propulsive mechanism of the scooter is mounted overhead. The propeller is the most difficult part to make, and possibly some experimentation will be necessary to get the most effective result. However, the important thing to remember is that it must be balanced accurately and lined up well to ensure smooth running. It is mounted on a wire shaft supported by a tin bracket. But before assembling the propeller in its bearing, a few beads or a few loose turns of wire should be slipped over the shaft, as indicated, to provide clearance. The actual power is furnished by a long rubber strip, or a number of rubber bands looped

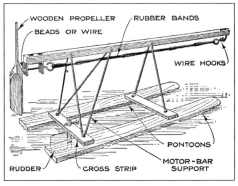

A WATER "SCOOTER" DRIVEN BY A RUBBER-BAND MOTOR, AND THAT CAN BE EASILY MADE FROM LIGHT STRIPS OF WOOD. IT IS CAPABLE OF GOOD SPEED FOR VOYAGES THAT AVERAGE ABOUT 50 FEET.

together. The rubber strip thus obtained being dusted with talcum powder and fastened at one end to the propeller, and at the opposite end to the overhead wooden strip, as shown. Powerful rubber bands can be cut from an old inner tube. If desired, a rudder may be added to the boat so that it can be made to travel in a circle instead of a straight line. Such a scooter, lightly constructed and with a sufficiently powerful rubber-band motor, will travel at good speed for about 50 ft.

— Building Model Boat Hulls —

The amateur naval constructor speedily learns that a boat hull is no simple thing to make, easy though it may look. However, by carving the bow and stern from blocks of wood and using tin or other sheet metal for extending the hull, a very satisfactory piece of work is obtained. After the bow and stern have been completed, they are joined together at the desired distance apart with wooden strips, one at the bottom and one at each side, as shown in the drawing. These strips fit flush into mortises that have been cut in the blocks to receive them. The open space between the stem and stern is closed by tacking a

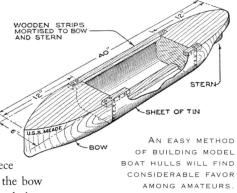

AN EASY METHOD OF BUILDING MODEL BOAT HULLS WILL FIND CONSIDERABLE FAVOR AMONG AMATEURS.

sheet of tin to the strips and wooden ends, with strips of rubber between to make watertight joints. A wooden deck may be provided and, if desired, masts, funnels, gun turrets, and other gear may be added, depending on whether one is building a battleship or a merchantman.

— Live Ballast for the Model Yacht —

When the skipper of a racing sailboat goes out for a speed trial he usually carries "live ballast." That is, two or three of his crew shift their weight to the windward side of the boat as may be necessary. This permits him to carry a greater

spread of canvas than would otherwise be possible.

The same effect can be obtained with a model yacht by using the attachment shown. A 1¼-in. length of brass tubing, large enough to slip over the mast, is obtained. A strip of sheet brass is bent around the tube and soldered, the end of the boom being lashed between the ends of the strip. A similar brass arm, about half the length of the beam, or width, of the boat is soldered to the tubing exactly opposite the boom. A ball of lead is soldered to the outer end of the second arm.

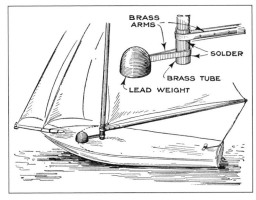

A SIMPLE COUNTERBALANCE APPLIED TO THE MAINSAIL BOOM OF A MODEL YACHT TAKES THE PLACE OF "LIVE BALLAST."

When completed, the tube is slipped over the mast and several turns of wire are made around the mast just above it to keep the boom from working up. The proper weight for the lead ballast must be found by testing the boat in water.

The action of the device is simple; when the boom is forced out by the wind, the ball of lead is swung out over the windward side, tending to balance the pressure of the wind on the sail.

— MODEL PADDLE-WHEEL BOATS —

Only a few boys have ponds of their own, in a pasture, perhaps. But there are miniature lakes in our city parks, pools at our summer camps, and old water holes in the woods. If all of these fail, a boy can still sail his ships on the bathtub sea.

A simple side-wheeler, built of wood, is shown in the sketch. It

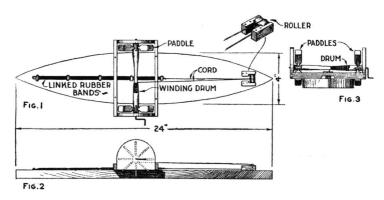

FIG. I

FIG. 3

FIG. 2

THE RUBBER-BAND MOTOR IS WOUND UP AT THE CRANK
AND PROPELS THE BOAT ABOUT 20 FEET.

winds up with a crank and runs 15 to 20 ft. A float is made by pointing the ends of a thick board, the dimensions of which are given in *Fig. 1*, the side view, *Fig. 2*, and the end view, *Fig. 3*. It is made of thin wood. A broom-handle section, just long enough to slip into this frame, is whittled to form a winding drum and fitted with paddles, wire axles, and a crank. A second, shorter section of the broom handle, set between blocks nailed to the stern, serves as a roller for the rubber bands. These, linked together and tied to a length of heavy cord, as shown in *Fig. 1*, are fixed to the bow

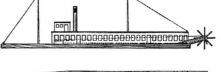

FIG. 5

THE STERN-WHEELER IS SIMILAR IN
CONSTRUCTION TO THE SIDE-WHEELER
AS TO DRIVING MECHANISM.

and run over the roller to the drum. The addition of a top, or lid, of cardboard, wood, or tin, and painted to resemble cabins and pilot house, and fitted with masts and a smokestack, completes the model. *Fig. 5* shows a similarly built stern-wheeler with the stern-wheel shaft set on brackets.

— A SPRING-DRIVEN TOY BOAT —

A boat that is propelled by springs, and that will furnish much amusement to children, may easily be made from no more elaborate materials than a piece of board, a pair of corset steels or hacksaw blades, and some pieces of tin.

The board is cut to approximately the outline of a boat, and a piece is cut from the stern to accommodate the paddle wheel, the latter being made by inserting pieces of tin into slots cut into a round wooden axle. Staples are used to secure the ends of the axle to the board. The two springs are mounted opposite each other, as shown, and a piece of stout string is attached to the free ends and to each side of the paddle-wheel axle. When the paddle wheel is wound up, the string will draw the springs up in

A SPRING-DRIVEN TOY BOAT THAT USES CORSET STEELS OR HACKSAW BLADES AS THE SOURCE OF POWER CAN BE DRIVEN IN A FORWARD OR BACKWARD DIRECTION, DEPENDING ON HOW IT IS WOUND UP.

arcs as illustrated, and as soon as the wheel is released, the tendency of the springs to resume their horizontal position will revolve the paddle wheel and cause the boat to move forward or backward, depending on which direction the wheel is turned when winding.

— HOW TO MAKE A "WATER SKATE" —

A novel little water craft, using a rubber band to furnish power, has a rudder at the stern that is swung from side to side to produce an effect similar to that obtained when a rowboat is culled forward with a single oar at the stern.

A short piece of light board is curved at the front end to form the hull of the boat, and a vertical keel is fastened to the underside. The rudder or, more properly in this case, the propeller is mounted in a bearing fastened to the rear end of the keel. The upper end of the rudder is provided with a slotted tiller that is engaged by the crankpin on the wooden flywheel. The method of supporting the flywheel and the shaft to which it is attached as well as the manner in which the rubber-band motor is

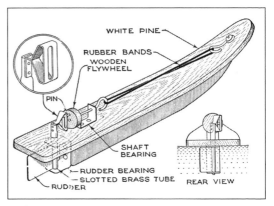

A WATER SKATE IS A TOY BOAT MADE FROM A PIECE OF LIGHT BOARD AND SCULLED FORWARD EXACTLY AS A ROWBOAT IS PROPELLED FROM THE STERN.

hooked up are so clearly shown in the drawing that a detailed description is unnecessary. The boat is made ready for operation by turning the flywheel so that the rubber band will be twisted tightly, producing sufficient tension to drive the little craft forward when it is placed in the water.

— SPRING-PROPELLED TOY BOAT —

A length of shade-roller spring forms the motive power for a model side-wheel boat, the hull of which is built along the usual lines for such craft.

The paddle wheels are mounted on a stiff wire shaft on which a cork pulley,

about ½ in. in diameter, is forced. The wheel assembly is mounted amidships. The pulley-and-shaft assembly, mounted at the stern, consists of a grooved pulley tacked to the end of a spool, the whole revolving smoothly on a shaft made from a wire nail.

The spring is cut to such a length that, when one end is secured at the stem, the other will reach halfway to the pulley axle at the stern. One end of a stout string is tied to the free end of the spring, the other end being fastened to the spool with a small brad. Power is transmitted to the paddle wheels by means of a string belt.

The craft is "wound up" by turning the paddles backward until the spring has been stretched to double its length. By using two or more pulleys to increase the ratio of revolutions of

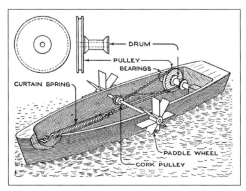

A SPRING-PROPELLED TOY BOAT THAT CAN BE EASILY MADE FOR THE ENTERTAINMENT OF THE CHILDREN. THERE ARE FEW PARTS TO BREAK OR GET OUT OF ORDER.

the paddles to the drive pulley such a boat can be made to develop considerable speed make quite extended voyages.

KEEP IT MOVING

— HOW TO MAKE A CHILD'S ROLLING TOY —

Secure a tin can or a pasteboard box about 2 in. in diameter and 2 in. or more in height. Punch two holes, *A, Fig. 1,* in the cover and the bottom, ¼ in. from the center and opposite each other. Then cut a curved line from one hole to the other, as shown

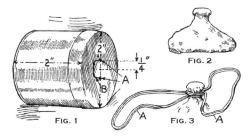

in *B.* A piece of wood, which can be procured from a woodworker, is cut

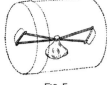

FIG. 4

FIG. 5

ROLLING CAN TOY

holes A are turned up, as in *Fig. 4,* and the ends of the bands looped over them. The flaps are then turned down on the band and the can parts put together as in *Fig. 5.* The can may be decorated with brilliant colored stripes, made of paper strips pasted on the tin. When the can is rolled away from you, it winds up the rubber band, thus storing the propelling power that makes it return.

in the shape shown in *Fig. 2,* the size being 1 by 1⅛ by 1¼ in. An ordinary rubber band is secured around the neck of the piece of wood, as shown in *Fig. 3,* allowing the two ends to be free. The pieces of tin between the

— SEMAPHORE SIGNALS FOR TOY RAILWAY —

With only a few simple and easily obtainable materials, a full set of electric semaphore signals can be built for the toy railroad. The semaphore mast is made of wood, while the arm may be of thin wood, cardboard, or metal. The mast is mounted on a small block, as shown. The signal is operated by a solenoid attached to the bottom of the mast with tape or a small metal clamp. The solenoid consists of several yards of bell wire, wound in a coil around a small brass tube. A light cord or thread is attached to the semaphore arm, and a small piece of iron or steel is attached to the opposite end and is

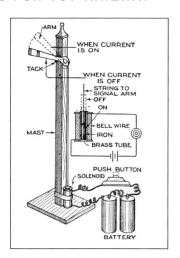

dropped into the hollow core of the solenoid. The string should be just long enough so that when the arm is raised the metal on the string will be drawn entirely inside the coil. By connecting the ends of the coil to a dry battery and pushbutton, the metal weight will be pulled to the bottom and the semaphore arm will fly up in the "clear" position shown by the dotted lines. As soon as the current ceases to flow, the arm will drop into the horizontal, or "danger," position. An automatic block-signal system can be arranged by insulating sections of the track from others and connecting the semaphores to the track circuit so that as soon as the train enters that "block," or section, the signals will operate.

— CHILDREN'S ADJUSTABLE PUSHCYCLE —

Boys between the ages of five and ten years old hate to do "girlish" things, such as riding three-wheeled velocipedes. Their chief ambition is to own a bicycle, which few boys are allowed to do, owing to the dangers of the streets and to the fact that they soon outgrow a bicycle suitable to their age. The pushcycle shown in the drawing will fill the gap and can be readily made from a pair of wheels from an old baby carriage and strips of wood. As shown in the drawing, this cycle has all the features of the regular article with

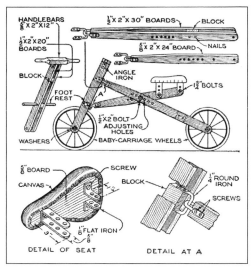

A PUSHCYCLE WILL FURNISH SPORT FOR THE SMALL BOY AND TEACH HIM TO BALANCE, IN ANTICIPATION OF THE DAY WHEN HE WILL OWN A REAL BICYCLE.

the exception of pedals, chain, and sprockets, the device being pushed along by the feet of the rider. As the owner grows older and larger, the height of the seat is readjusted by removing the bolt at the center and putting it in another hole. For smaller children, the seat is brought nearer the ground in the same manner.

— A CHILD'S PLAYHOUSE —

The child's playhouse is an expensive luxury if it is purchased ready to set up. But by following the instructions given herewith a large and inexpensive one may be constructed.

Procure about 100 ft. of 1¾ by 1½-in. boards, and saw out pieces, as shown. It will be much easier to construct using iron corner brackets rather than using mortises, nails, and glue. The frame will also be much stronger.

When the frame is completed, burlap is tacked on to make the covering. The burlap can be purchased cheaply, and the best color to use is green, red, or brown. This material should be fastened on the different sections before they are hinged together. To prevent the burlap from unraveling, turn the edges under before tacking them down.

A piece of wire screen is used for

THE COVERED FRAMEWORK CAN BE USED IN- OR OUTDOORS, AS DESIRED, AND WHEN SET UP AND THE WINGS SWUNG BACK, IT PRESENTS THE APPEARANCE OF A HOUSE.

the door. An old piece will do, if it is well coated with black or dark-green paint. It is then tacked on the inside of the door. Fasten the different parts together with the hinges. The hinges are fastened on the inside of

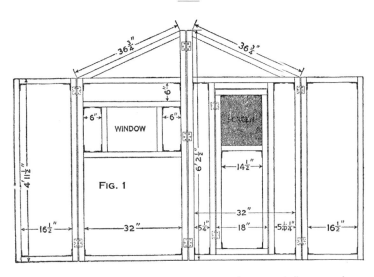

FIG. 1

36¾″ 36¾″

6″ 6″ 6″

WINDOW

SCREEN

14½″

6′2½″

32″

4′11½″

16½″ 32″ 5¼″ 18″ 5¼″ 16½″

THE ENTIRE FRAMEWORK IS HELD TOGETHER WITH BRACKETS AND IS HINGED AT THE JOINTS SO IT CAN BE FOLDED UP AND PUT INTO A SMALL SPACE. THE SECTIONS ARE COVERED WITH COLORED BURLAP TO MAKE THEM APPEAR SOLID. ON THE RIGHT IS SHOWN THE AWNING-FRAME CONSTRUCTION.

1′ 8″

8″

HINGE HINGE

FIG. 2

AWNING FRAME   WINDOW FRAME

HINGE

FIG. 3

the side wings and on the outside of the two front pieces. With the hinges placed in this manner, the house can be folded into a small space.

For the one built for this article, green burlap was used. By trimming the door and window frames along the edges with white paint, a very pretty effect was produced.

A small awning was made over the window, which improved the appearance very much. Roller shades on the door and window, and an electric doorbell, completed a very neat and practical playhouse.

— HOMEMADE TOY BANK —

The little bank illustrated is not exactly burglar-proof, but once put together it cannot be opened except by the destruction of one of the units of which it is composed. It requires but little skill to make, and would be a good problem for manual training, as it offers an excellent opportunity for teaching certain rudiments of woodworking by the application method.

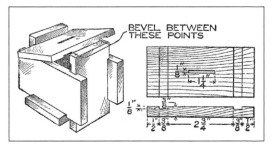

SIX PIECES OF WOOD AS THEY ARE PUT TOGETHER TO FORM A TOY BANK.

Its construction requires six pieces of hardwood of the dimensions shown in the sketch. White wood will do if there is no hardwood at hand. The coin slot is ⅛ in. wide by 1¼ in. long, and is cut in only one piece.

The first five pieces should be easy to put together, but the sixth, or top, piece shown in the sketch, will not go in, because the bottom edge of the raised side will strike the inside of the piece to the right. By beveling this edge with a chisel from top to bottom between the dadoes, or grooves, it can be forced down quite a distance. It can be sprung in place by placing a block of wood on the high side and striking it a sharp blow with a heavy hammer.

— HOW TO MAKE A MINIATURE WINDMILL —

The following description outlines how a miniature windmill is made. This will produce considerable power for its size, even in a light breeze. Its smaller parts, such as blades and pulleys, were constructed of 1-in. sugar pine on account of its softness.

The eight blades were made from pieces 1 by 1½ by 12 in. Two opposite edges were cut away until the blade was about ⅛ in. thick. Two

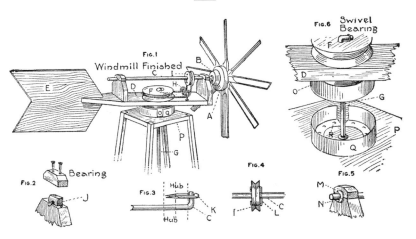

DETAILS OF MINIATURE WINDMILL CONSTRUCTION

inches were left uncut at the hub end. They were then nailed to the circular face plate, *A, Fig. 1,* which is 6 in. in diameter and 1 in. thick. The center of the hub was lengthened by the wooden disk, *B, Fig. 1,* which was nailed to the face plate. The shaft, *C, Fig. 1,* was ¼-in. iron rod, 2 ft. long, and turned in the bearings detailed in *Fig. 2. J* was a nut from a wagon bolt and was placed in the bearing to ensure easy running. The bearing blocks were 3 in. wide, 1 in. thick and 3 in. high without the upper half. Both bearings were made in this manner.

The shaft *C* was keyed to the hub of the wheel by the method shown in *Fig. 3.* A staple, *K,* held the shaft from revolving in the hub. This method was also applied in keying the 5-in. pulley, *F,* to the shaft, *G, Fig. 1,* which extended to the ground. The 2½-in. pulley, *I, Fig. 1,* was keyed to shaft *C,* as shown in *Fig. 4.* The wire, *L,* was put through the hole in the axle and the two ends curved so as to pass through the two holes in the pulley. They were then given a final bend to keep the pulley in place. The method by which the shaft *C* was kept from working forward is shown in *Fig. 5.* The washer, *M,* intervened between the bearing block and the wire *N,* which was passed through the axle and then bent to prevent its falling out. Two washers were placed on shaft *C,* between the forward bearing and the hub of the wheel to lessen the friction.

The bed plate, *D, Fig. 1*, was 2 ft. long, 3 in. wide, and 1 in. thick and was tapered from the rear bearing to the slot in which the fan, *E*, was nailed. This fan was made of ¼-in. pine 18 by 12 in., and was cut to the shape shown.

The two small iron pulleys with screw bases, *H, Fig. 1*, were obtained for a small sum from a hardware dealer. Their diameters were 1¼ in. The belt that transferred the power from shaft *C* to shaft *G* was top string, with a section of rubber in it to take up slack. A rubber band was placed in the grooves of each of the two wooden pulleys to prevent it from slipping.

The point for the swivel bearing was determined by balancing the bed plate, with all parts in place, across the thin edge of a board. There, a ¼-in. hole was bored in which shaft *G* turned. To lessen the friction, washers were placed under pulley *F*. The swivel bearing was made from two lids of baking-powder cans. A section was cut out of one to permit its being enlarged enough to admit the other. The smaller one, *O, Fig. 6*, was nailed top down, with the sharp edge to the underside of the bed plate, so

that the ¼-in. hole for the shaft *G* was in the center. The other lid, *G*, was tacked, top down also, in the center of the board *P*. The lid was attached with brass-headed furniture tacks, *R, Fig. 6*, which acted as a smooth surface for the other tin to revolve upon. Holes for shaft *G* were cut through both lids. Shaft *G* was only ¼ in. in diameter, but to keep it from rubbing against the board *P*, a ½-in. hole was bored for it, through the latter.

The tower was made of four 1-by-1-in. strips, 25 ft. long. They converged from points on the ground forming an 8-ft. square to the board, *P*, at the top of the tower. This board was 12 in. square and the corners were notched to admit the strips as shown, *Fig. 1*. Laths were nailed diagonally between the strips to strengthen the tower laterally. Each strip was screwed to a stake in the ground so that by disconnecting two of them the other two could be used as hinges and the tower could be tipped over and lowered to the ground. This is necessary in certain instances as, for instance, when the windmill needs oiling. Bearings for the shaft *G* were placed 5 ft. apart in the tower. The power was put to various uses.

— Decorative Toys and Boxes Made at Home —

Homemade toys and gifts, as well as the "treasure boxes" in which they are contained, have an added interest both to the one making and the one receiving them. The holiday season makes this work especially attractive, which affords opportunity for individuality in construction and design limited only by the skill of the worker. The decorated toys and the box described in detail this article are suggestive only, and may be adapted to a large variety of forms and designs. The gorgeously colored parrot and the gaily caparisoned rider and horse suggest a host of bird and animal forms, those having possibilities for attractive coloring being most desirable. The decorated box shown in *Fig. 7* may be adapted as a gift box, to be used where its decoration may be seen, as in a nursery. It can be made in forms as varied as cardboard boxes are. Plant, animal, or geometrical forms may be used to work out designs, and appropriate color schemes applied to them. A

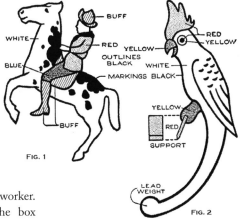

THE OUTLINES FOR THE HORSE AND RIDER AND THE PARROT MAY BE MADE BY ENLARGING THESE SKETCHES. THE COLOR SCHEME INDICATED IS SUGGESTIVE ONLY AND MAY BE VARIED TO SUIT INDIVIDUAL TASTE.

good plan in determining a color scheme is to use the colors of the flower or other motif. If the design is not associated with objects having varied colors—a geometrical design, for instance—harmonious colors should be chosen. These may be bright and contrasting, such as red and green, and violet and orange, or they can be more subdued in tone.

A brightly colored design for a horse and rider is shown in *Fig. 1.* The form is cut out of thin wood and the color applied. The painted figure is mounted on the curved wire, weighted at one end, as shown in *Fig. 6.* The toy adds a touch of novelty to a room when suspended from the corner of a mantel, a shelf, or other suitable place. Balanced in a striking attitude, forefeet upraised, even grown-ups can hardly resist tipping the rider to see his mount rear still higher. The parrot shown in *Fig. 2* is made similarly and is weighted at the end of its tail. The point of balance is at the feet, which may be fastened to a trapeze, or can be arranged to perch on a convenient place, like that suited to the horse and rider.

The tools and equipment necessary for the making of such toys are simple and are generally available in most boys' workshops or tool chests. A coping saw, like that shown in *A, Fig. 3,* is suitable for cutting the wood. A fretsaw, operated by hand, foot, or power, may be used. Such a tool makes this work proceed rapidly. To use the coping saw to the best advantage, particularly if the work is to be done on a table that must not be marred, a sawing board

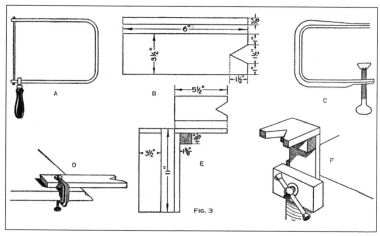

THE TOOLS REQUIRED ARE FOUND IN MOST BOYS' WORKSHOPS, AND A SATISFACTORY SAW TABLE MAY BE MADE EASILY, AS SHOWN IN DETAIL.

should be made. In its simplest form, this consists of a board as shown in *B*, about ⅞ in thick, 3½ in. wide, and 6 in. long, with one end notched. This is clamped to the end of the table, as in *D*, with a clamp. An iron clamp of the type shown in *C* is best. Another form of sawing table, especially useful when the woodworker wants to stand up at the work, is shown in *E* in detail, and clamped in the vise in *F.* It consists of a notched board, 3½ in. wide, fixed at right angles to a board of similar width, 11 in. long, and braced at the joint with a block about 1⅜ in. square. In using the coping saw with either of these saw tables, the wood is held down on the support, as shown in *Fig. 5.* The saw is drawn

downward for each cutting stroke, thus tending to hold the board more firmly against the saw table. It is, of course, important that the saw be inserted in the coping-saw frame with the teeth pointing toward the handle so that the method of cutting described may be followed. The wood must be sawed slowly, especially at the beginning of a cut. The operator soon learns the kinks in handling the saw and wood to the best advantage and can then make rapid progress.

An outline drawing of the form to be cut out of the wood must first be made to the exact size the object is to be. It can be very satisfying to work out the form of the animal or other figure, especially for the boy or girl

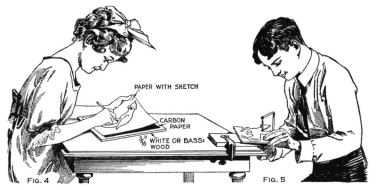

THE DESIGN IS TRACED CAREFULLY ONTO THE WOOD AND THEN CUT OUT WITH THE COPING SAW, ON THE SAW TABLE.

who has the time necessary to do good work. If desired, the figure may be traced from a picture taken from a book, magazine, or other source. Cut a piece of wood to the size required for the design and place a sheet of carbon paper over it. Or if none is available, rub a sheet of paper with a soft pencil, and use this as a carbon paper, the side covered with the lead being placed on the surface of the wood. The carbon paper and the sheet bearing the design should then be held in place on the wood with thumbtacks or pins, and the transfer made with a pencil, as shown in *Fig. 4*. The design should be placed on the wood so that the weaker parts, such as the legs of the horse, will extend with the length instead of across the grain of the wood.

In some instances, where a complicated form is cut out, it is necessary to use wood of several plies. Where this type of wood is available it is worthwhile to use it for all of this work. For smaller objects, wood 3/16 in. thick is suitable, and stock up to ½ in. in thickness may be used. Whitewood, basswood, poplar, and other soft, smooth-grained woods are suitable.

When the design has been satisfactorily outlined, place the piece of wood on the saw table with the design on the upper side. Holding the wood down firmly, as shown in *Fig. 5,* and sawing in the notch of the saw table, cut into the edge slowly. Apply light pressure on the downstroke only, as the upstroke is not intended to cut. Turn the piece to keep the saw on the line and in the notch. It is important that the saw be held vertically so that the edge of the cutout portion will be square. With proper care and a little practice, the edges may be cut so smoothly that only a light sandpapering will be required to produce a smooth edge. When the figure has been cut out, smooth the edges by trimming them carefully with a sharp knife, if necessary. Sandpaper them lightly to remove sharp corners. A fine sandpaper, about No. 1/2, is suitable for this purpose. The figure is then ready for painting. The white is put on first and, when dry, the other colors applied over it.

Oil paints may be used, and a varnish or shellac applied over them to give a high-grade appearance. But this process requires much care, considerable skill, and long drying time between coats to prevent "runs" in the colors.

Watercolor paint, which can be

purchased in powder form at paint stores and mixed with water to the consistency of cream, is a satisfactory coloring material and is easy to apply. A small amount of each of the colors used—yellow, red, blue, black, and white—will be sufficient for several toys. Mix each color in a separate saucer and use a small watercolor brush to apply the paint. In painting the horse and rider, the horse is first painted entirely white, and then the black spots are applied after the color is dry. The rider's coat is painted red; the trousers blue; the hat and leggings buff, as indicated in *Fig. 1*. For buff, mix a brushful of yellow with a brushful of red and add about three brushfuls of white. A half

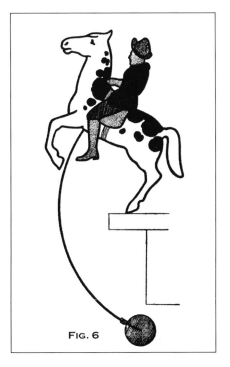

FIG. 6

brushful of black may be added to dull the color, if desired. The flesh tone for the rider's face is made by mixing a little red with white. When the colors are dry, all edges are outlined with a heavy line of black, not less than ⅛ in. in width. This outline may be evenly applied with the point of the brush.

The method of making the parrot is similar to that described for the

horse and rider, and the color scheme is suggested in *Fig. 2*.

It should be obvious that no attempt is made to secure a lifelike, or realistic effect in painting these toy shapes. All colors are flat, that is, without light and shade. The toys are really decorative designs, and the maker is at liberty to use any colors desired, whether natural or not.

The horse and rider construction

is balanced on the hind foot, as shown in *Fig. 6*, by attaching a lead weight to a 1/16-in. wire as a counterweight. The wire should be set into the body of the horse, behind the foreleg, to a depth of ¾ in. The weight of the metal and the curve of

the wire should be adjusted to obtain the proper balance. The parrot is balanced in the same way, except that the weight is fixed to the end of the tail, which is curved like the wire.

These and other homemade toys

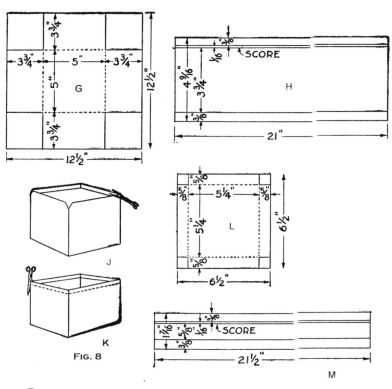

THE VARIOUS STEPS IN THE PROCESS OF MAKING AND COVERING A RECTANGULAR CARDBOARD BOX ARE SHOWN IN DETAIL. THE METHOD OF MAKING A PATTERN FOR THE DESIGN IS SHOWN ABOVE.

or gifts may be sent or contained appropriately in boxes decorated to match them. They may be made complete, or commercial boxes of suitable sizes may be covered and decorated. If good materials are used, such a box makes a pretty and useful gift in itself. The complete process of making a typical box is described for those who prefer to make one of special size. The dimensions given are thus only suggestive and may be adapted to suit particular needs.

The materials necessary are: cardboard, cover paper, lining paper, bond paper, paste, and watercolors. The latter should be of the opaque variety, since white or other light shades may then be used on darker-colored paper. A sharp knife, a scissors, a metal-edge ruler, and bookbinder's paste are also needed. Suitable substitutes for the various kinds of paper may usually be obtained in the home, if they are not readily available at local stationery stores or printing establishments.

The box is made as follows: Decide on the proper size and select cardboard and colored paper to use as cover material to carry out the design. Cut out a square of the cardboard, with sides 12½ in. long, as shown in *G*. Then mark it as indicated and cut on the full line to remove the square corners. Crease it on the dotted lines and fold to form a box. To hold the cardboard in box shape, strips of bond paper—ordinary writing paper—are cut, 3¾ in. long and 1 in. wide, then creased along their centers and pasted to the corners. The paste should be applied to the paper strip first, then on the corners of the box. Apply the piece of paper over the corner of the box on the outside, pressing it to make a snug fit. Repeat this operation on the other corners.

Lay off the dimensions given on the selected color of cover paper—which will be the background color for your design—and score the lines indicated. Spread paste smoothly over the surface of the colored paper, between the lines drawn ⅜ in. from the long edges, and then spread a thin layer of paste over the outer surface of one of the sides of the box. Apply the paper to the pasted surface and press it down, rubbing gently out from the center to remove air bubbles. Fold the ⅜-in. laps at the top and bottom over the upper edge of the box and around the lower corner. Repeat this process, covering the four sides. To form a smooth fold at the corners, it is best to miter the paper as shown at *J* and *K,* before pasting it down. Then paste a square of the same paper 4⅞ in. wide on the bottom of the box, taking care to match the edges evenly all around.

Line the box with a strip of lining paper, 20 in. long and 4 in. wide. Try the lining by folding it into the box so that its upper edge is about ⅛ in. from the edge of the box, and crease it carefully into the corners. Remove it, apply paste, and press it well into the corners when pasting it down. Paste a square of the same paper, 4⅞

in. wide, in the bottom of the box.

The cover is made by the same process as the main portion of the box. The dimensions of the cardboard are shown in *L,* and the covering in *M.* Notice that the cover is slightly wider than the box, so that it will fit easily.

When the box is thoroughly dry, it is ready to receive decorations on the top and sides. The design may be created in different colored papers and adapted from a leaf, flower, or similar form, as well as from geometric or animal forms.

— Miniature Metal-Bound Chests —

Boys in shop class became very enthusiastic over the making of small chestlike boxes, bound with ornamental metal, and adapted them to a great variety of uses. The boxes were designed to suit the taste of the maker and for use as glove, handkerchief, jewelry, treasure, and other boxes. The boxes were lined with silk and finished in wax and varnish, in various stains. Oak was used for most of these, and the metals employed were largely copper and brass, although silver is suitable for small boxes. They are simple in con-

struction, as shown in the working drawings, and can be made in the home workshop. The photograph reproduced shows a group of boxes, for various purposes, and in several styles of metal binding. The long box at the top is for gloves or ties; the larger ones are for boys' personal use, caring for collars, handkerchiefs, etc.; the smaller boxes are for the dresser, providing a place for jewelry and similar small articles. The boxes proved great favorites as gifts, and the monogram of the recipient may be etched into the metal.

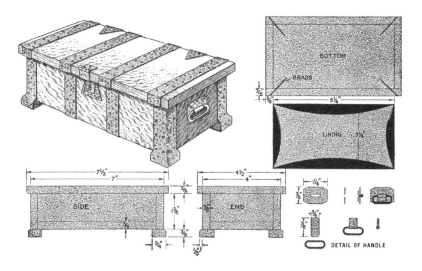

THE CONSTRUCTION OF THE JEWELRY BOX IS TYPICAL OF THE OTHERS.
THE HANDLE IS SHOWN IN DETAIL. THE NAILING OF THE BOTTOM AND
THE FITTING OF THE LINING ARE SHOWN AT THE RIGHT.

Well-seasoned oak is the most suitable material for the making of the boxes, as it harmonizes well with the plain metal trimmings. The quarter-sawn variety is preferable, being more ornamental and less likely to warp or twist. For most of the boxes, stock ⅜ in. thick is suitable, although this may be cut down to ⁵/₁₆ in. for the smaller boxes, if convenient. The method of joining the pieces is similar in all the varieties of boxes, and the jewel box illustrated in the working drawings will be

taken as a specimen. The sides of the box are butted against the ends, lapping over them, flush, and nailed with small brads. The bottom is fitted between the sides and ends, and nailed so that the nails are concealed by the metal bands at the four corners and at other points, if bands are placed near the middle. The stock for the box is cut and finished on all sides to the following dimensions: all pieces to be ⅜ in. thick, top, 4½ by 7½ in.; two sides, 1⅞ by 7 in.; two ends, 1⅞ by 4 in.; bottom, 3¼ by 6¼ in.

All the pieces should be scraped carefully to a smooth finish. Nails should be started with an awl or a slightly flattened nail of the same size, fitted into a hand drill. Extreme care must taken in nailing to ensure that the surface of the wood is not marred. Damage is likely to occur if the nails are driven into the wood too rapidly or without guide holes. The feet are cut from a strip, ⅜ in. thick and ¾ in. wide, the cut edges being sandpapered smooth without destroying the squareness of the sharp corners. They are nailed to the bottom of the box with brads, care being taken to have the end grain of each block at the end of the box—particularly if the metal trimmings do not cover the blocks.

The cover is fixed in place with small plain butts. The butts are countersunk into the wood, one leaf into the top and the other into the back of the box. A simpler method is to set both leaves of the hinge into the edge of the back. Care must be taken in fitting the hinges so that they are set in line with the back of the box. Holes should be made for the screws before driving them into place. Excessive care should be taken with the fitting of the hinges, because the proper fitting of the lid—both as to resting level and being in line with the edges of the box—depends on the fitting of the hinges.

After the construction work and nailing are completed, the box may be sandpapered carefully. Sand in the direction of the grain and be careful not to round off the edges. Excessive sanding of the woodwork marks the work of the careless novice. The box should be handled as little as possible while the metal trimmings are being fitted and, before the finish is applied, should be sanded lightly to remove dirt. When the metal pieces are fitted and ready to be fastened in place, the finish may be applied to the box. Warm browns or other dark oak finishes are best suited to the simple style of chest and the metal fittings. A coat of stain should be applied and followed, when dry, with a coat of filler, rubbed well into the pores of the wood. The filler should be permitted to dry hard, and the surface then sanded very lightly with a fine grade of paper—No. 00 is best. Do not rub through the filler or stain, particularly at the corners. Wax is the most commonly applied outer finish. Several coats may be used to give a substantial finish. For a high-gloss finish, apply a coat of shellac followed by coats of rubbing varnish. Allow each coat to dry well and sand between coats with No. 00 sandpaper. This is a more involved process and requires that the varnish be rubbed down with pumice stone and water and finished with an oil polish.

No. 20 gauge or lighter copper or brass is suitable for the trimmings. The details of the handles are shown in the sketch. Cut a back plate, ⅞ in. by 1¼ in., and fit the handle of wire to it by means of a strap bent from a strip of metal, ⅜ in. by ⅞ in. The other bands are merely strips, ½ to ¾ in. in width and fitted to the size of the box, where applied. Strap hinges of the same metal may be made, but the most convenient method for the amateur is to fit the metal strips into place at the hinges merely as ornamental features. Various types of locks may be fitted to the box. For the worker who has the skill, a hasp can be a very interesting feature, as indicated in the sketch.

The designing and making of the metal trimmings affords unlimited opportunity for originality. It's wise to test-fit the desired strips cut from paper before making them of metal. Also keep in mind that the simple bands and forms are better suited to the plain box than ornate trimmings.

Having decided upon suitable patterns for the metal strips, cut them from the sheet with snips or tinner's shears, being careful to produce a smooth edge. A file may be used to smooth and round the edges of the metal slightly. The metal is fastened with escutcheon pins, which add to the ornamental effect if properly spaced. Holes for them must be drilled or punched through the metal.

The metal may be left smooth and polished or hammered with the round end of a ball-peen hammer to produce the dented effect shown on several of the boxes in the group. This, as well as other finishing of the metal, must be done before it is fixed in place. Beautiful colors may be given to the metal by heating it and observing the colors as they "run." A trial will enable one to judge the proper heat for the various colors, which "run" from a light straw to a deep purple, with various reddish intermediate tones. A brown oxidized finish, or a verd-antique—greenish—finish may also be obtained. The metal should be polished with wax to preserve the finish if other than the latter type is used.

The boxes are lined with silk or other suitable material. The method is as follows: Cut cardboard pieces to fit against the inner sides of the bottom, sides, and ends. Pad one side of them with cotton batting, and cover with silk, gluing the edges of it on the back of the cardboard, as shown in the sketch. By bending the pieces slightly, they may be inserted and glued in place. Be careful in handling the glue that the silk is not soiled. Pads of felt, or chamois skin, may be glued to the bottom of the feet of the box to ensure that the box does not mar the surface upon which it rests.

The most popular boxes, which are especially suitable for gift purposes, are the jewelry, glove, and handkerchief boxes. Their dimensions are: jewelry box, 2¾ by 4 by 7½ in.; glove box, 3¼ by 5 by 13 in.; handkerchief box, 4 by 6 by 10 in. Other sizes suited to special purposes may, of course, be readily designed. They can be made in walnut, mahogany, or other cabinet woods.

JUST *for* FUN

— A WHIRLIGIG CLAPPER —

A good noisemaker for Halloween—or any other occasion—can be made by carefully following the directions given here. The box is the first thing to make. It is constructed of wood pieces, ½ in. thick, and consists of two ends and two sides. The ends are each 1½ in. square and the sides 1½ in. wide and 6 in. long. These parts are nailed together with the ends lapping the sides.

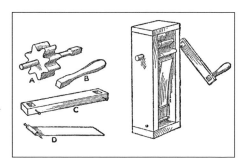

DETAIL OF THE PARTS AND HOW THEY ARE ASSEMBLED TO MAKE THIS CLAPPER.

The ratchet wheel *A* is a disk of hardwood, 1½ in. in diameter. Its rim is divided into eight equal parts and notched with a knife as shown. It is placed in the forward end of the box on a wood axle of ⅜-in. diameter to which it is glued. One end of this axle is squared and projects 1 in. beyond the side of the box. The squared end passes through a square hole in the end of the crank *C*, which is a piece of wood ¾ in. thick, 1 in. wide and 4 in. long, and is fastened with brads and glue. At the other end of the crank, a similar hole connects with a handle whittled to the shape shown in *B*.

A flat piece of steel spring, ½ in. wide and long enough to reach from the rear end of the box to the teeth of the ratchet wheel, is shaped as shown in *D*. The spring may be made from a stiff piece of corset steel or bicycle trousers guard. The spring is fastened with a nail through the end and box sides and a second nail passes through the sides over the spring, about 2 in. forward of the first nail. This is to give the spring tension on the teeth.

To operate the clapper, allow it to hang straight down. The right hand grasps the handle and whirls the box in a circle around to the left.

— Making and Using the "Bandilore" —

An East Indian toy, known as a "bandilore," is made from a piece of spool, about ½ or ¾ in. thick, and two tin disks, about 4 in. in diameter.

The section of spool is tacked between the two disks, exactly in the center. Tie one end of a 3- or 4-ft. length of stout cord to the spool. The bandilore is operated by winding the cord around the spool and holding the free end of the string in the hand. The toy is dropped and descends with great speed; just before the end of the cord is reached, the whole thing is given a quick upward jerk. This

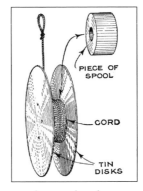

PIECE OF SPOOL

CORD

TIN DISKS

increases the speed and momentum of the disks so that the cord is wound in the opposite direction, and the bandilore climbs upward, the process being repeated as often as desired.

— A Perpetual Whirligig —

Camphor is the motive power that drives the device shown in the illustration. It will cause the whirligig to revolve for several days, or until the camphor is consumed.

The whirligig is made of a piece of cork, ½ in square, with a needle stuck into each of its four sides. Smaller pieces of cork, to which pieces of camphor have been attached with sealing wax, are stuck on the ends of the needles. Take care to keep the needles and cork free from oil or grease, because this will retard their movement. As soon as the device is placed in a dish of water it will start whirling and continue to do so as long as motive power is supplied. A small flag or other ornament may be attached to the center cork.

— ❖ ❖ ❖ —

CHAPTER 5

FUN *for* OLDER KIDS

—

CLEVER AMUSEMENTS

— JUMPING TOYS FROM MAGAZINE PICTURES —

Jumping jacks without boxes will provide endless entertainment for the juvenile members of the household. These can be made from no more elaborate materials than a few strips of pasteboard and some rubber bands. Three strips of stiff cardboard, of uniform size, are required to make one of the toys. Two of the strips are placed together and slits, about ½ in. deep, are cut in both ends, as shown in the drawing. Two long rubber bands are required. These are cut open at one end and

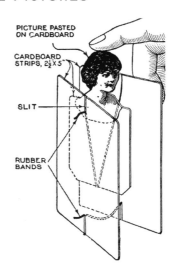

PICTURE PASTED ON CARDBOARD

CARDBOARD STRIPS, 2½ X 5"

SLIT

RUBBER BANDS

the ends are inserted in the slits of the opposite cards, as shown. Only one rubber band is used at a time, the other one being provided in case the first breaks. This will allow the toy to be turned upside down and used without interruption. The third card has a suitable picture pasted at one end, and the cardboard is cut away around the edges of the picture. Hold the toy in the hand and insert the strip containing the picture at the top. Press down against the rubber band in the manner indicated. When the pressure of the hand is relieved, the tension of the rubber band causes it to jump out above the upper edge of the strips.

— A Toothpick "Popper" —

This particular "popper" is made from six toothpicks and is entirely harmless. The toothpicks are arranged as shown in the drawing. The center slivers put the others under considerable tension, and at the same time hold them together. To "touch off" this popper, it is held in the hand, and one corner lit with a match. As the corner ends are weakened by the flame, the toothpicks will fly apart with considerable force. The experiment should be per-

TOOTHPICKS

formed only in a place where there is no danger of fire, and the "popper" artist should be careful of his eyes.

— How to Make Paper Balloons —

This project involves using flammable materials to create a miniature hot-air balloon, and because of the danger of fire, the balloon should be ignited and flown only under the supervision of adults and with the appropriate safety precautions including a fire extinguisher. The balloon should be flown only over water.

This type of balloon, made spherical or designed like the regular aeronaut's hot-air balloon, are the best kind to make. Those having an odd or unusual shape will not make good ascensions, and in most cases, the paper will catch fire from the torch and burn before they have flown very far. The following description is for making a tissue-paper balloon about 6 ft. high.

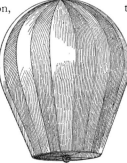

FIG. 1

PAPER BALLOON.

top. The bottom of the gore is one-third the width of the widest point. The dimensions and shape of each gore are shown in *Fig. 2*.

The balloon is made up of 13 gores pasted together, using about ½-in. lap on the edges. Any good paste will do—one that is made up of a well-cooked mixture of flour and water will serve the purpose. If the gores have been put together correctly, the pointed ends

The paper may be selected in several colors. The gores cut from these and pasted in alternately will produce a pretty array of colors when the balloon is in flight. The shape of a good balloon is shown in *Fig. 1*. The gores for a 6-ft. balloon should be about 8 ft. long or about one-third longer than the height of the balloon. The widest part of each gore is 16 in. The widest place should be 53½ in. from the bottom end, or a little over halfway from the bottom to the

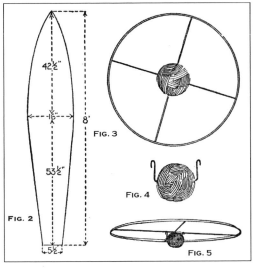

PATTERN AND PARTS TO MAKE BALLOON.

will close up the top entirely and the wider bottom ends will leave an opening about 20 in. in diameter. A light wood hoop having the same diameter as the opening is pasted to the bottom end of the gores. Two cross wires are fastened to the hoop, as shown in *Fig. 3*. These are to hold the wick ball, *Fig. 4*, so that it will hang as shown in *Fig. 5*. The wick ball is made by winding wicking around a wire, with the wire ends bent into hooks as shown.

The balloon is filled with hot air in a manner similar to that used with the ordinary cloth balloon. A small trench or fireplace is made of brick with a chimney over which the mouth of the paper balloon is placed. Use fuel that will make heat with very little smoke. Hold the balloon so it will not catch fire from the flames coming out of the chimney. Have some alcohol ready to pour on the wick ball, saturating it thoroughly. When the balloon is filled with hot air, carry it away from the fireplace, attach the wick ball to the cross wires, and light it under the supervision of an adult.

In starting the balloon on its flight, take care that it leaves the ground as nearly upright as possible.

— HOW TO MAKE A FLUTTER RING —

The flutter ring is for enclosing in an envelope and to surprise the person opening it by the revolving of the ring. The main part is made of a piece of

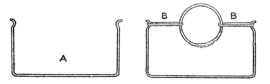

THE SHAPE OF THE WIRE AND MANNER OF ATTACHING THE RUBBER BANDS TO THE RING.

wire, *A*, bent so that the depth will be about 2 in. and the length 4 in. Procure or make a ring 2 in. in diameter. The ring should be open like key ring. Use two rubber bands, *BB*, in connecting the ring to the wire.

To use it, turn the ring over repeatedly until the rubber bands are twisted tightly, and then lay it flat in a paper folded like a letter. Hand it to someone in this shape or after first putting it into an envelope. When the paper is opened up, the ring will do the rest.

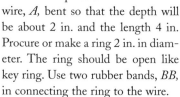

— PAPER CUBES THAT "PUFF UP" —

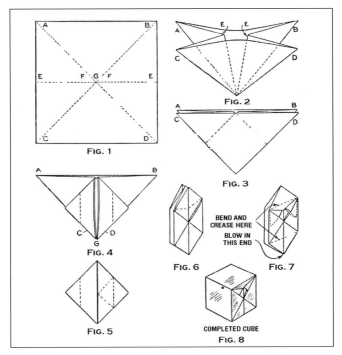

PAPER CUBES, OR BOXES, THAT EXPAND ARE EASILY MADE
FROM SQUARE PIECES OF PAPER. THE ILLUSTRATION
SHOWS THE VARIOUS STEPS IN CONSTRUCTION.

Paper cubes, or boxes, that will provide considerable amusement for the children are easily made. A square piece of paper is folded, as shown by the dotted lines in *Fig. 1,* from points *A* to *D* and from *B* to *C.* The paper is spread out and folded on the opposite side from points *E* to *F.* The square of paper is again spread out and folded into the form shown in *Figs. 2* and *3.* The corners *A, B, C,* and *D* are folded on the dotted lines shown in *Fig. 3,* to the center *G* in *Fig. 4.* When all four corners have been folded, the paper will appear as shown in *Fig. 5*. The four corners are folded toward the center, as indicated by the dotted lines in *Fig. 5*. When this is done the paper will appear as in *Fig. 6*. The corners *A, B, C,* and *D* are bent on the dotted lines in *Fig. 6* and folded inside the flap, as in *Fig. 7*. When the paper has been folded into the form shown in *Fig. 7*, a hole will be left at one end and the cube, or box, is expanded by blowing into it. The inflated cube is shown in *Fig. 8*.

— AN ARMY IN A SMALL BOX —

A play device that will afford much amusement and is interesting for boys to make is shown in the sketch. To make the peephole cabinet, obtain a box of suitable size. Fasten a piece of looking glass inside, at each end. Make

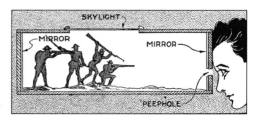

WITH THE HELP OF THE MIRRORS, A FEW SOLDIERS ARE MADE TO APPEAR AS AN ARMY.

a peephole at one end of the box and rub the silvering from the back of the looking glass at the hole. Place a few metal soldiers, horses, etc., along the sides of the box 1 or 2 in. apart, one being set to hide the reflection of the hole. When a boy looks through the hole, he'll see an endless army. Light is provided through the skylight at the top, which is fitted with ground glass or tissue paper. This device perplexes most people who are not familiar with its construction.

— A RECORDING ANNUNCIATOR TARGET —

In rifle practice it is often desirable to provide a target that will indicate to the marksman when the bull's-eye is struck. The device shown in the sketch, arranged behind an ordinary card target, has given satisfactory results on a private range and can easily be adapted to other uses.

Referring to *Fig. 1, A* indicates a wooden base, 4-by-8-by-½ in., on which is mounted a strap hinge, *B,* 6½ in. long, by means of a block, 1⅜ in. high. An opening, *C,* 1½ in. in diameter, is provided in the base. A plate, *D,* 1¾ in. square, is riveted to the strap hinge opposite to the opening. An electromagnet, *E,*

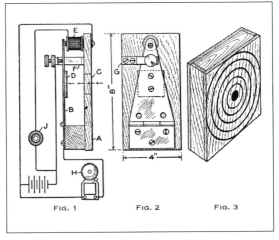

FIG. 1   FIG. 2   FIG. 3

THE BULLET FORCES THE HINGE AGAINST THE THUMBSCREW, CAUSING THE BELL TO RING.

obtained from an electric bell, is mounted upon the base under the small end of the hinge. A standard, *F,* provided with a cross arm, *G,* is secured upon the base between the opening and the magnet. A thumbscrew with a locknut extends through the cross arm, engaging the rear side of the strap hinge, and permits adjustment of distance between the core of the magnet and the surface of the hinge. A bell or buzzer, *H,* is connected as indicated, through the battery circuit. The electromagnet is connected through the battery and push button *J.*

The strap hinge normally rests against the electromagnet. The force of any projectile passing through the opening against the plate closes the bell circuit and indicates to the marksman that the bull's-eye has been hit. By the closing the magnetic circuit, the strap hinge is drawn again into normal position and the bell circuit is broken. *Fig. 2* shows a front view of the circuit-closing device. The device may be mounted in any suitable box, as suggested in *Fig. 3.* The front of the box is covered with sheet metal, ¹⁄₁₆ in. thick, and the standard target card is mounted thereon.

— THE SOMERSAULTING "BUNNY" TARGET —

The somersaulting "bunny" target shown in the drawing is intended for target practice with the bow and arrow. But, by substituting sheet-iron parts for the wooden ones described, it may be used as well for small-caliber rifle practice.

The rabbit is outlined on a 10-by-24-in. board with the rings and bull's-eye of the target a trifle off center to the right; the bull's-eye is formed by drilling a 1½-in. hole through the board.

A 2-by-6-in. post is used for supporting the target, which is mounted on a shaft so as to revolve freely. A piece of gas pipe, about 12 in. long, will answer for the shaft. This is inserted through a hole drilled in the post and is attached to the back of the target with a floor flange. A washer on each side of the post, together with cotter pins driven through holes in the shaft, serve to maintain the proper space between the post and target for operation of the trigger.

The trigger is made by fastening two blocks of wood

to the opposite ends and sides of a piece of spring steel. One of the blocks is nailed to the post in such a position as to bring the other block directly behind the bull's-eye block and, by bearing against a nail in the back of the target, to hold the rabbit vertically until the trigger is released by a properly placed shot.

The somersaulting effect is produced by the weight arrangement

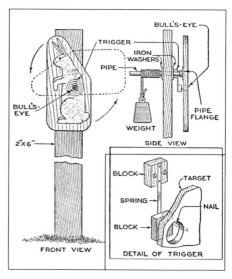

WHENEVER THE MARKSMAN MAKES A BULL'S-EYE ON THIS TARGET THE "BUNNY" MAKES A COMPLETE SOMERSAULT, AND TURNS AGAIN TO AN UPRIGHT POSITION READY FOR ANOTHER SHOT.

shown in the drawing. A piece of stout twine is wound around the projecting end of the shaft, behind the post, and a weight is attached to the free end. The target remains stationary until a lucky shot springs the trigger. The weight then unwinds the rope, and the rabbit makes a complete revolution, the nail striking the block again and stopping the target when it is in an upright position.

From 10 to 20 bull's-eyes may be recorded by the somersaulting bunny before it has to be rewound, depending on the number of turns of rope around the shaft.

— SHOOTING GALLERY FOR TOY PISTOLS —

Skill in shooting toy pistols, blowguns, and similar harmless weapons that use peas, marbles, or wooden darts for ammunition can be easily honed by practicing on a target of the type shown in the drawing. Clothespins, spools, and some wire are about the only materials required. The clothespins are placed on a stiff wire or small rod with a spool between each pair. The wire is then fitted in a box, as shown. In back of the clothespins and a little above their lower ends is a second wire that holds them upright. This wire should be placed so that the pins will lean forward a little. When these targets are

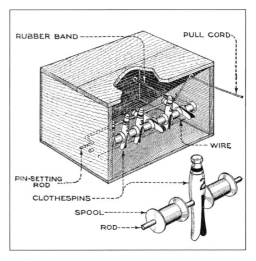

RUBBER BAND

PULL CORD

WIRE

PIN-SETTING ROD

CLOTHESPINS

SPOOL

ROD

A PISTOL FOR INDOOR USE, BY MEANS OF WHICH THE YOUNG MARKSMAN CAN IMPROVE HIS "SHOT" WITH HARMLESS AMMO SUCH AS MARBLES, PEAS, AND DARTS.

knocked over by an expert—or lucky—shot, they are caught by the pin-setting rod at the back. This rod is bent from a piece of stiff wire and is held horizontally by a rubber band. When all the targets have been knocked over, or after each marksman's turn is over, the pins are reset by a pull on the cord tied to the pin-setting rod. If desired, the clothespins can be painted and designated by numbers.

— An Illuminated Indicating Target Box —

The joys of target practice are often hampered by the delays in the settlement of hits. It takes time and is annoying to be constantly advancing to the target to examine it. To do away with this, an illuminated target was

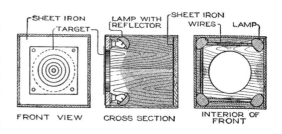

FRONT VIEW   CROSS SECTION   INTERIOR OF FRONT

THE LOCATION OF HITS IS RECORDED BY A BEAM OF LIGHT STREAMING THROUGH THE HOLE SHOT IN THE PAPER TARGET.

constructed that enables the shooter to locate every hit without leaving his post. To make the device, a square wooden box of convenient size is obtained. In one side of this, cut a round hole as large as the largest ring on the targets used. The side opposite this is fitted with a piece of sheet iron to stop the bullets. Paint this iron and the interior white. Inside the box, arrange four electric lights so their rays will be thrown on the hole, as shown. Candles may be used, if necessary. The lamps must be out of range of the bullets that hit the target, and protected by an iron plate. The targets are painted on thin paper and fastened over the front of the hole. The lights are turned on while shooting. Each shot punctures the paper, and the light streaming through the hole will show the location of the hit.

— GOLD FISH TRAVEL
FROM BOWL TO BOWL —

An interesting and entertaining arrangement—permitting goldfish in one bowl to travel to another—is created as shown in the drawing. An extra fish bowl is provided and filled with water to the same height as the one containing the fish. Then a piece of glass tube, of large diameter, is made into an elongated U by heating where the bends are to be and slowly bending. After it has cooled, this U-shaped tube is filled with water and one end

is placed in each bowl. The water will remain in the glass tube, even though above the level of the two bowls, so long as the water in both is kept above the ends of the tube.

AN ARRANGEMENT THAT PERMITS GOLDFISH IN ONE BOWL TO SWIM TO ANOTHER THROUGH A GLASS TUBE.

NOISEMAKERS

— A HOMEMADE HAWAIIAN UKULELE —

The one-string banjo, the cigar-box guitar, and similar vaudeville favorites are giving way to the tantalizing ukulele. The home mechanic, to be up to date in his musical craftsmanship, must fall in line. The size of this instrument makes it especially suited to the cigar-box type of body construction,

as detailed in the several sketches. This neat ukulele was made inexpensively by careful selection of materials form the shop scrap stock.

A cigar box of good-quality Spanish cedar, about 2½ by 6 by 9 in., as shown in *Fig. 1*, is used for the body. Remove the paper carefully so as not to mar the surface, soaking it if

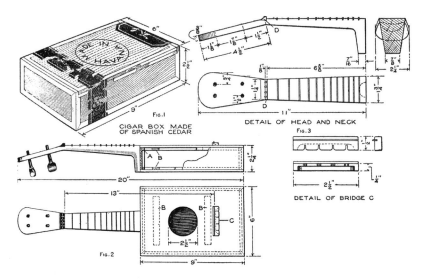

TO KEEP IN FASHION HIS MUSICAL CRAFTSMANSHIP, THE HOME MECHANIC
MAY MAKE A CIGAR-BOX UKULELE AS DETAILED.

necessary. Take it apart; if the nail holes are too numerous or broken out, trim off the edges. Fit the parts of the body together, as shown in *Fig. 2.* The top and bottom pieces should rest against the side and end pieces, and the latter between the sides. Cut the 2½-in. hole in the top piece, as shown, 3¾ in. from the neck end. To reinforce the body make strips, *A,* ¼ in. square, and fit them to be glued into the corners at the top and bottom. Make strips, *B,* ¼ by ⅝ by 4½ in., and glue them under the top and on the bottom as

indicated in *Fig. 2.* The final assembling and gluing of these parts, using animal glue, should be done after the bridge *C* is in place, and the other parts are made. The bridge is of hardwood hollowed underneath the notched edge, as detailed, and is fitted with a metal string contact.

Spanish cedar or mahogany is suitable for the neck, as detailed in *Fig. 3.* A single piece is best, but the extension for the pegs and the wide end at the body may be joined and glued to the main portion of the neck. Dowels should then be used to reinforce the joints. The outline of the parts of the neck are shown in detail in *Fig. 3.* In the sectional view, the shape of the neck at the thinnest and thickest parts is shown by the two upper curved, dotted lines. The nut, *D,* is made of mahogany, walnut, or other hardwood, the grain extending lengthwise, and the notches for the strings spaced as shown.

The making and spacing off the frets must be done very carefully. They are aluminum, although brass and other metals are suitable. Make the frets $1/16$ by $3/16$ in. and cut grooves $1/8$ in. deep for them. The spacing of the frets is determined as follows, a standard practice: The distance from the metal string contact on the bridge to the nut should be measured carefully. The first fret, near the head, is $1/18$ of this distance from the nut, the total length being in this instance, 13 in. The second fret is set $1/18$ the distance from the first fret to the bridge; the third $1/18$ from the second fret to the bridge, etc. The frets must fit tightly in the grooves, requiring no special fastening. The tuning pegs may be bought or made.

In assembling the parts, fasten the end of the body to the neck with glue and reinforce with screws. Set its upper edge parallel with the fingerboard and so that the latter is flush with the top of the body when fitted to it. Assemble the body, without the top, gluing it to the end fixed to the neck. When this portion is thoroughly dried, fit the top into place finally and glue it. The whole construction is then cleaned, sandpapered, stained, and shellacked or varnished. The stringing of the instrument is simple, and the strings may be purchased in sets.

— A GUITAR THAT IS EASY TO MAKE —

A guitar having straight lines, giving it an old-fashioned appearance, can be made by the home mechanic. If care is taken in selecting the material and having it thoroughly seasoned, the finished instrument will have a fine tone. The sides, ends, and bottom are made of hardwood, preferably hard maple, and the top should be made of a thoroughly seasoned piece of soft pine. The materials required are listed in the materials list.

Cut the fingerboard tapering and fasten pieces cut from hatpins with small wire staples for frets. All

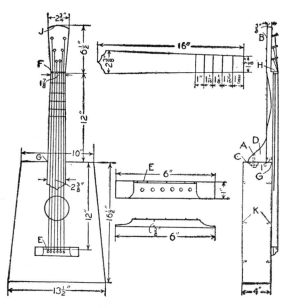

DETAILS OF GUITAR

dimensions for cutting and setting are shown in the sketch. The neck is cut tapering from *F* to *F* and *J* to *F,* with the back side rounding. A drawknife is the proper tool for shaping the neck. Cut a piece of hardwood, ¼ in. square and 1⅞ in. long, and glue it to the neck at *F.* Glue the fingerboard to the neck and hold it secure with clamps while the glue sets.

The brace at *D* is 1 in. thick, cut to any shape desired. The sides are glued together and then the front is glued on them. Place some heavy weights on top and give the glue time to dry. Fasten pieces of soft wood in the corners for braces. Glue the neck to the box, making it secure by the addition of a carriage bolt at *A.* A small block *C* is glued to the end to reinforce it for the bolt. Glue strips of soft wood, as shown by *K,* across the front and back to strengthen them. The back is then glued on and the outside smoothed with sandpaper.

Make the bottom bridge by using an old hatpin or wire of the same size used for *E* secured with pin staples.

Glue the bridge on the top at a place that will make the distance from the bridge *F* to the bottom bridge *E* just 24 in. This dimension and those for the frets should be made accurately. Six holes, ³⁄₁₆ in. in diameter, are drilled in the bottom bridge for pins. The tuning plugs *B* and strings can be purchased at any music store.

List of Materials

1 top, ³⁄₁₆ by 14 by 17 in.
1 bottom, ³⁄₁₆ by 14 by 17 in.
2 sides, ³⁄₁₆ by 3⅝ by 16¾ in.
1 end, ³⁄₁₆ by 3⅝ by 13⅛ in.
1 end, ³⁄₁₆ by 3⅝ by 9⅝ in.
1 neck, 1 by 2 ⁵⁄₁₆ by 18½ in.
1 fingerboard, ³⁄₁₆ by 2⅝ by 16 in.

— A MUSICAL WINDMILL —

Make two wheels out of tin. They may be of any size, but wheel A must be larger than wheel B. On wheel *A* fasten two pieces of wood, *C,* to cross in the center, and place a bell on the four ends, as shown. The smaller wheel, *B,* must be separated from the other with a round piece of wood or an old spool. Tie four buttons with split rings to the smaller wheel, *B*. The blades on the wheels should be bent opposite on one wheel from the others so as

to make the wheels turn in different directions. When turning, the buttons will strike the bells and make them ring constantly.

GAME DAY

— A SNAKE GAME —

Ask any Canadian Native American what a snow snake is, and he will tell you that it is a piece of twisted wood, such as wild grape vine, about 5 or 6 ft. long, and 1 in. or more in thickness, stripped of its bark and polished. It is grasped with one hand in the center and given a

THROWING THE SNOW SNAKE IN TRACKS MADE THROUGH THE SNOW WITH A LOG. EACH PLAYER TRIES TO GET HIS SNAKE FIRST OUT AT THE END OF THE TRACK MORE TIMES THAN HIS OPPONENTS.

strong forward throw at the tail end by the other hand, while at the same time the hold in the center is loosened. With a hard bottom and about 1 in. or more of light snow on top—ideal conditions for playing the game—the snake will travel for long distances when thrown by an expert. To a novice seeing the snake traveling along at a rapid speed, raising and lowering its head as the wood vibrates from side to side, its resemblance to the real reptile is perfect.

When the Native Americans have tests of skill with the snake they make tracks through the snow by drawing a log in it. Sometimes as many as dozen tracks are made side by side, and a dozen snakes are sent along at once. The one who makes his snake emerge from the end of the track first the most times out of a certain number of throws takes the prize. The trick of throwing the snake is not at all hard to acquire, and it makes for an exciting game.

— A MARBLE-UNDER-BRIDGE GAME OF SKILL —

The object of this game is to pass a marble from one end to the other of the "roadway," under the "bridges," and over the "inclines," without dropping it. A stop must be made at each hole. The device is made as follows: Cut two pieces of wood, ¼ by 1¾ by 12 in., and join them to form a right angle. Cut pieces of cardboard, 4 each, 1¾ by 2½ in. wide, with a ¾-in. hole in the center, for inclines *B*, and 1¾ by 3 in., for bridges *A*. Also cut two pieces 1¾ in. square for stops *C*. Fasten them with tacks as shown. The marble should be large enough so that it will rest in the holes at *B*.

— MAGNETIZED CHECKERMEN —

Anyone who has played checkers knows how easy it is to have the pieces become disarranged, usually at the most interesting point of the game. Two methods of preventing this are illustrated in the accompanying drawing. One of these ideas requires small magnets made from clock springs, which are attached to the bottom of the checker men. A metal

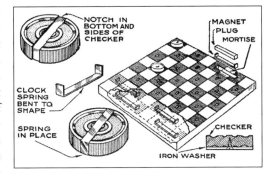

MAGNETISM IS CALLED UPON TO PREVENT CHESS AND CHECKER MEN FROM BECOMING DISARRANGED ON THE BOARD.

board is required. Three or four of the checkers are clamped in a vise, and grooves are filed on opposite edges and one side, as shown. Some pieces of clock spring of good thickness—but not more than ¼ in. wide—are cut into pieces of the proper length and bent to fit neatly and snugly into the filed grooves, and flush with the face of the checker. These pieces are magnetized by bringing them into contact with an ordinary horseshoe magnet. The checkerboard used with these checkers may be an ordinary board with a covering of galvanized iron, or tin plate, on which the squares are painted. Chessmen are fitted with magnets in the same manner as checkers.

The second idea is to embed the magnets in the checkerboard, and is preferred because heavier magnets may be used. This means they will be stronger and longer-lived. As shown in the drawing, mortises are cut into the board so that the ends come at the centers of two black squares. The magnets are formed and magnetized in the manner described, and put in place, after which the opening is plugged up with wood to match the rest of the board. After all the magnets have been put in place, the surface of the board is finished smooth so that the ends of the magnets will just come flush with the top. The checkers are held to the magnets by means of soft-iron washers that are attached to one side with small screws, as indicated.

— AN INDOOR BASEBALL GAME —

An indoor game of baseball may be played on a board 5 ft. long and 4 ft. wide. A diamond is laid off at one end of the board and pins representing the hits are attached to the board so they will project above the surface. The locations of the players are designated by holes bored partway in the wood with an expansive bit.

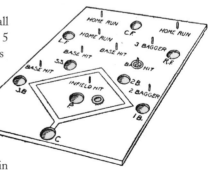

BASEBALL DIAMOND ON A BOARD.

These holes should be large enough to receive the rings easily. The rings may be gaskets or they may be made of rope, and should have an inside diameter of about 3 in.

Only two people can play this game. The distance from the board to the thrower may be from 10 to 100 ft., according to the size of the room. This distance should be marked and each thrower stands at the same place.

If the ring is thrown over one of the "base-hit" or "two-bagger" pegs, it shows the number of bases secured. Throwing a ring over one of the "home run" pegs means a score, of course. The "infield hit" secures a base. If the ring slips into a hole, that counts as one out. A player must throw until he has three outs. The score is kept for the runs made.

— A BUCKET-BALL GAME —

This is a new indoor game that follows out in principle a regular game of baseball. It is an exciting and interesting pastime. And while a certain amount of skill is required to score runs, a person who cannot play the regular game can score as many runs, and as often as the best players in the professional leagues.

THE PLAYER MUST THROW THE BALL SO THAT IT WILL ENTER AND STAY IN ONE OF THE BUCKETS, WHICH DESIGNATES THE BASE HITS BY THE NUMBER IN ITS BOTTOM.

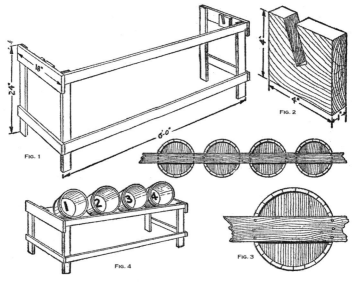

THE FRAME IS MADE UP WITHOUT A BACK, TO HOLD THE BUCKETS
AT AN ANGLE THAT MAKES IT DIFFICULT TO TOSS THE BALL
SO THAT IT WILL STAY IN ANY ONE OF THEM.

Anyone that is just a little handy with tools can make the necessary parts for this game. The tools required are a hammer and a saw. The materials consist of some finishing nails; three strips of wood, 6 ft. long, 2 in. wide, and 1 in. thick; two strips, 18 in. long, 4 in. wide, and 1 in. thick; four strips, 24 in. long, 2 in. wide, and 1 in. thick; two strips, 18 in. long, 2 in. wide, and 1 in. thick; two blocks, 4 in. square, and 1 in. thick; and four wood buckets.

A frame is built up as shown,

6 ft. long, 18 in. wide, and 24 in. high, without a back. One of the long pieces is fastened to the bottoms of the buckets as shown, spacing the latter equally on the length of the piece. This piece is then set in notches cut in the blocks of wood at an angle of 45 degrees. These blocks are fastened to the upper crosspieces at the ends of the frame. The upper part of the buckets rest on the upper front piece of the frame.

The rules for playing the game are as follows: Three baseballs are used.

The players stand about 10 ft. away and in front of the buckets. Each player, or side, is permitted to throw only three balls an inning, irrespective of the number of runs scored. Any kind of delivery is permitted, but an underhand throw will be found most successful. The buckets are numbered from 1 to 4, and represent, respectively, one-, two-, and three-base hits, and home runs. The one in which the ball stays designates the run.

Plays are figured as in a regular ballgame. For instance, if a ball should stay in bucket *No. 2* and the next in bucket *No. 3*, the first man would be forced home, counting one run, and leaving one man on third base. If the next ball stays in bucket *No. 4*, the man on third base is forced home, as well as the one who scored the home run, making three runs for that inning. The runs should be scored as made.

— Pin Setter for the Home Tenpins —

Bowling with a set of small tenpins, which can be purchased at a department store, is a very interesting game. The chief drawback, however, is the setting of the pins. With a little rack like the one shown in the illustration, the interest in the game may be increased considerably. It not only helps in setting the pins rapidly but also ensures a good setting with the proper spacing between the pins. It is very simple to make, because it consists of a triangular piece of wood with ten holes bored into it at the proper places, the dimensions of which will be governed by the size of

All the tenpins are quickly set, and each in its proper place.

the pins, and three supports. The pins are dropped in the holes and the rack lifted from them.

— Electric Scoreboard for Indoor Games —

A very good electric scoreboard, for use in scoring basketball and other games played indoors, is shown in the illustration. It is constructed entirely of wood but should be lined with backing board or sheathing. The dimensions are a matter of choice, but one 4 ft. long, 2 ft. wide, and 18 in. deep is a good size. The back of the box is provided with two cleats, each 2½ ft. long, fastened at each end. This allows a projection of 3 in. at the top and bottom, for fastening the scoreboard to the wall. The manner of construction is shown in *Fig. 1,* and a cross section of the box, in *Fig. 2.*

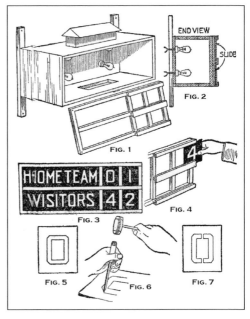

ELECTRIC INDOOR SCOREBOARD, SHOWING ITS CONSTRUCTION AND MANNER OF CUTTING OUT THE LETTERS AND NUMBERS.

The front of the box should be fastened with screws to make its removal easy in case of repairs. This part of the box carries the frame for inserting the numbers and the words "Home Team" and "Visitors,"

as shown in *Fig. 3*. Because the words are a permanent fixture, the cards carrying them are fastened to the front. At the end of these words a frame is constructed as shown in *Fig. 4,* in which the cards having the numbers are inserted in slides.

Numerals and letters can be cut

out of heavy cardboard or tin. The design of a letter having sharp angles and straight edges, as shown in *Fig. 5,* is very easily cut out with a chisel. The method of cutting is shown in *Fig. 6.*

Because portions of the letters and numerals, such as the center in an O, would fall out if cut entirely around, some way must be provided to hold the parts in place. The way to prepare stencils is to leave a portion uncut, which is known as a tie, and the letter will appear as shown in *Fig. 7.*

The best method of making these letters and figures is to cut out the letter entirely, then to paste thin paper over the back and replace the parts removed by the cutting in their original position.

— MARBLE-AND-CHECKERS "BASEBALL" GAME —

A light 8-by-16-in. board is elevated at one end by means of a square stick and drilled with five holes, about 1 in. in diameter, in the positions shown in the drawing. The two upper holes are called "singles," the hole just below this is a "double," the next a "triple," and the last one is a "home run." Small wire brads are driven into the board around these holes. The brads are placed irregularly but with sufficient space between them to allow a marble to pass. The outline of a ball diamond is drawn

AN INDOOR BASEBALL GAME THAT MAY BE PLAYED BY TWO PLAYERS, AND IS MADE ONLY OF TWO PIECES OF WOOD AND SOME NAILS.

upon a card, and the three bases and home plate are indicated on it. Each of the two players is provided with nine checkers that correspond to the players on his team.

When the game is on, one of the players places a checker on the home plate as a batter. Then, the marble is placed between the two nails at the top center of the inclined board and allowed to roll. If it falls into the "single" hole, the "batter" is advanced to first base, and another checker is put up. The game is played just as the regular game, and when three men are out, the second player's team of checkers comes to bat, and the other team takes the field. If the marble lodges in the tacks below the horizontal line on the board, it is a "base on balls" and if the marble stops above the line, it counts as a "strikeout." Should the marble roll entirely off the board without entering any of the holes, it counts as an "out." Scorecards can be prepared and the game made almost as exciting as a real game.

— A PARLOR CUE ALLEY —

Parlor cue alley is really a game of bowling except that it is played on a small raised board. Instead of throwing the balls by hand, an ordinary billiard cue is used, the balls being about 1¼ in. in diameter. The automatic feature of this new game saves the time usually required to set up the pins, and assures that they will be set absolutely true each time.

To build this alley, first procure

A CUE IS USED TO SHOOT THE BALL ON THIS ALLEY.

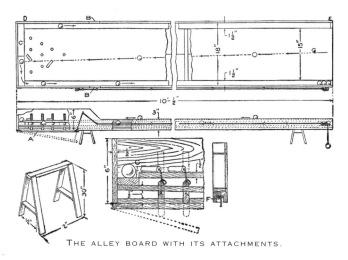

THE ALLEY BOARD WITH ITS ATTACHMENTS.

three planed boards. Use hardwood even though it is more difficult to work. Two of the boards should be 10 ft. long, 9 in. wide, and ½ in. thick, and the other 10 ft. long, 15 in. wide, and ½ in. thick. Place the first two boards side by side and fasten them with cleats, the first cleat being placed 18 in. from the end to be used for the pins. The cleats should be of ¾- or ⅞-in. material and cut as long as the upper board is wide, or 15 in. These are placed on top of the lower boards, or between the two. By placing the first one 18 in. from the end, clearance is obtained for the trap *A*. The other board is placed on the cleats and fastened, after it has been centrally

located, with screws from the underside. The screws must not come through or the surface of the upper board marred in any way that might prevent the balls from rolling freely. The difference in width of the lower board and the upper one provides a 1½-in. clearance on each side as grooves for the return of the balls.

Enclose the alley with boards, 3 in. wide and ½ in. thick, to the point *B*, and from there around the pin end with boards, 6 in. wide. The upper board should be cut to such a length that a space of 2 in. at the end *C* will be provided. Into this space is fitted a block of wood, about ⅞ in. thick, with its upper surface slightly pitched toward the sides of the alley to start the balls back to the front of the board. From the ends of this block two 1½ in. wide strips are fitted into the side grooves, from *D* to *E*. They should be set on an incline, to return the ball after each shot.

The location of each pin is marked on the end of the upper board. Small holes are drilled just large enough to allow pieces of stout cord, like a fish line, to pass through freely. The pins are made of hardwood and are carefully balanced; one end should not be heavier than the other. The lower end of each pin is drilled to make a recess, *F*, in which the cord is fastened with a screw or nail. Holes are bored through the bottom board, ⅜ in. in diameter, to correspond to the 10 small holes made through the upper one. Lead weights of about 2 oz. are fitted in the holes and attached to the strings from the pins. The ends of the weights should extend about ½ in. from the underside of the alley.

Attach a board, 18 in. square, with hinges to the end of the alley so that it will hang under the weights. A stout cord is run along the underside of the alley to the front end through screw eyes, and attached to the swinging board. By letting the board swing down the weights are released and they draw the pins into a standing position, accurately set for the next break. When set, the line is drawn, and the swinging board pushes the weights up and releases the pins.

The balls used are made of hardwood. If it is not possible to make them, they can be purchased from a toy store. They are 1¼ in. in diameter. Each player has three shots. The ball is placed on the spot *G* and shot with a billiard cue, the object being to knock down as many pins as possible. The score is kept as in bowling.

Horses can be made of metal and wood, as shown, for holding the alley at the proper height. The alley can be used on a large table, but horses are more convenient.

GOOD SPORTS

— A CIRCULAR SWING —

Many a farm or country house features a circular swing like the one constructed, which proves very attractive to boys and their friends. The circular swing will be far more popular than the regular version, becoming a favorite with all the younger people, boys and girls alike.

To make the one in the illustration, a 10-ft. length of chain was looped around a branch of a large elm and 18 or 20 ft. from the tree trunk. To the hanging end of this chain a 1-in. rope nearly 10 ft. longer than was needed to reach the ground was made fast.

Directly beneath the point where the chain went around the limb, as determined by a plumb bob, was set a 6-in. piece of cedar post 3½ ft. above the ground. Into the top of this post was set a ½-in. rod, to serve as a pivot for the swing. It was set in

THE CIRCULAR SWING WILL BE FOUND VERY SAFE AND PLEASURABLE. BUT, AS IN THE CASE OF AN ORDINARY SWING, ANYONE CARELESS ENOUGH TO GET IN THE WAY OF IT WILL GET BADLY BUMPED.

firmly about 6 in. and projected about 3 in. from the top of the post.

A straight-grained piece of pine board, 15 ft. long, 8 in. wide, and 1 in. thick, was procured and a hole bored in one end large enough to make it turn freely on the pin in the upper end of the post. Two holes were bored in the other end of the board large enough to admit the rope. The first hole was 6 in. from the end, and the second hole, 3 ft. The hanging end of the rope was passed down through one of these holes and back up through the other and then made fast to itself about 3 ft. above the board after the board had been adjusted so that it would swing throughout its length at the height of the post, or 1½ ft. from the ground. The swing was then complete except for a swivel, which was put in the rope within easy reach of one standing on the board, so that it could be oiled.

One good push would send the board with a boy on the end three or four times about the 90-ft. circle. The little fellows would like to get hold of the board in near the post and shove it around. Once started, it could be kept going with very little effort.

In putting up such a swing, make sure to set the post solidly in the ground, because it has a tendency to work loose. Tie all the knots tightly. Do not look upon the swivel as unnecessary. The first swing put up was without one, and the rope twisted off in a few days.

It is not necessary to climb a tree; just throw a stout cord over the limb by means of a stone or nut tied to the end. Then haul the rope and chain up over the limb with the cord. Before the chain leaves the ground, loop the end of it and pass the cord through the loop. The higher the limb from the ground, the better the swing will work, but 25 ft. will be about right.

— AN ADJUSTABLE PUNCHING-BAG PLATFORM —

A punching-bag platform, suitable for the tall athlete as well as the small boy, is shown in the accompanying sketch. The platform is securely fastened to two strong wooden arms or braces, which in turn are nailed to a 2-by-12-in. plank as long as the diameter of the platform. This plank, as shown in the small drawing at the upper left-hand corner of the sketch, is placed in grooves or slots fastened against the side of a wall. The plank with the platform attached may be raised or lowered to the desired height and held there by a pin or bolt put through the bolt-hole of the plank and into a hole in the wall.

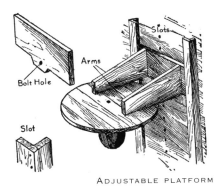

ADJUSTABLE PLATFORM

— TO PRACTICE BATTING FOR BASEBALL PLAYING —

A boy with a very great desire to make a good ballplayer found that he could not hit a ball tossed to him. Try as he might, the bat never hit the ball. Someone suggested that a ball hung by a cord would help to a great extent, and it was tried out with excellent results. An inexpensive ball was suspended from the limb of a tree so that it would be at the proper height for the batter. In striking at the ball it was not necessary to hit home runs, as this is liable to break the cord, or get it tangled to its support. If the strikes are made properly, the ball will swing out and come back in a perfect curve, or can be made to come back bounding and in no straight line. This will teach the eye

to locate the ball and make hits where it cannot be taught by having someone toss the ball to the striker.

THRILLS *in* MOTION

— HOMEMADE OVERHEAD TROLLEY COASTER —

The accompanying sketch shows a playground trolley line that furnished a great deal of amusement to many children at a minimum cost. The wire, which is 3/16 in. in diameter, was stretched between a tree and a barn across vacant quarter block. The strength of the wire was first tested by a heavy man. When not in use the wire is unhooked from the tree and hauled into the barn and coiled loosely in the hay loft. The wire was made taut for use by a rope that was fastened to the beams in the barn. The trolley was made, as shown in *Figs. 1* and *2*, of strips of wood bolted with stove bolts on two grooved pulleys. The middle wide board was made of hardwood. The wheels were taken from light pulley blocks and stove bolts were purchased from a local hardware store to accurately fit the hubs. Because it was necessary to keep the bearings greased, we used Vaseline. This coaster made great sport for the youngsters and at no time were they in danger of a serious fall because the line was hung low and the slant of the wire was moderate.

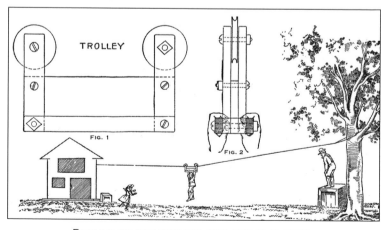

DETAILS OF THE TROLLEY AND HOW IT IS USED.

— EASILY RENEWED COASTER BRAKE —

The brake that forms a part of most models of children's toy wagons and coasters of various kinds is usually unsatisfactory because of its short life. The wooden lever wears down rapidly, and an iron brake wears the tires, and there is usually no way to renew either.

The drawing and photograph illustrate an iron brake handle that has provision made at its lower end for holding a wooden-block brake shoe. As soon as there is any amount of wear, a new block can be inserted, and the brake will be as good as new. The brake lever is forged from a piece of round iron, with one end flattened to accommodate the brake-shoe holder, to which it is riveted. The brake lever is fastened to the wagon by means of a stud attached to the underside of the wagon box.

— A BOY'S MOTOR CAR —

Even though the home-built "bearcat" roadster or other favorite model does not compare in every detail with the luxurious manufactured cars, it has an individuality that puts it in a class by itself. The amateur mechanic, or the ambitious boy who is fairly skilled with tools, can build at least the main parts for his own small car of the simple, practical design shown in the sketch and detailed in the working drawings. If necessary, he can call more skilled mechanics to his aid. A motorcycle engine or other small gasoline motor is used for the power plant. The control mechanism of the engine and the electrical connections are similar to those of a motorcycle. They are installed to be controlled handily from the driver's seat. The car is built without springs, but these may included, if desired. Or the necessary comfort may provided—in part, at least—by a cushioned seat. Strong bicycle wheels are used, the 1½-by-28-in. size being suitable. The hood may be of wood, or of sheet metal, built over a frame of strap iron. The top of the hood can be lifted off, and the entire hood can also be removed, when repairs are to be made. The toolbox on the rear of the frame can be replaced by a larger compartment, or rack, for transporting loads, or an extra seat for a passenger.

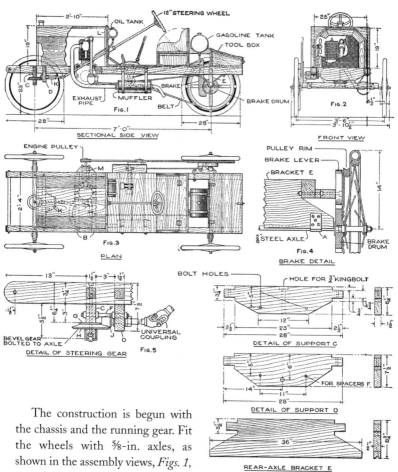

12" STEERING WHEEL

OIL TANK

GASOLINE TANK

TOOL BOX

BRAKE

EXHAUST PIPE

MUFFLER

BRAKE DRUM

BELT

FIG. 1

28"   7'-0"   28"

SECTIONAL SIDE VIEW

25"

19"

FIG. 2

3'-6"
3'-10½"

FRONT VIEW

ENGINE PULLEY

PULLEY RIM

BRAKE LEVER

BRACKET E

14"

STEEL AXLE

A

BRAKE DRUM

FIG. 3

PLAN

FIG. 4

BRAKE DETAIL

13"   1½"   3"   1½"

BEVEL GEAR BOLTED TO AXLE

UNIVERSAL COUPLING

DETAIL OF STEERING GEAR   FIG. 5

BOLT HOLES

HOLE FOR ¾" KINGBOLT

2½"   23"   2½"
12"
28"

DETAIL OF SUPPORT C

14"
11"
28"

FOR SPACERS F

DETAIL OF SUPPORT D

36"

REAR-AXLE BRACKET E
FIG. 6

The construction is begun with the chassis and the running gear. Fit the wheels with ⅝-in. axles, as shown in the assembly views, *Figs. 1, 2,* and *3,* and detailed in *Fig. 4.* Fit the ends of the axles to the hubs of the wheels, providing the threaded ends with lock nuts. Make the wooden supports for the frame, as

detailed in *Fig. 6.* The axles are fastened into half-round grooves cut in the bottoms of the supports and secured by iron straps, as shown in

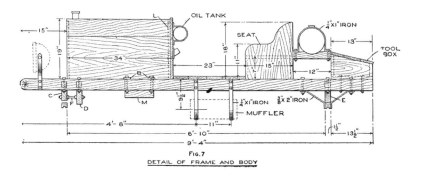

Fig.7

DETAIL OF FRAME AND BODY

A, Fig. 4. Make the sidepieces for the main frame 2½ by 3¼ in. thick, and 9 ft. 4 in. long, as detailed in *Fig. 7.* Mortise the supports through the sidepieces, and bore the holes for the bolt fastenings and braces. Glue the mortise-and-tenon joints before the bolts are finally secured. Provide the bolts with washers, and lock the nuts with additional jam nuts where needed. Keep the woodwork clean, and apply a coat of linseed oil, so that dirt and grease cannot penetrate readily.

Finish only the supporting structure of the chassis in the preliminary woodwork. Set the front-axle and steering-rigging supports *C* and *D,* and adjust the spacers *F* between them. Bore the hole for the kingbolt, as detailed in *Fig. 6.* Fit the bevel gears and the fifth wheel *G,* of ¼-in. steel, into place, as shown in *Fig. 5.*

The gear *H* is bolted to the axle support. The pinion J is set on the end of a short ¾-in. shaft. The latter passes through the support *D,* and is fitted with washers and jam nuts, solidly, yet with sufficient play. A bracket, *K,* of ¼-by-1¾-in. strap iron, braces the shaft, as shown in *Fig. 3.* The end of this short shaft is joined to one section of the universal coupling, as shown, and, like the other half of the coupling, is pinned with a 3/16-in. riveted pin. The pinion is also pinned, and the lower end of the kingbolt provided with a washer and nut, guarded by a cotter pin. Suitable gears can be procured from old machinery. A satisfactory set was obtained from an old differential of a well-known small car.

Before fitting the steering column into place, make the dashboard, of ⅞-in. oak, as shown in the assembly view, and in detail in *Fig. 7*. It is 19½ in. high and 2 ft. 4 in. wide, and set on the frame and braced to it with 4- by 4- by 1½-in. angle irons, ¼ in. thick. Fit a ⅞-in. strip of wood around the edge of the dashboard, on the front side, as a rest for the hood, as shown in *L, Figs. 1* and *7*. A brass edging protects the dashboard, and gives a neat appearance. Lay out carefully the angle for the steering column, which is of ⅞-in. shafting, so as to be convenient for the driver. Mark the point at which it is to pass through the dashboard, and reinforce the hole with an oak block, or an angle flange of iron or brass, such as is used on railings or boat fittings. A collar at the flange

counteracts the downward pressure on the steering post. The 12-in. steering wheel is set on the column by a riveted pin.

The fitting of the engine may next be undertaken. The exact position and method of setting the engine on the frame will depend on the size and type. It should be placed as near the center as possible, to give proper balance. The drawings show a common air-cooled one-cylinder motor. It is supported, as shown in *Figs. 1* and *3* and detailed in *Fig. 8*. Two iron strips, *B*, riveted to 1½-by-1½-in. angle irons, extend across the main frame, and support the engine by means of bolts and steel clamps, designed to suit the engine. Cross

TO SIMPLIFY THIS SMALL BUT SERVICEABLE MOTOR CAR FOR CONSTRUCTION BY THE YOUNG MECHANIC, ONLY THE ESSENTIAL PARTS ARE CONSIDERED. OTHER USEFUL AND ORNAMENTAL FEATURES MAY BE ADDED AS THE SKILL AND MEANS OF THE BUILDER MAKE POSSIBLE.

strips of iron steady the engine, and the clamps are bolted to the crank case. The center clamp is a band that passes under the crankcase.

The engine is set so that the crankshaft extends across the main frame. Other methods may be devised for special motors, and the power transmission changed correspondingly. One end of the crankshaft is extended beyond the right side of the frame, as shown in *Fig. 3*. This extension is connected to the shaft by means of an ordinary setscrew collar coupling. A block *M, Figs. 3* and *7*, is bolted to the frame, and a section of heavy brass pipe fitted as a bearing.

The ignition and oiling systems, carburetor, and other details of the engine control and allied mechanism are the same as those used on the motorcycle engine originally, fitted up as required. The oil tank is made of a strong can, mounted on the dashboard, as shown in *Figs. 1* and *2*. It is connected with the crankcase by copper tubing. A cut-out switch for the ignition system is mounted on the dashboard. The controls used

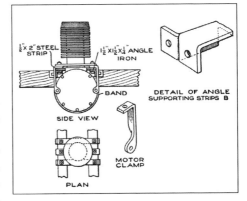

DETAIL OF THE MOTOR SUPPORT. THE ENGINE IS MOUNTED ON REINFORCED ANGLE IRONS, AND SECURED BY CLAMPS AND A SUPPORTING BAND UNDER THE CRANKCASE.

for the engine of the motorcycle can be extended with light iron rods, and the control handles mounted on the dashboard or other convenient position. The throttle can be mounted on the steering column by fitting an iron pipe around the post and mounting this pipe in the angle flange at the dashboard. A foot accelerator may also be used, suitable mountings and pedal connections being installed at the floor.

In setting the gasoline tank, make only as much of the body woodwork as is necessary to support it, as shown in *Figs. 1, 3,* and *7*. The tank should be made and properly fitted in the same way and with the same materials as gasoline tanks in commercial cars. The feed is through a copper tube, as shown in *Fig. 1.* A small vent hole, to guard against a vacuum in the tank, should be made in the cap. The muffler from a motorcycle is used, fitted with a longer pipe, and suspended from the side of the frame.

The transmission of the power from the motor shaft to the right rear wheel is accomplished by means of a leather motorcycle belt. This is made by fitting leather washers close together over a bicycle chain, oiling the washers with neat's-foot oil. A grooved iron pulley is fitted on the end of the motor shaft, and a grooved pulley rim on the rear wheel as shown in *Figs. 1* and *3,* and detailed in *Fig. 4.* The motor is started by means of a crank, and the belt drawn up gradually, by the action of a clutch lever and its idler, detailed in *Fig. 9.* The clutch lever is forged, as shown, and fitted with a ratchet lever, *N,* and ratchet quadrant, *O.* The idler holds the belt to the tension desired, giving considerable flexibility of speed.

The brake is shown in *Figs. 1* and *3,* and detailed in *Figs. 4* and 9. The fittings on the rear wheel and axle are made of wood, and bolted, with a tension spring, as shown. The brake drum is supported on iron bands, riveted to the wheel, and to the pulley rim. The brake arm is connected to the brake wheel by a flexible wire. When the pedal is forced down, the wire is

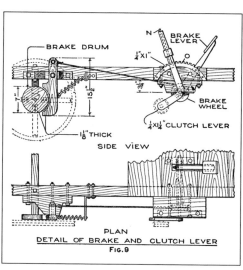

DETAIL OF BRAKE AND CLUTCH LEVER
FIG. 9

THE BRAKE IS CONTROLLED BY A PEDAL, AND A CLUTCH LEVER IS MOUNTED ON THE CENTRAL SHAFT, AND SET BY MEANS OF A RATCHET DEVICE AND GRIP-RELEASE ROD.

wound on the brake wheel, thus permitting adjustment. The pedal is of iron and fixed on its shaft with a setscrew. An iron pipe is used as a casing for the central shaft. The shaft carrying the clutch lever, and the pipe carrying the brake pedal and the brake wheels. The quadrant *O* is mounted on a block, fastened to the main frame. The central shaft is carried in wooden blocks, with iron caps. A catch of strap iron can be fitted on the floor, to engage the pedal, and lock the brake when desired.

The engine is cooled by the draft through the wire-mesh opening in the front of the hood, and through the openings under the hood. If desirable, a wooden split pulley, with grooved rim and rope belt, may be fitted on the extension of the engine shaft, and connected with a two-blade metal fan, as shown in *Fig. 2.*

The lighting arrangement may finally be installed. Use gas or electric lamps, run on batteries. Mudguards are desirable if the car is to be used on muddy roads. Strong bicycle mudguards can be installed with the guard braces bolted on the axles. A strong pipe, with a draw bolt passing through its length, is mounted across the front of the frame. The body is built of ⅞-in. stock, preferably white wood, and is 2 ft. 4 in. wide. A priming coat should be applied to the woodwork, followed by two coats of the body color, and one or two coats of varnish. The metal parts, except at the working surfaces, may be painted or enameled.

— A Cyclemobile —

The cyclemobile is a three-wheeled vehicle that can easily be constructed in the home workshop with ordinary tools. The main frame is built up of two side-pieces, *AA, Fig. 1,* each 2 in. thick, 4 in. wide, and 7 ft. long. These are joined together at the front end with a crosspiece, *B,* of the same material, 17 in. long. The sides are made to be slightly tapering so that the rear ends are 11 in. apart at the point where they are joined together with the blocks and rear-wheel attachments. A crosspiece, *C,* 13 in. long, is fastened in the center of the frame.

The place for the seat is cut out off each sidepiece, as shown by the notches in *D.* These notches are 2 ft. from the rear ends. Two strips of

wood, *E,* ½ in. thick, 4 in. wide, and 22 in. long, are nailed to the rear ends of the sides, as shown. The rear wheel is a bicycle wheel, which can be taken from an old bicycle or may be purchased cheaply at a bicycle store. It is held in place with two pieces of strap iron, *F,* shaped similar to the rear forks on a bicycle. Each piece is bolted to a block of wood 3 in. thick, 4 in. wide, and 6 in. long, fastened to the sidepiece with the same bolts that hold the strap iron in place. The blocks are located 20 in. from the rear ends of the sidepieces.

The pedal arrangement, *Fig. 2,* consists of an ordinary bicycle hanger with cranks and sprocket wheel set into the end of a piece of wood, 2 in. thick, 4 in. wide and 33 in. long, at a point 4 in. from one end. The pieces *GG* are nailed on across the frame at the front end of the car to hold the hanger piece in the center between sidepieces, as shown in *Fig. 1.* A small pulley, *H,* is made to run loosely

THREE-WHEELED CYCLEMOBILE PROPELLED LIKE A BICYCLE
AND STEERED AS AN AUTOMOBILE.

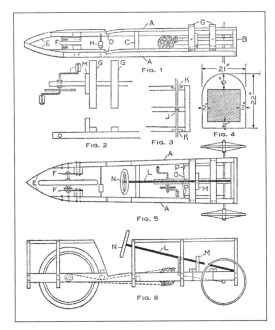

are taken from a discarded baby carriage and are about 21 in. in diameter.

A good imitation radiator can be made by cutting a board to the dimensions given in *Fig. 4*. A large-mesh screen is fastened to the rear side to imitate the water cells.

The steering gear *L, Fig. 5*, is made of a broom handle, one end of which passes through the support *M* and fits into a hole bored into the lower part of the imitation radiator board. A steering wheel, *N*, is attached to the upper end of the broom handle. The center part of a rope, *O*, is given a few turns around the broom handle, and the ends are passed through the openings in screw eyes, *PP*. They are then turned in to the inner surfaces of the sidepieces *AA*, and tied to the front axle.

The seat is constructed of ½-in. lumber and is built in the notches cut into the main frame shown in *D,*

on a shaft fastened between the sidepieces. This is used as an idler to keep the upper part of the chain below the seat.

The front axle is 30 in. long, pivoted as shown in *J, Fig. 3*, 6 in. from the front end of the main frame. Two small brass plates, *KK*, are screwed to the under edge of each sidepiece, as shown, to provide a bearing for the axle. The front wheels

Fig. 1. The body frame is made of lath, or other thin strips of wood, that can be bent in the shape of the radiator and nailed to the sidepieces, as shown in *Fig. 6.* These are braced at the top with longitudinal strip. The frame is then covered with canvas and painted as desired.

— HAND CAR MADE OF PIPE AND FITTINGS —

Although it appears complicated, the construction of the car shown in the accompanying illustration is very simple. With a few exceptions all the parts are short lengths of pipe and common tees, elbows, and nipples.

The wheels were manufactured for use on a baby carriage. The sprocket wheel and chain were taken from a discarded bicycle, which was also drawn upon for the cork handle used on the steering lever. The floor is made of 1-in. white pine, 14 in. wide and 48 in. long, to which are bolted ordinary flanges to hold the framing and the propelling and steering apparatus together. The axles were made from ⅜-in. shafting. The fifth wheel consists of two small flanges working on the face surfaces. These flanges and the auxiliary steering rod are connected to the axles by means of holes stamped in the piece of

BOY'S HAND CAR.

sheet iron that encases the axle. The sheet iron was first properly stamped and then bent around the axle. The levers for propelling and steering the car work in fulcrums made for use in lever valves. The turned wooden handles by which these levers are operated were inserted through holes drilled in the connecting tees. The working joint for the steering and hand levers consists of a ½-by-⅜-by-⅜-in. tee, a ½-by-⅜-in. cross and a piece of rod threaded on both ends and screwed into the tee. The cross is reamed and, with the rod, forms a bearing.

The operation of this little hand car is very similar in principle to that of the ordinary tricycle. The machine can be propelled as fast as a boy can run. It responds readily to the slightest movement of the steering lever.

— A HOMEMADE ROLLER COASTER —

The popular roller coaster that furnishes untold amusement for the multitudes that patronize amusement parks during the summer can be easily duplicated in a smaller way on a vacant lot or backyard for the children of the home. Alternatively, the boys of the neighborhood could contribute to a fund and construct quite an elaborate affair, on the same lines as described, for the combined use of the owners. The one described was built with a track, 90 ft. long, 5 ft. high at one end and 3 ft. at the other, the track between being placed on the ground.

In coasting from the high end to the low one, the coaster will run up on the incline, then drift back to within 24 ft. of the starting end. The car was built to seat four children or two adults. The cost of all the materials was modest.

The track is of simple construction and requires but little description. It is necessary to make it straight and nailed firmly to the cross ties on the ground and to the trestles where it is elevated. The ties and trestles are placed about 6 ft. apart. The two trestles for the starting platform should be set so that there is a slant to the

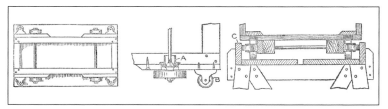

DETAIL OF THE CAR, WHEELS, AND THE TRESTLE,
WHICH IS ATTACHED TO A TIE.

track of about 6 in. for starting the car without pushing it. The car can be carried back for starting by adults, but for children a small rope can be used over the platform to draw it back on the track, or a small windlass may be arranged for the purpose.

The main frame of the car is 3 ft. long and about 13 in. wide, firmly fastened at the corners. The axles for the wheels are machine steel, 19 in. long, turned up on the ends and threaded in

INEXPENSIVE BACKYARD ROLLER COASTER, SUITABLE FOR THE ENJOYMENT OF THE YOUNG AS WELL AS THE OLDER PERSON.

and 1 in. thick, and are set on the bicycle cone of the ball cup, after they are properly adjusted, and securely fastened between washers with a nut on the end of the axle. Guide wheels, *B*, are placed on the sides in the manner shown. These wheels are ordinary truck casters—not the revolving kind— 2 in. in diameter.

About ½-in. clearance should be provided between the guide wheels *B* and the guardrail *C*, on the track.

the manner of a bicycle axle to fit parts of bicycle hubs, attached to the main frame as shown in *A*. The wheels are solid, 4 in. in diameter

When the car is made in this manner it runs close to the track and there is no place where a child can get a foot or hand injured under or at the sides of the car. The one described has been used by all the children, large and small, for a year without accident.

— HOW TO MAKE A FLYMOBILE —

The boy owning a pushmobile, or even a power-driven auto car, is often very much disappointed because motion soon stops when the power is not applied. The car illustrated is of a little different type, being equipped with a flywheel that will propel the car and carry the rider a considerable distance after pedaling is stopped. The flywheel also aids the operator, as it will steady the motion and help him over a rough place or a bump in the road.

The main frame of the flymobile is made up a few pieces of 2-by-4-in. timbers. The pieces *A* are 6 ft. 4 in. long, and the end crosspieces, *B,* 24 in. long. These are jointed, glued, and screwed together, as shown in *Fig. 1.* The frame that supports the driving parts consists of a piece, *C,* 6 ft. 2 in. long, and a piece, *D,* 2 ft. 11 in. long. These are fitted in the main frame and securely fastened to the end crosspieces *B.* Two other crosspieces, *E* and *F,* are used to strengthen the driving parts frame.

The entire hanger *G,* with its bearings, cranks and pedals, can be procured from a discarded bicycle and fastened to the piece *C.* The barrel holding the bearings is snugly fitted into a hole bored in the piece with an expansive bit. The location will depend on the builder and should be marked as follows: Place the hanger on top of the piece *C,* then put a box or board on the frame where the seat is to be and set the hanger where it will be in a comfortable position for pedaling. Mark this location and bore the hole.

The transmission, *H,* consists of a bicycle coaster-brake hub, shown in detail in *Fig. 2.* A split pulley, *J,* 6 in. in diameter, is bored out to fit over the center of the hub between the spoke flanges. The halves of the pulley are then clamped on the hub with two bolts run through the holes in opposite directions. Their heads and nuts are set into coun-

tersunk holes so that no part will extend above the surface of the pulley. The supports for the hub axle consist of two pieces of bar iron, 4 in. long, drilled to admit the axle ends, and screws for fastening them to the frame pieces *C* and *D*. This construction is clearly shown in *Fig. 2.*

The arrangement of the coaster-brake hub produces the same effect as a coaster brake on a bicycle. The one propelling the flymobile may stop the foot-power work without interfering with the travel of the machine. A little back pressure on the pedals will apply the brake in the same manner.

The flywheel, *K,* should be about 18 in. in diameter with a 2-in. rim, or face. Such a wheel can be purchased cheaply from any junk dealer.

The flywheel is set on a shaft, turning between the pieces *C* and *D* and back of the coaster-brake wheel *H.* Two pulleys, *L,* about 3 in. in diameter, are fastened to turn with the flywheel on the shaft and are fitted with flanges to separate the belts. The ends of the shaft should run in good bearings, well oiled.

Another pulley, *M,* 6 in. in diameter, is made of wood and fastened to the rear axle. An idler wheel, shown in *Fig. 3,* is constructed of a small pulley or a large spool attached to an L-shaped piece of metal, which in turn is fastened on the end of a shaft controlled by the lever *N.* The function of this idler is to tighten up the belt or release it, thus changing the speed in the same manner as on a motorcycle.

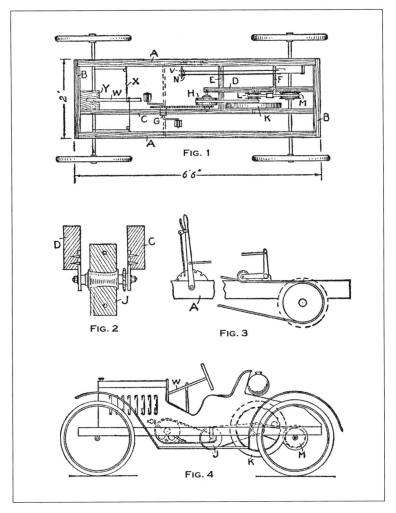

FIG. 1

FIG. 2

FIG. 3

FIG. 4

PLAN AND ELEVATION OF THE FLYMOBILE, SHOWING THE LOCATION OF
THE WORKING PARTS, TO WHICH, WITH A FEW CHANGES, A MOTORCYCLE
ENGINE CAN BE ATTACHED TO MAKE IT A CYCLE CAR. ALSO DETAILS OF
THE BRAKES, BELT TIGHTENER, AND COASTER-BRAKE HUB.

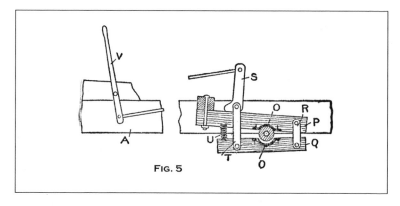

FIG. 5

The elevation of the flymobile is given in *Fig. 4,* which shows the arrangement of the belting. The size of the pulleys on the flywheel shaft causes it to turn rapidly, and, for this reason, the weight of the wheel will run the car a considerable distance when the coaster hub is released.

The rear axle revolves in bearings. Half of the axle is recessed in the under edges of the pieces *A,* while the other half is fastened to a block, screwed on over the axle. A simple brake is made as shown in *Fig. 5.* Two metal pieces (preferably brass), *O,* are shaped to fit over the shaft with extending ends for fastening them to the pieces *P* and *Q* as shown. These pieces are hinged with strap iron, *R,* at one end. The other end of the piece *P* is fastened to the crosspiece *F, Fig. 1,* of the main frame. The lower piece *Q* is worked by the lever *S* and side bars, *T.* A small spring, *U,* keeps the ends of the pieces apart and allows the free turning of the axle until the brake lever is drawn. The lever *S* is connected by a long bar to the hand lever *V.*

The steering apparatus, *W, Figs. 1* and *4,* is constructed of a piece of gas pipe, 3 ft. 4 in. long. It has a wheel at one end and a cord, *X,* at the other. The center part of the cord is wound several times around the pipe and the ends are passed through screw eyes in the main-frame pieces, *A,* and attached to the front axle. The axle is pivoted in the center under the block *Y.* The lower end of the pipe turns in a hole bored slanting in the block. A turn of the steering wheel causes one end of the cord to wind and the other unwind, which turns the axle on the center pivot.

The wheels are bicycle wheels, and the ends of the front axle are turned to receive the cones and nuts, instead of using the regular hub axles. The ends of the rear axle are turned to closely fit the hubs after the ball cups have been removed. A large washer and nut clamp each wheel to the axle so that it will turn with it.

The body can be made up as desired, from sheet metal, wood, or cloth stretched over ribs of wood, and painted in the manner of an automobile. A tank and tires can be placed on the back to add to the appearance. Fenders and a running board can be attached to the main frame.

With the addition of some cross-pieces in the main frame at the front and a motorcycle engine fastened to them so that the driving sprocket will be in line with the sprocket on the coaster hub, the builder will have a real cycle car.

CHAPTER 6

THE TOY WORKSHOP

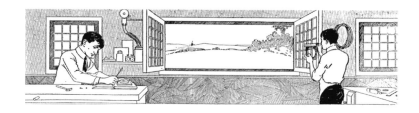

— A HOMEMADE VISE —

While making a box a woodworker had some dovetailing to do, and because there was no vise on the bench the clever mechanic rigged up a substitute. He secured a board ¾ in. thick, 3 in. wide, and 20 in. long and bored a ½-in. hole through it, 1 in. from each end. He then attached the board to the bench by driving two screws through washers and the holes in the board into the bench top. The screws

VISE ON BENCH.

should be of a length suitable to take in the piece to be worked.

— GAUGE FOR WOODWORK —

A convenient gauge can be quickly made by using a block of wood and an ordinary nail, or several nails for different widths can be placed in one block. Drive the nails straight into the block until the distance between the head and block is the required distance to be gauged. The rim of the nail head makes the mark as the block is drawn over the wood surface.

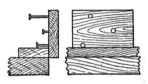

— NAIL CABINET WITH MUFFIN-PAN TRAYS —

M uffin-pan trays used by the housewife in baking make serviceable containers for nails, screws, and other small articles used in the shop. The illustration shows the pans fitted into a box and sliding in grooves cut into the sides with a saw.

The box is made with the end pieces overlapping at top and bottom, this being a better construction to carry the weight of the trays. The wood used in the sides is ⅞ in. thick, so that a saw cut may be made to the depth of ¼ in. without weakening the support. Thinner wood may be used if instead of saw cuts small

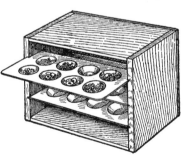

THE METAL TRAYS ARE SUBSTANTIAL AND MAY BE REMOVED READILY FOR USE ELSEWHERE.

strips of wood are nailed against the sides as tray slides.

— A Workbench for the Amateur —

The accompanying detail drawing shows a design of a portable workbench suitable for the amateur woodworker. This bench can be made easily by anyone who has a few sharp tools and a little spare time. If the stock is purchased from the mill ready planed and cut to length, much of the hard labor will be saved. Birch or maple wood makes a very good bench, and the following pieces should be ordered:

Materials

4 legs, 3 by 3 by 36 in.
2 side rails, 3 by 3 by 62½ in.
2 end rails, 3 by 3 by 20 in.
1 back board, 1 by 9 by 80 in.
1 top board, 2 by 12 by 77 in.
1 top board, 1 by 12 by 77 in.
2 crosspieces, 1½ by 3 by 24 in.
1 piece for clamp, 1½ by 6½ by 12 in.
1 piece for clamp, 1½ by 6½ by 14 in.
4 guides, 2 by 2 by 18 in.
1 screw block, 3 by 3 by 6 in.
1 piece, 1½ by 4½ by 10½ in.

Make the lower frame first. Cut tenons on the rails and mortise the posts, then fasten them securely together with ⅜-by-5-in. lag screws as shown. Also fasten the 1½-by-3-by-24-in. pieces to the tops of the posts with screws. The heads should be countersunk or else holes bored in the top boards to fit over them. Fasten the front top board to the crosspieces by lag screws through from the underside. The screws can be put in from the top for the 1-in. thick top board.

Fasten the end pieces on with screws, countersinking the heads of the vise end. Cut the 2-in. square holes in the 1½- by 4½- by 10-in. pieces for the vise slides, and fit it in place for the side vise. Also cut square holes in the one end piece of the end vise slides as shown. Now fit up the two clamps. Fasten the slides to the front pieces with screws. Countersink the heads of the screws to they will not be in the way of the hands when the vise is used. The two clamp screws should be about 1½ in. in diameter. They can be purchased at a hardware store. A block should be fitted under the crosspiece to hold the nut for the end vise. After you have the slides fitted, put them in place and bore the holes for the clamp screws.

263

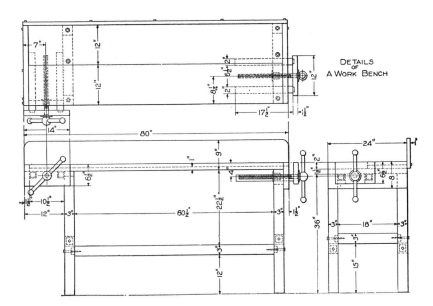

DETAILS
of
A WORK BENCH

DETAIL OF THE BENCH

WORKBENCH COMPLETE

The back board can now be fastened to the back with screws as shown in the top view. The bench is now complete, except for a couple of coats of oil that should be applied to give it a finish and preserve the wood. The amateur workman, as well as the patternmaker, will find this a very handy and serviceable bench for his workshop.

Because the amateur workman does not always know just what tools he will need, a list is given that will serve for a general class of work. This list can be added to as the workman becomes more proficient in his line and has need for other tools. Only the better grade of tools should be purchased, as they are the cheapest in the long run. If each tool is kept in a certain place, it can be easily found when needed.

Tools

1 bench plane or jointer
1 jack plane or smoother
1 crosscut saw, 24 in.
1 ripsaw, 24 in.
1 claw hammer
1 set of gimlets
1 brace and set of bits
2 screwdrivers, 3 and 6 in.
1 countersink
1 compass saw
1 set chisels
1 wood scraper
1 monkey wrench
1 2-ft. rule
1 marking gauge
1 pair pliers
1 nail set
1 pair dividers
1 pocket level
1 6-in. try square
1 oilstone
No. 1, 2, and 00 sandpaper

— CONVENIENT TOOL DRAWER UNDER CHAIR SEAT —

For the homeowner who does small repairing occasionally at home, a sliding drawer under his working chair will be an exceptional convenience. The tools are always handy when he sits down to his

work, and he can put them away again without arising from the chair. This arrangement is also useful in small shops where a chair or stool is used for tinkering or light bench work.

— Useful Tool
for Home Mechanics —

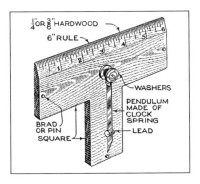

Combining a square, plumb, and rule, the tool illustrated is well worth the slight time and trouble required in making it. Wood is used for the T-shaped piece, the long edge of which is graduated into inches and fractions, while the angles formed at the corners are used as squares. The plumb consists of a weighted pendulum, made from a piece of clock spring. Brads, or pins, are inserted at the proper points on the three ends of the device to indi-cate the true plumb line, when using the tool to test the level of a surface.

INDEX